STOCKPORT

THROUGH TIME

Coral Dranfield

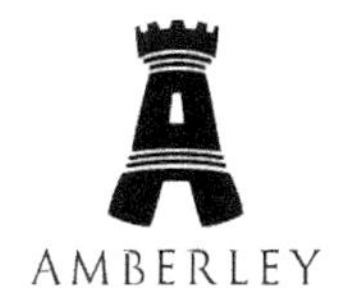

AMBERLEY

First published 2011

Amberley Publishing
Cirencester Road, Chalford,
Stroud, Gloucestershire GL6 8PE

www.amberleybooks.com

ISBN 978-1-4456-0115-1

British Library Cataloguing in Publication Data.
A catalogue record for this book is available from the British Library.

Typeset in 9.5pt on 12pt Celeste.
Typesetting by Amberley Publishing.
Printed in the UK.

Introduction

Since Stockport was granted a market charter in 1260, it has grown from a small hilltop town to the bustling metropolis that we know today. It owed its early existence to the River Mersey and the ford that crossed it. The ford was replaced by a bridge in the thirteenth century; the bridge linked Cheshire to Lancashire, and particularly to Manchester.

What was once an unspoilt wooded valley with salmon-laden rivers became an industrial town whose mills brought prosperity when work was plentiful and poverty when times were hard and unemployment high.

Like many other cotton towns, Stockport has been left with a legacy of buildings dating from that time; they overshadow its earlier history, but much of the town's past is still there if you know where to look for it – many buildings have a story to tell.

Over the centuries, Stockport has been viewed by various people in differing ways. 'One of the darkest and smokiest holes in the whole industrial area,' was how Friedrich Engels described it in the 1840s. Eighty years earlier, Daniel Defoe had witnessed a town with prosperity and employment for all. Unfortunately, a purely photographic history cannot tell the full story of this fascinating place.

Change is something we live with constantly, and often do not notice. The pictures in this book are merely snapshots in time, but whether they are from the 1900s, the 1960s or the 2000s, they have equal value in telling us what was happening at that particular period in the town's development.

Some of the colour photographs are taken at different angles to the old ones, on account of street furniture and my efforts to avoid being mowed down by traffic. Many Edwardian photographers seemed to like standing in the middle of the road, but the A6, especially, is not a place to linger long.

In these pages I hope to show you not only how the town has changed for the better, but also what is still there if you look for it.

Acknowledgements

I would like to thank the following people and organisations for their contribution to this book: Stockport Heritage Library, Stockport Heritage Centre, Grace Collier, Tony Steel, Kevin Dranfield, Ray and Wendy Dranfield.

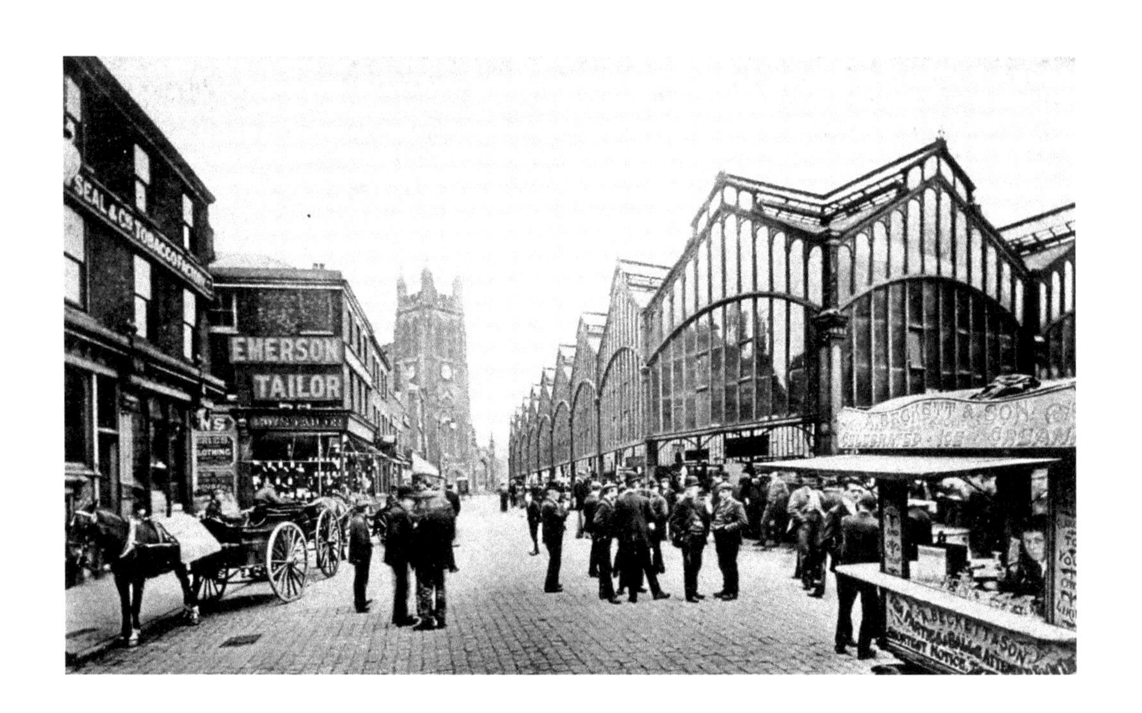

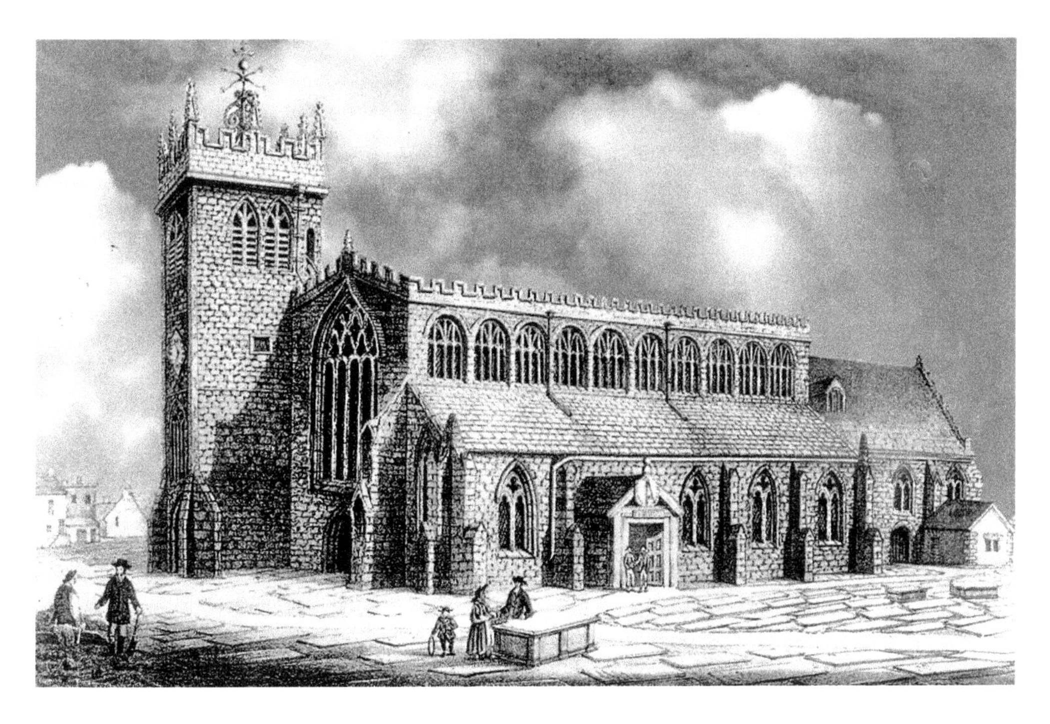

St Mary's Church

No doubt located on the site of an earlier wooden church, St Mary's, as seen in this drawing of around 1800, was built by the rector of Stockport, Richard de Vernon, between 1306 and 1334. Due to poor foundations, the main body of the building had to be demolished in 1810 and replaced in 1817 by the present church of Gothic style. However, the original fourteenth-century chancel, the oldest architecture in the town, still remains as can be seen in the later photograph.

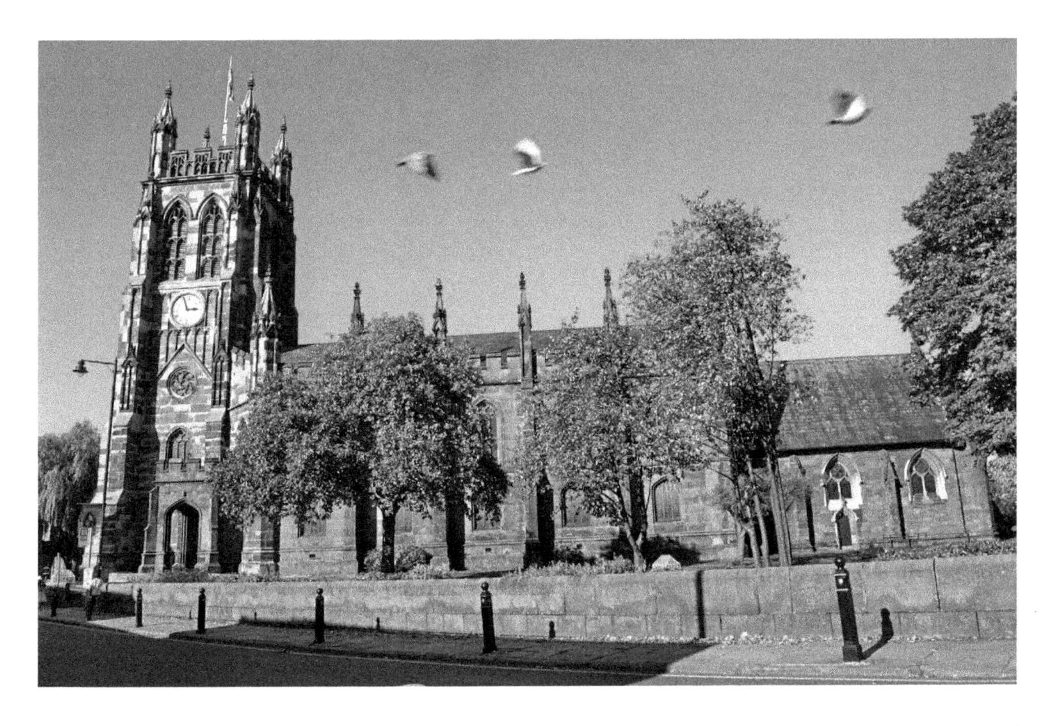

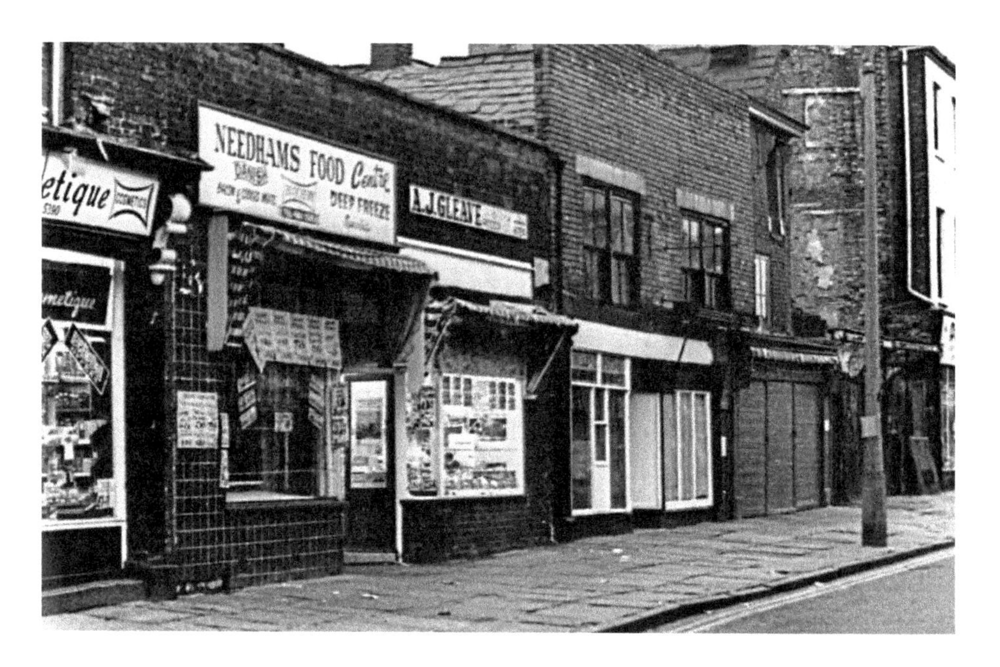

Staircase House

The Market Place was originally surrounded by shops and houses, most of which have been swept away by rebuilding. A remarkable survivor is Staircase House, the town house of the Shallcross family, saved from demolition by the efforts of Steve and Jean Cliffe with the support of Stockport Heritage Trust. Our earlier photograph shows the Georgian brick frontage, which concealed the original 1460 cruck-framed house and an amazing caged newel staircase – hence its name. Now it is a museum that never fails to surprise visitors after they have passed the rather plain frontage.

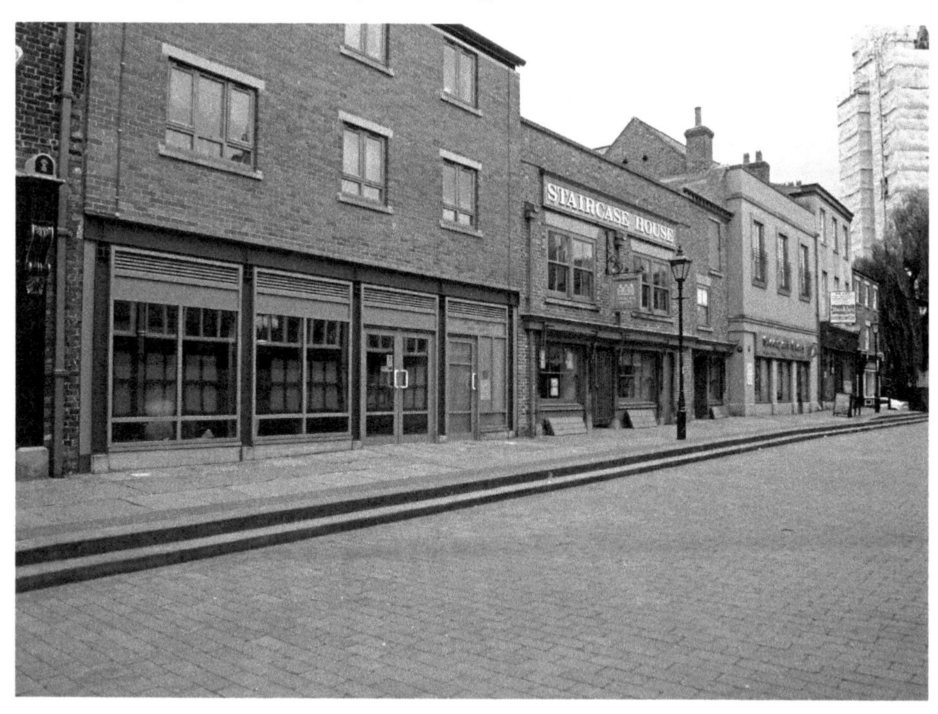

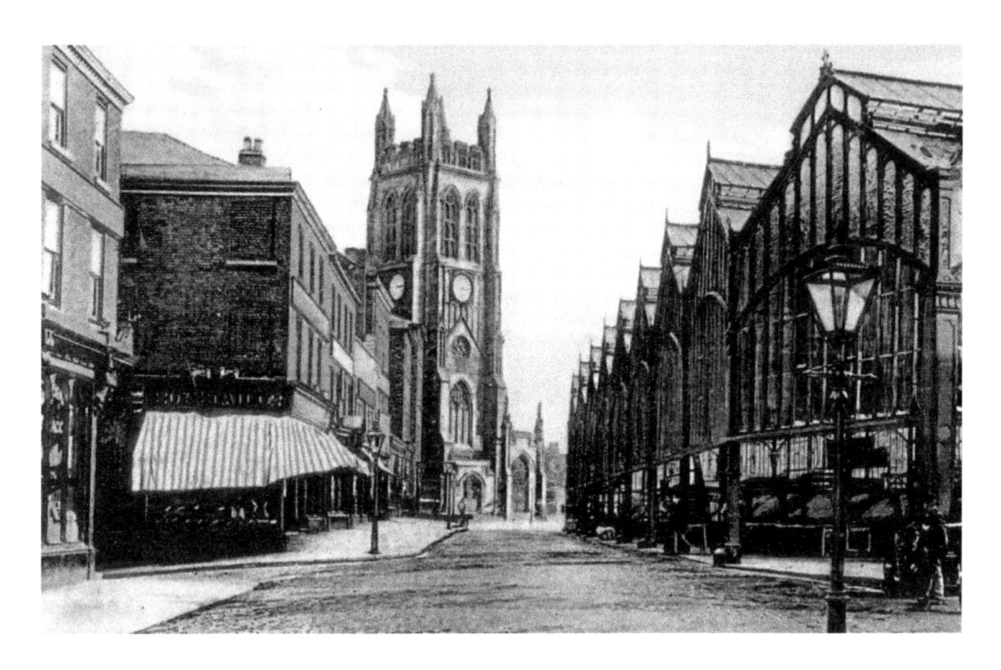

Market Hall

In 1850 the Stockport Corporation bought the manorial rights from Lord Vernon and immediately commenced a range of improvements to the market. The large glass and iron Market Hall was part of these works and opened in 1862. Because it was originally open-sided, it was soon nicknamed 'the glass umbrella'. The traders, led by Ephraim Marks of the Marks & Spencer families, complained of draughts, and the sides were progressively boarded in. Amazingly, demolition was proposed in the 1970s; only a vigorous public campaign saved it for the wonderful market of today.

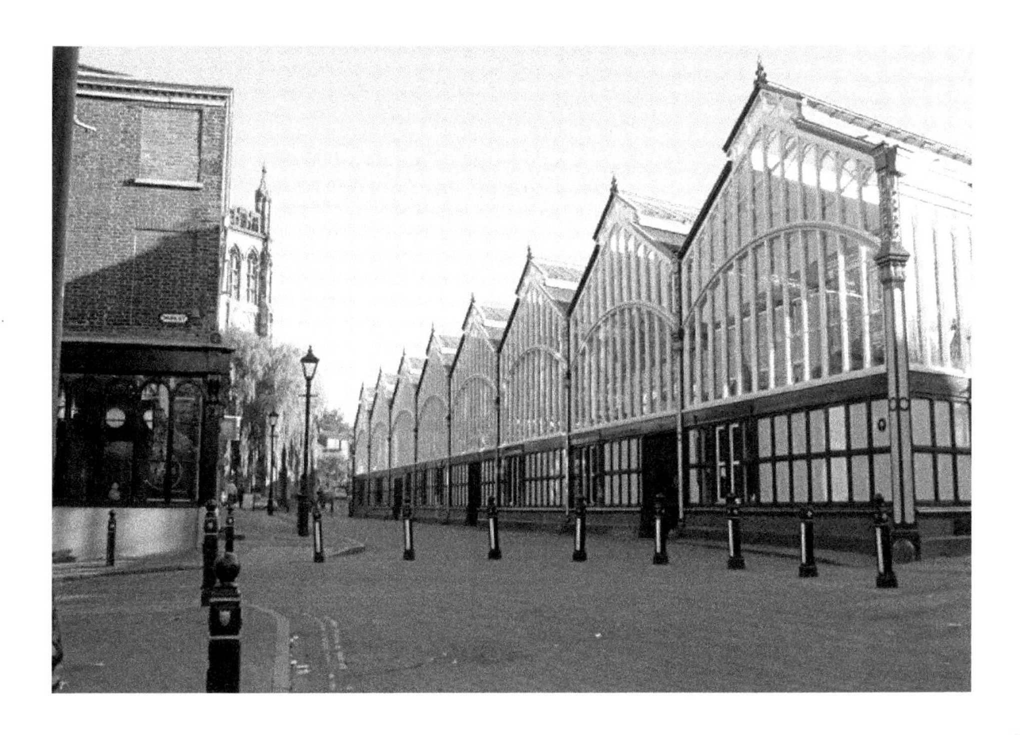

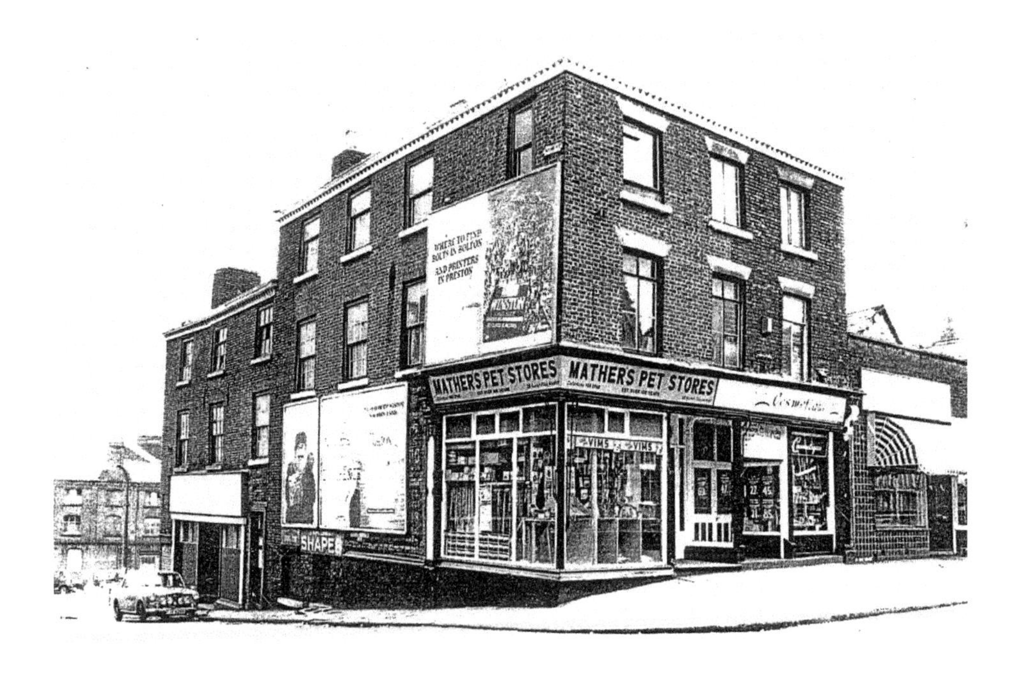

Mather's Pet Stores

The road alongside the Market Hall and Staircase House is now called 'The Mile' and at one end was Mather's Pet Stores, where, in the window, could be seen puppies and kittens for sale. Regeneration of the area of Shawcross Fold saw Mather's become Blackshaw's Café and the installation of a wonderful shop window. This window was recovered during the demolition of a baker's shop on Hillgate (Blackshaw's, appropriately) and was stored by the council for thirty years waiting for a suitable development to reuse it.

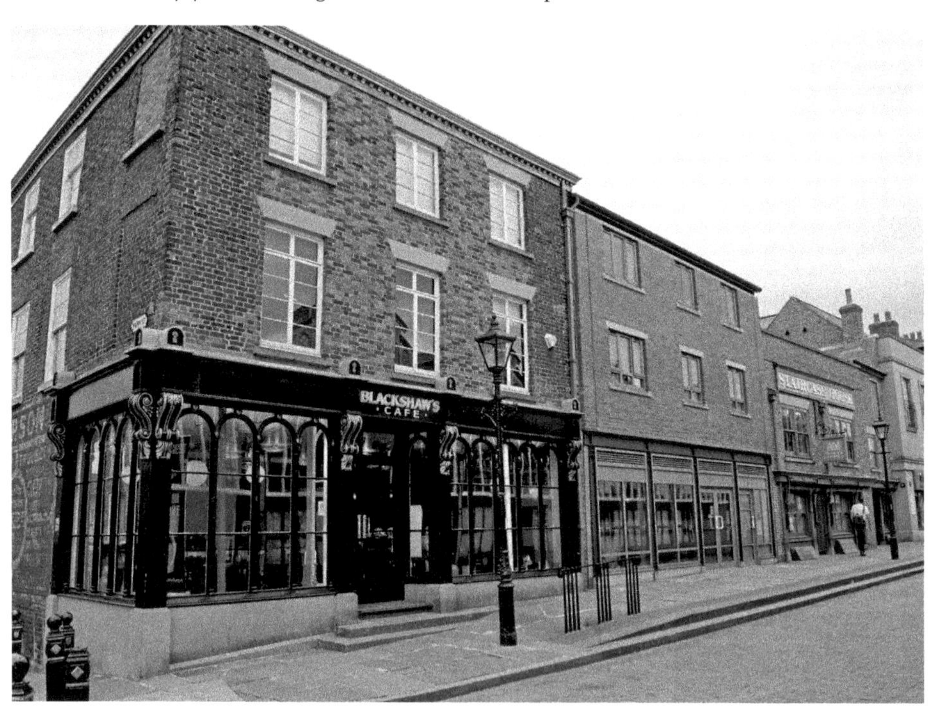

Boars Head Hotel

One of the oldest hostelries in the Market Place, the hotel's name reflects its situation on the corner of the brow that led down to the town's pig market. Legend says that butchers, needing a drink, would take their newly purchased pigs into the pub to avoid having them stolen. The door, blocked off in the modern picture, gave the hotel an address in the Market Place, and thereby considerable prestige. The lattice post was used by a short-lived trolleybus system that extended to Offerton Fold. Today it has been replaced by a CCTV mast.

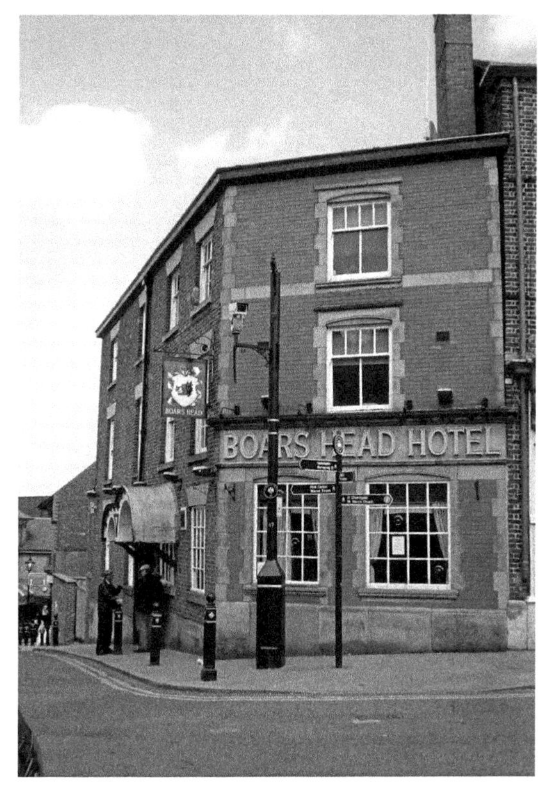

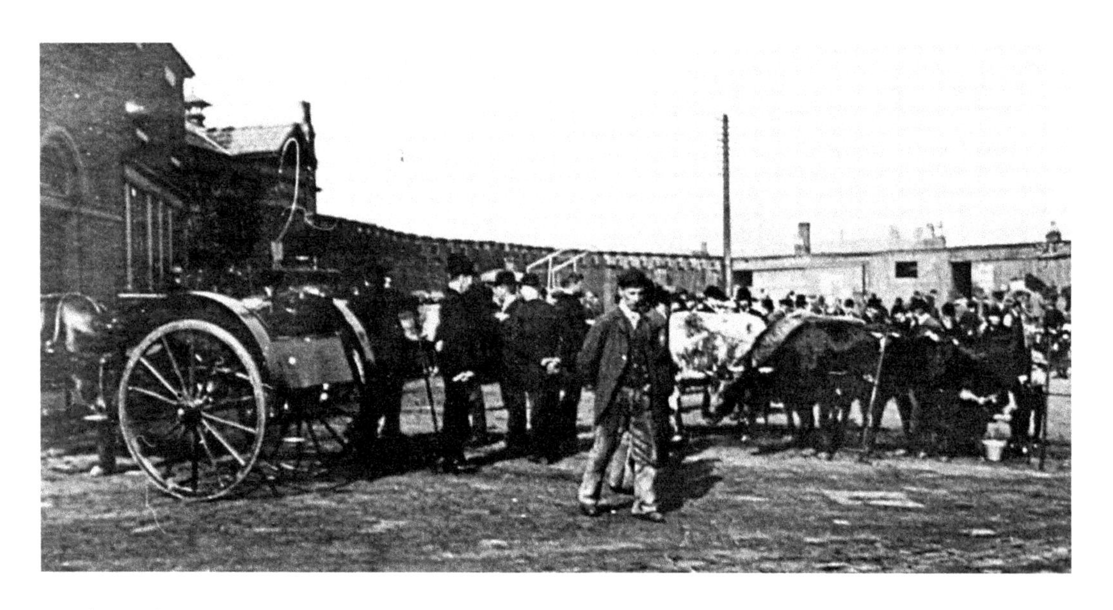

Castle Yard

This was the site of Stockport Castle, which overlooked the river and guarded the bridge across to Lancashire. It was swept away in the 1770s to allow construction of the town's first powered cotton mill. In 1827 there was much excitement when a balloon ascent was made from its yard. Unsuited to changes in cotton production and underpowered, the mill was demolished in 1841. The extra space was initially used for a potato market and then for cattle. Today the new Courts development overlooks Castle Yard, its profile echoing the Market Hall.

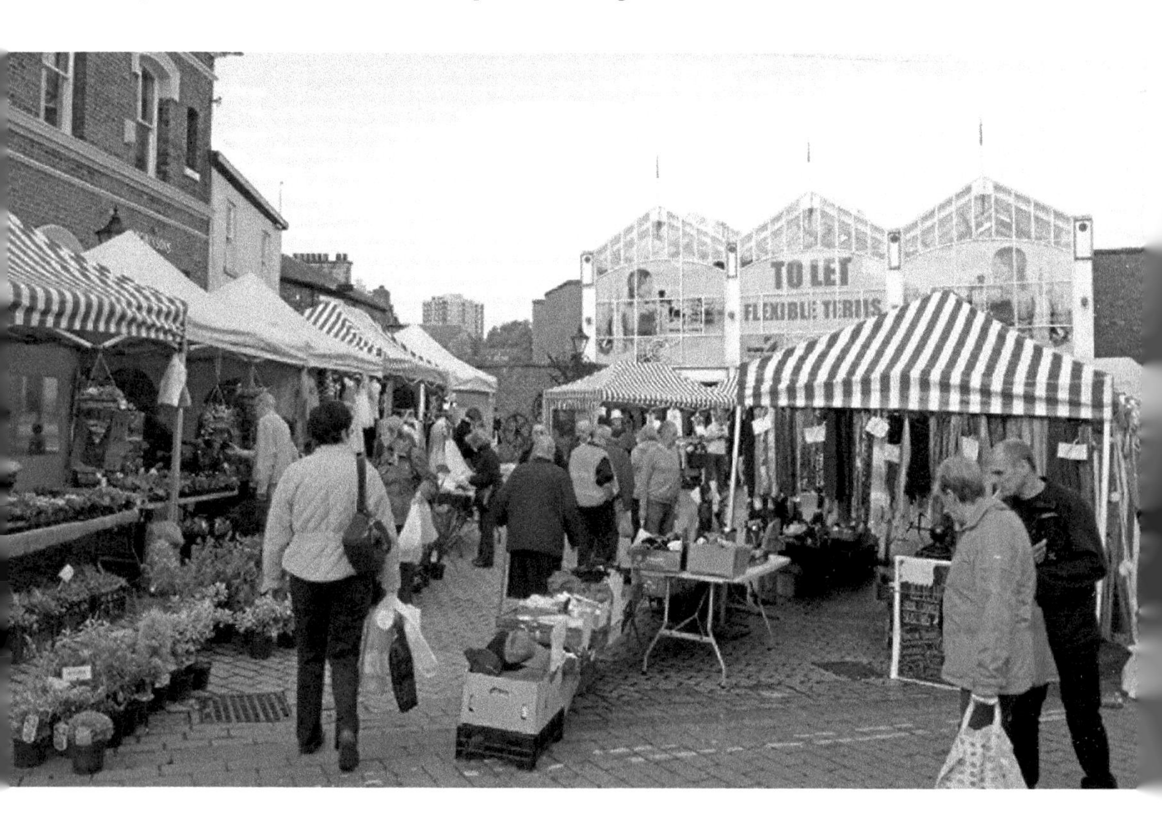

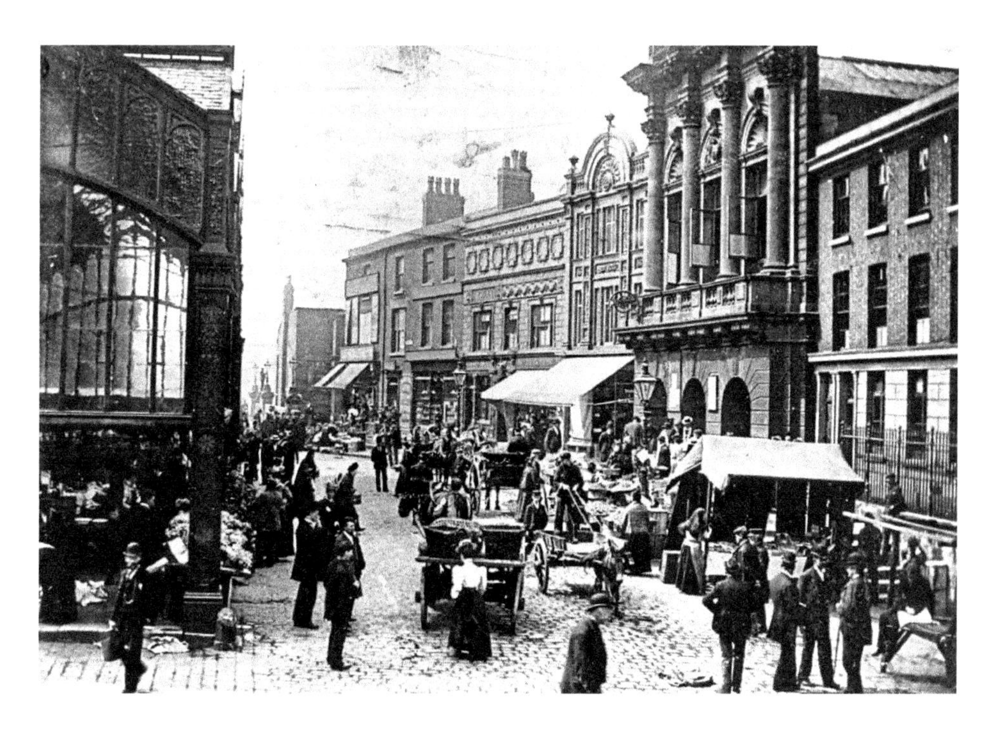

Market Hall and Lost Bay

Close scrutiny of the two photographs reveals the loss of one of the hall's bays. In the busy scene of about 1900 gable windows are evident, but today all signs of the bay have disappeared apart from a row of brackets along the gutter. This was due to 'the trackless tram' (a trolleybus system to Offerton), which opened in 1913. The tight bend at the corner of the hall was widened by the removal of the offending bay, in hindsight a mistake as by 1920 the fragile trolleybuses had finished.

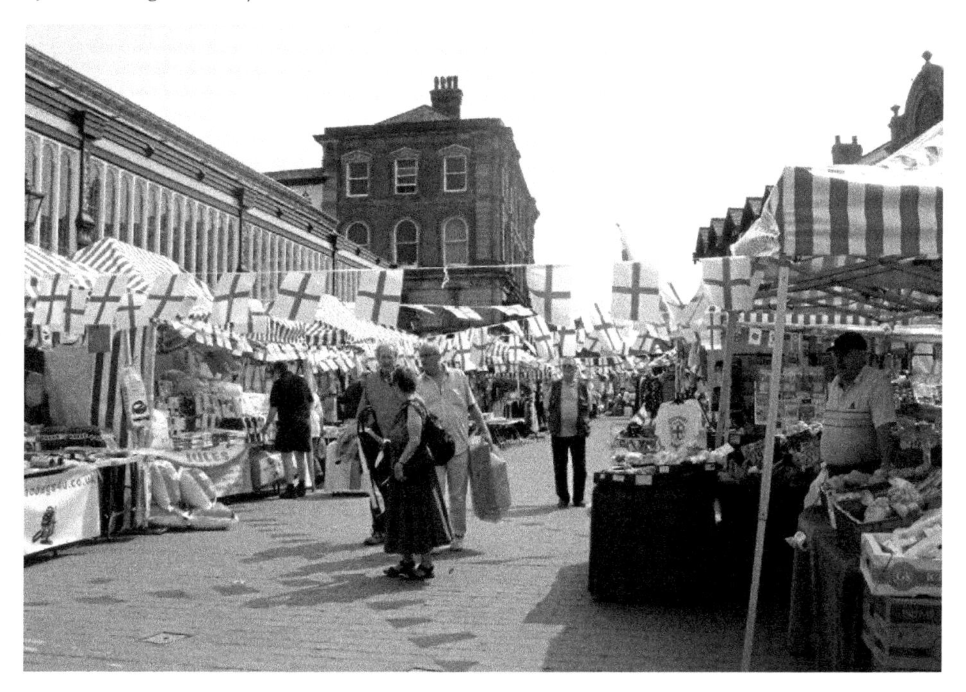

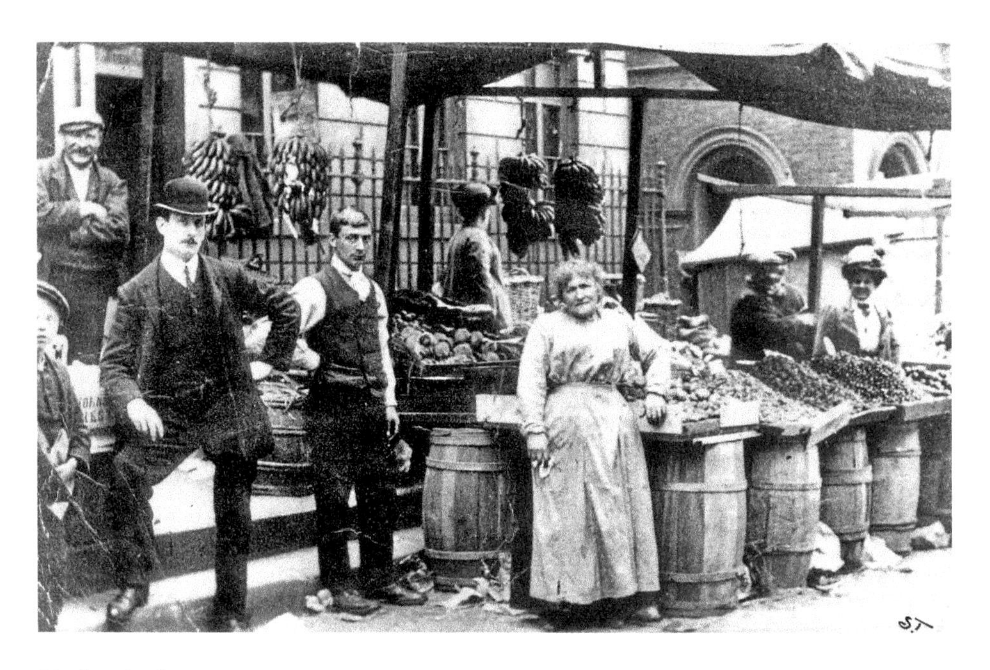

Market Stall

Any picture collection of the market would not be complete without an example of market stalls, in this case fruit and vegetables. Compare the makeshift counter of around 1910, with upturned barrels that have been used to bring the produce in, to today's purpose-built staging and colourful awning. But scrutiny shows an even greater unexplained contrast: the earlier scene has four huge hands of bananas hanging up on the railings. Today, there is a single bunch! Don't we eat bananas anymore?

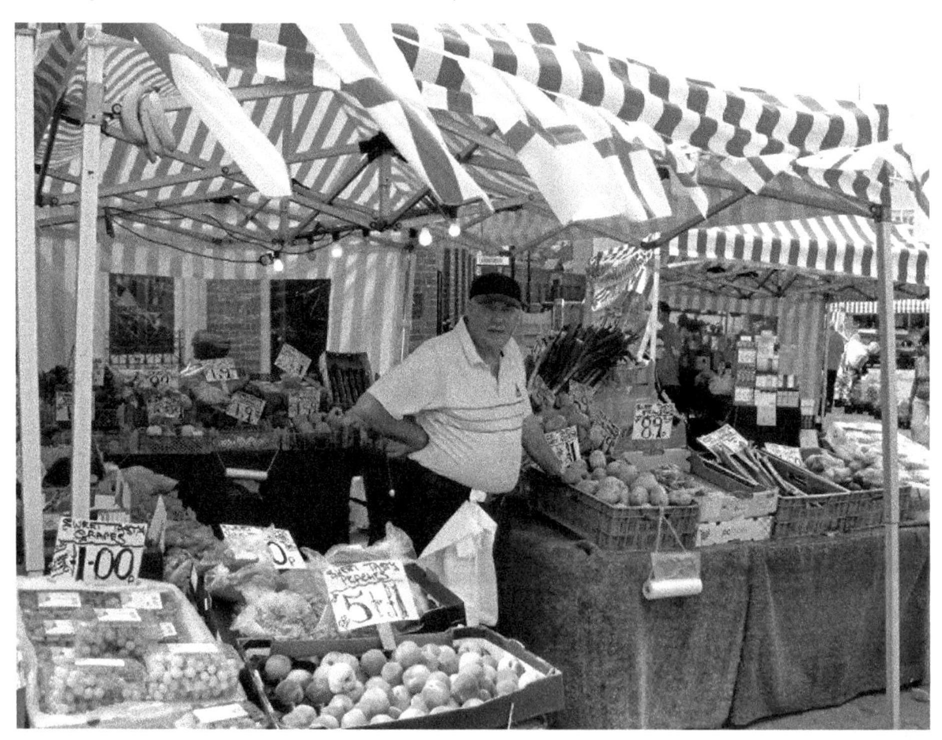

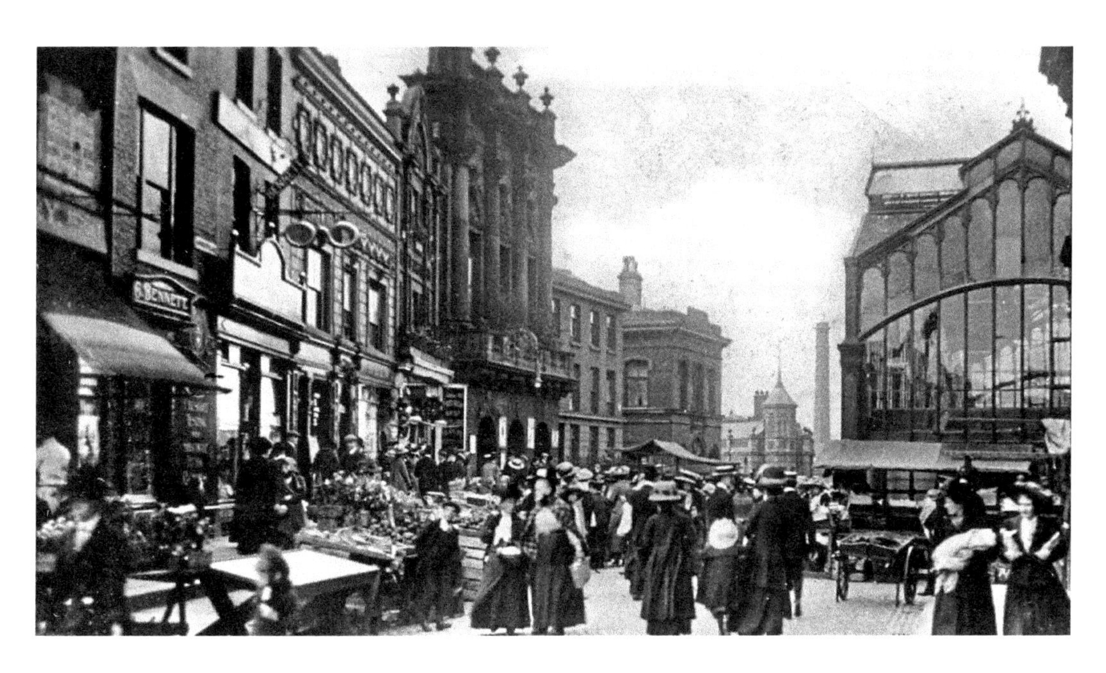

Produce Hall

This hall was one of the first improvements made by the Stockport Corporation after it acquired the market rights. It was opened in 1852 as a cheese exchange but use was also made of the balustraded balcony at the base of the columns for formal announcements. Our earlier scene shows the largest spectacles in Stockport that led myopics to Bennett's the opticians. In the modern regeneration of this row of buildings, the white-faced former Angel Inn stands out. A very early inn in the Market Place, it is more notable as the location of one of the first theatres in the town.

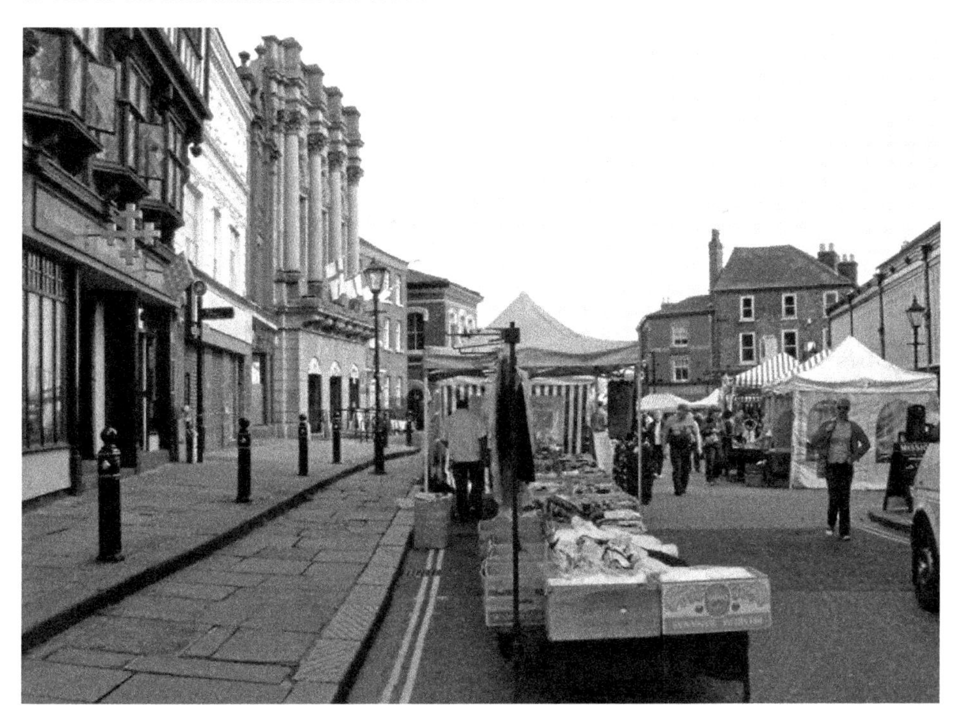

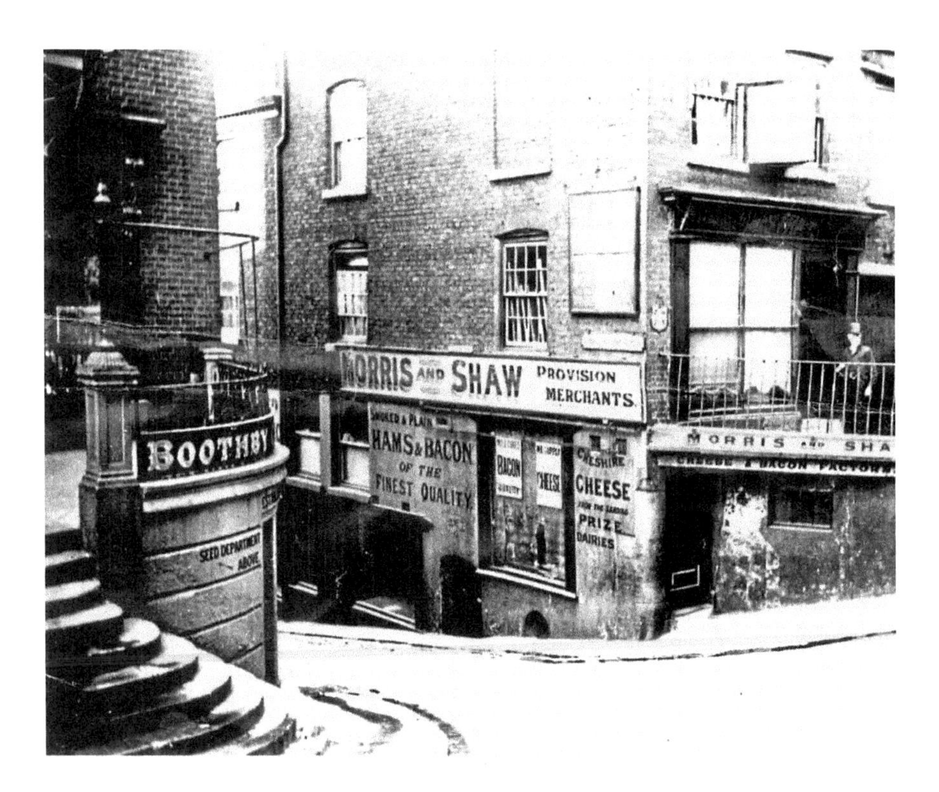

Mealhouse Brow

One of the ancient tracks into the Market Place, Mealhouse Brow is so named because the town's grain was kept, in earlier times, in a building at the top of the slope. Ideally placed at the bottom of the brow were the town's bakehouse and the Lord of the Manor's ovens, which no doubt yielded another worthwhile income for his manor. The gentleman on the pavement, in our later scene, stands outside the location of an early 'fish and chips' shop in Stockport, its proprietor of 1896 being one John Porter.

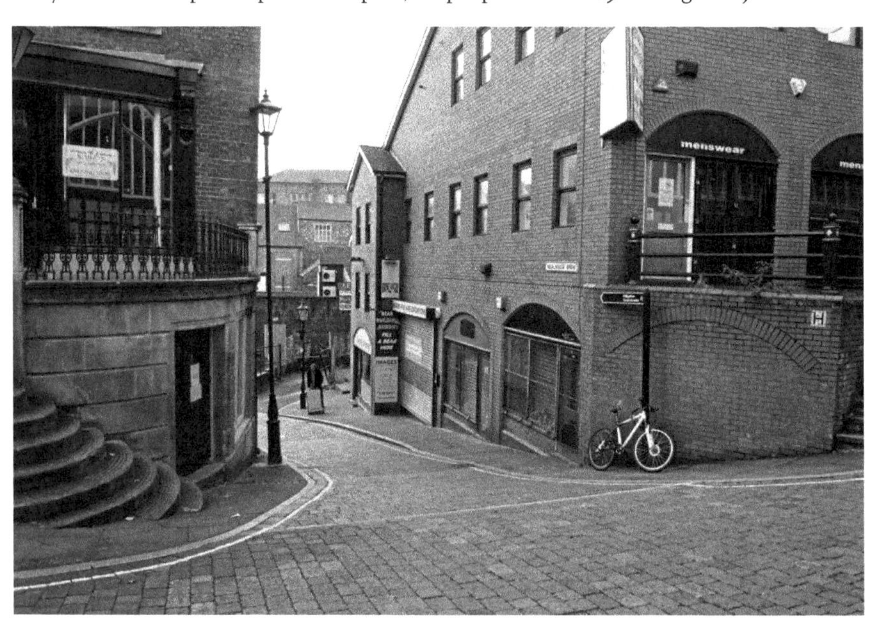

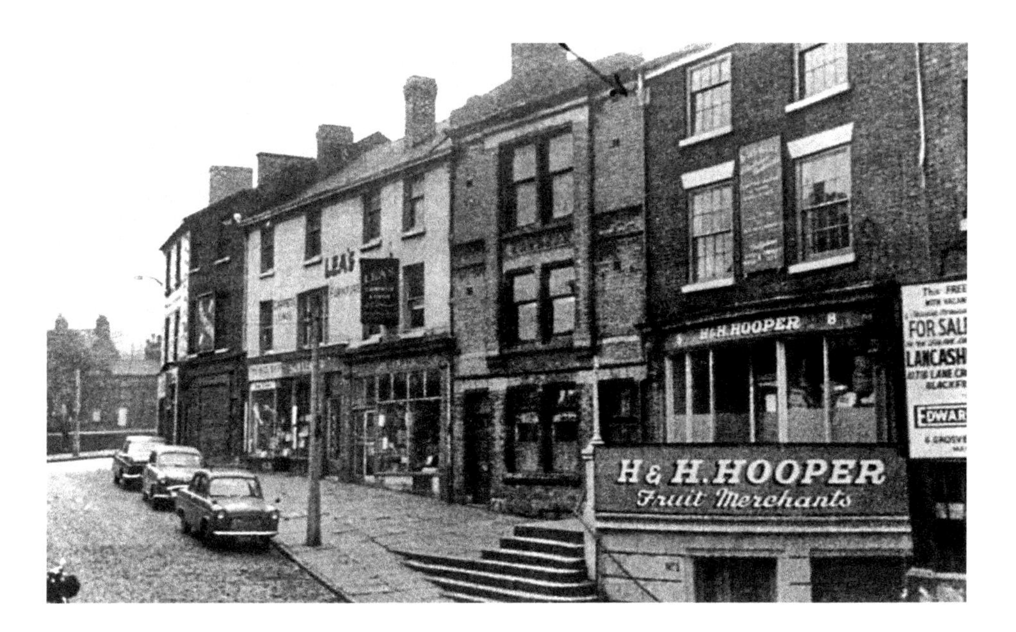

Court Leet and Dungeon

In the 1950s, Hooper's occupied a building, the town's old Court Leet, where burgesses would have met to run the town. Here the town's justice was carried out; below were several cells for locking up miscreants before they faced magistrates. It is Stockport's oldest municipal building, dating to the fifteenth century, and by 1790 the functions had moved to more suitable premises. Every now and again the members of Stockport Heritage Trust open up the 'dungeon', whose history, despite its later frontage, never ceases to amaze visitors both young and old.

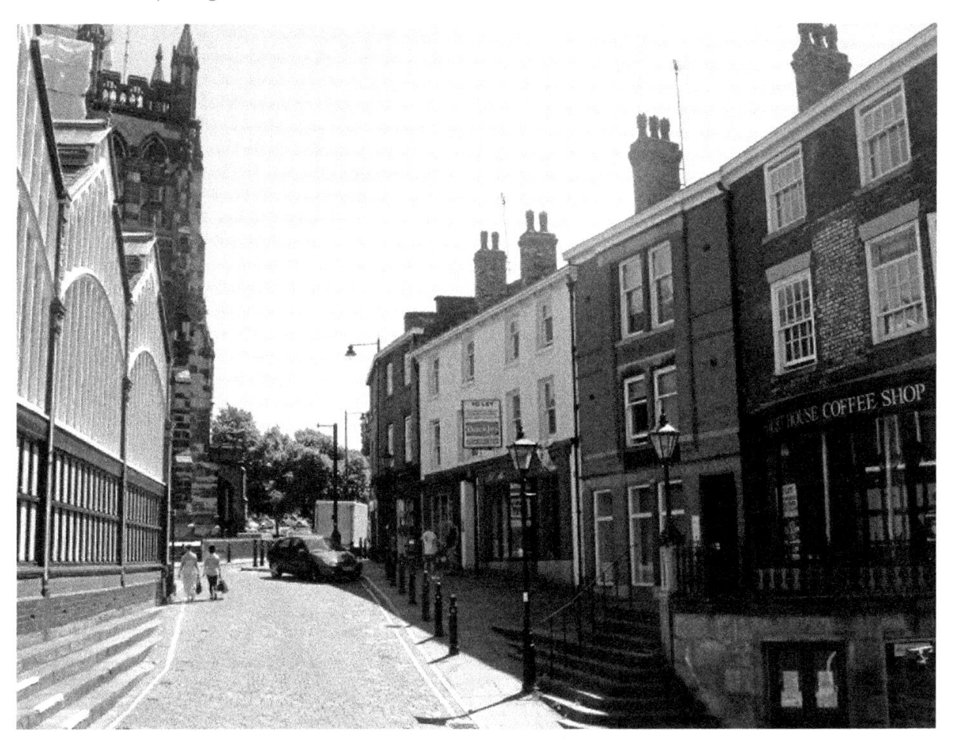

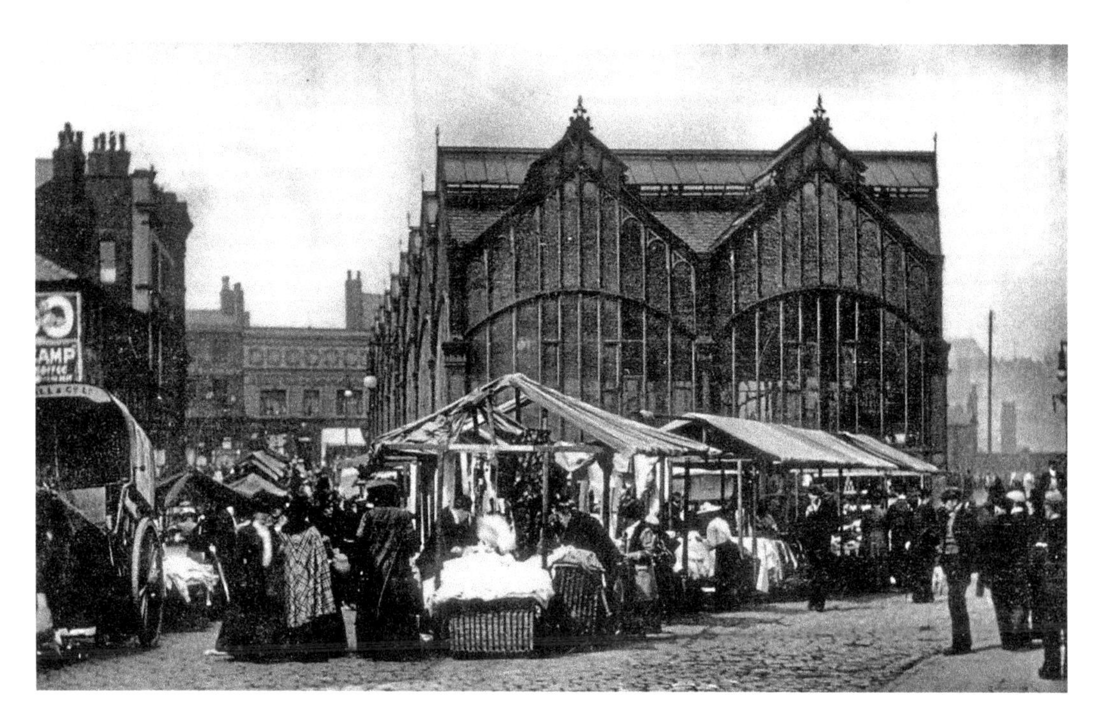

Market Hall

This magnificent hall narrows to two bays at the south end due to the irregular shape of the Market Place. The four missing gables at the north end were the same as the ones shown here. It is sad to see the reduced scale of the market – emphasised by the disappearance of stalls along Churchgate and past Mealhouse Brow. Trading from No. 3 in the Market Place was the wholesale grocer W. J. Hall, whose smart delivery cart on the left, with patient horse, waits for its next delivery.

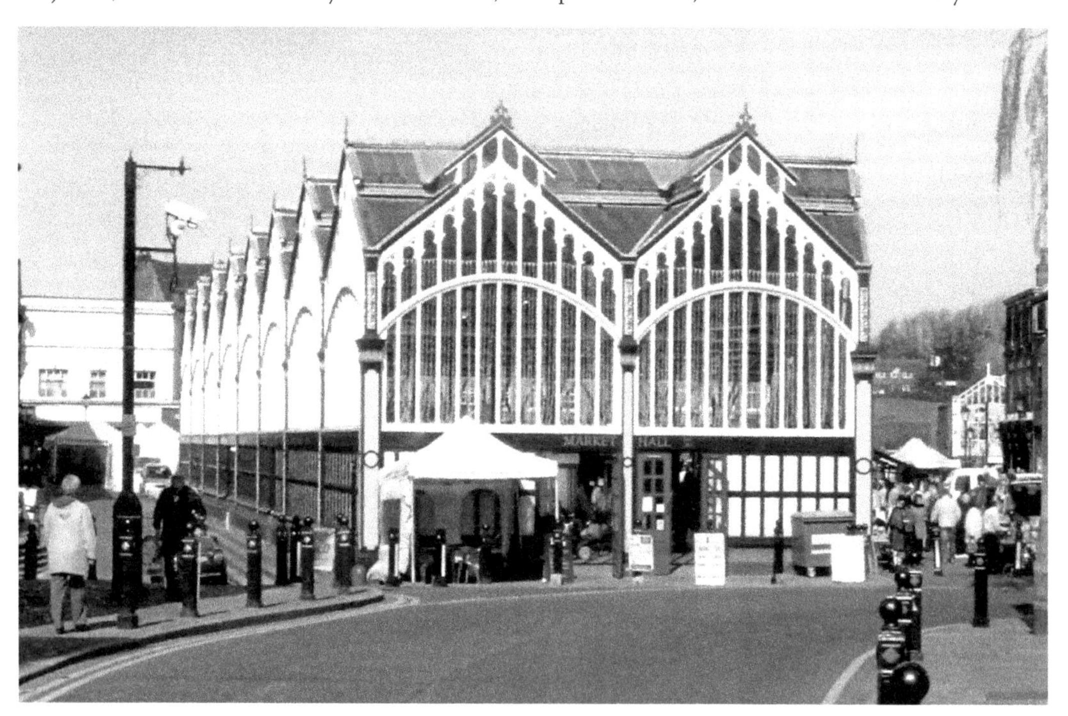

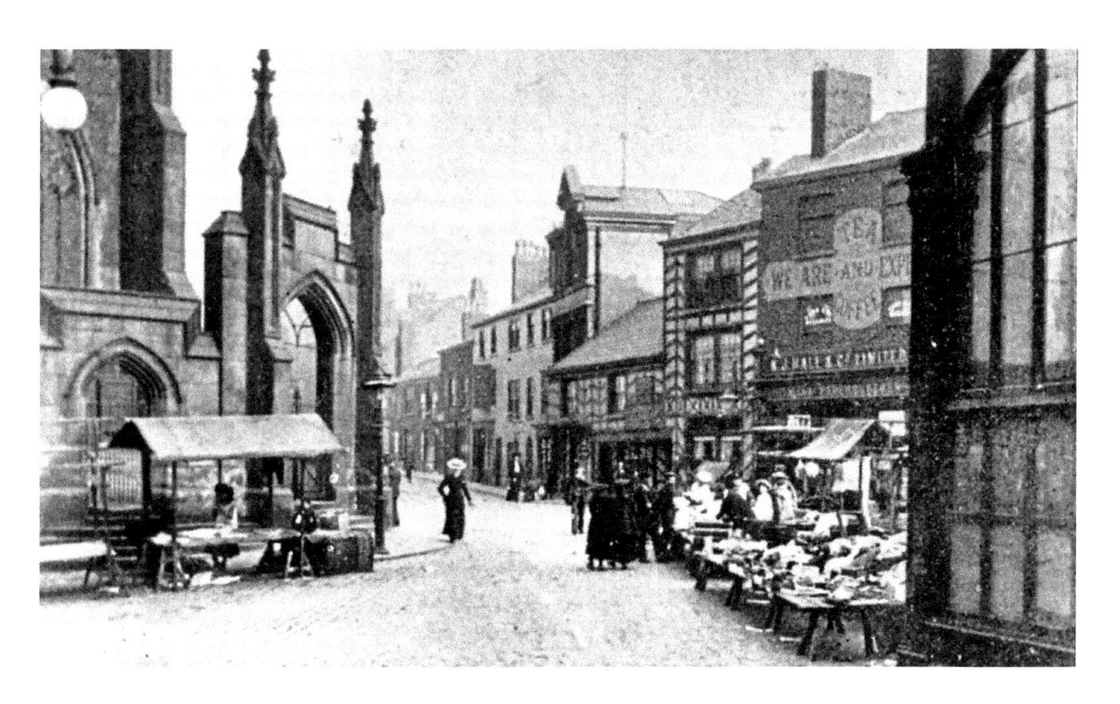

Church Gates and the Packhorse

W. J. Hall's emporium specialised in tea and coffee. The building was constructed in about 1850, replacing the Rose and Crown, the only pub in Stockport with a much-abused twenty-four-hour licence for market users. Next door lies the black-and-white Packhorse Hotel, pleasingly rebuilt in a similar style in 1931. The Gothic-style church gates date back to the 1817 rebuild. The nineteenth century was a more leisurely time for pedestrians, judging by the elegantly dressed lady strolling in the middle of the road compared with today's car dodging.

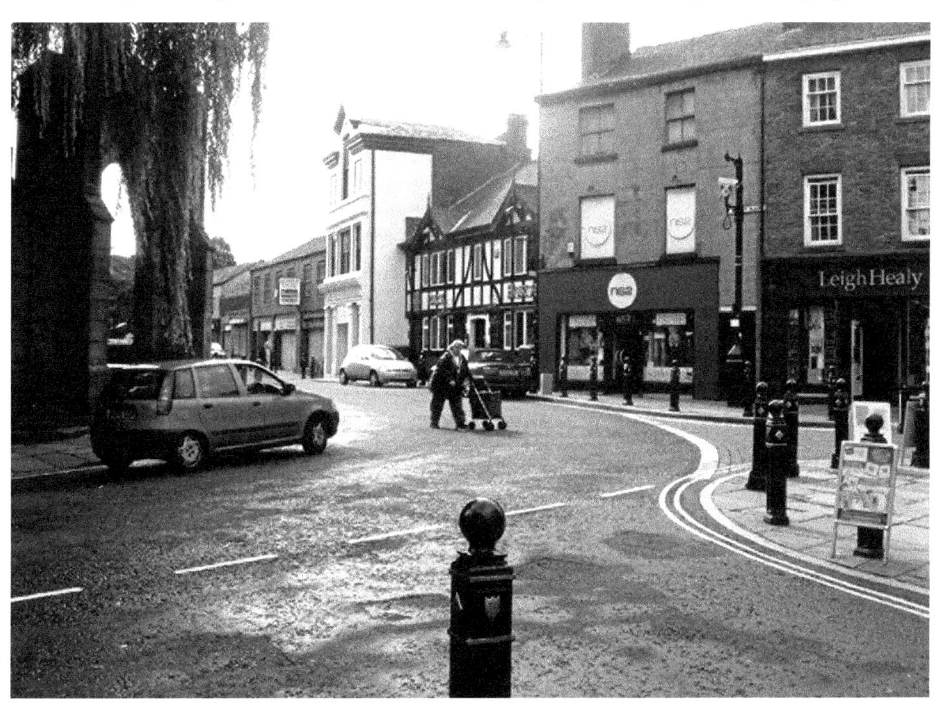

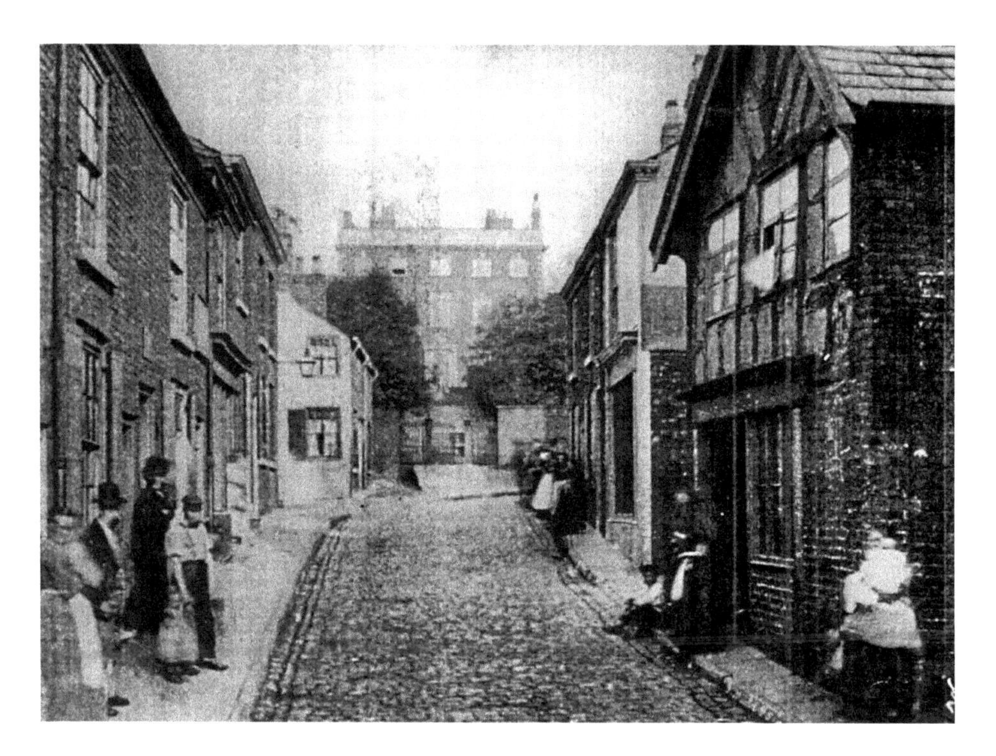

Churchgate

Thought to be part of the Roman road from Manchester to London, Churchgate had the appearance of an ancient thoroughfare until its widening in the nineteenth century. The mean-looking buildings on the right were demolished as part of the road improvements, but on the other side they remained until the 1960s. In the distant gloom can be seen the rectory, rebuilt in 1744, its elevation enabling the rectors and later the bishops of Stockport to look down on the town. It survived demolition proposals to become an impressive restaurant.

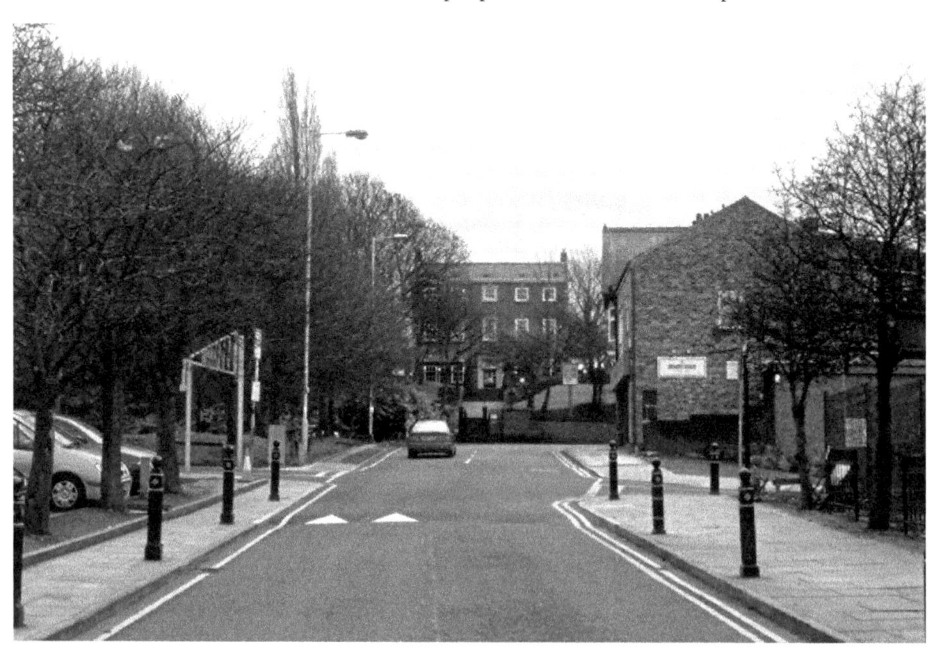

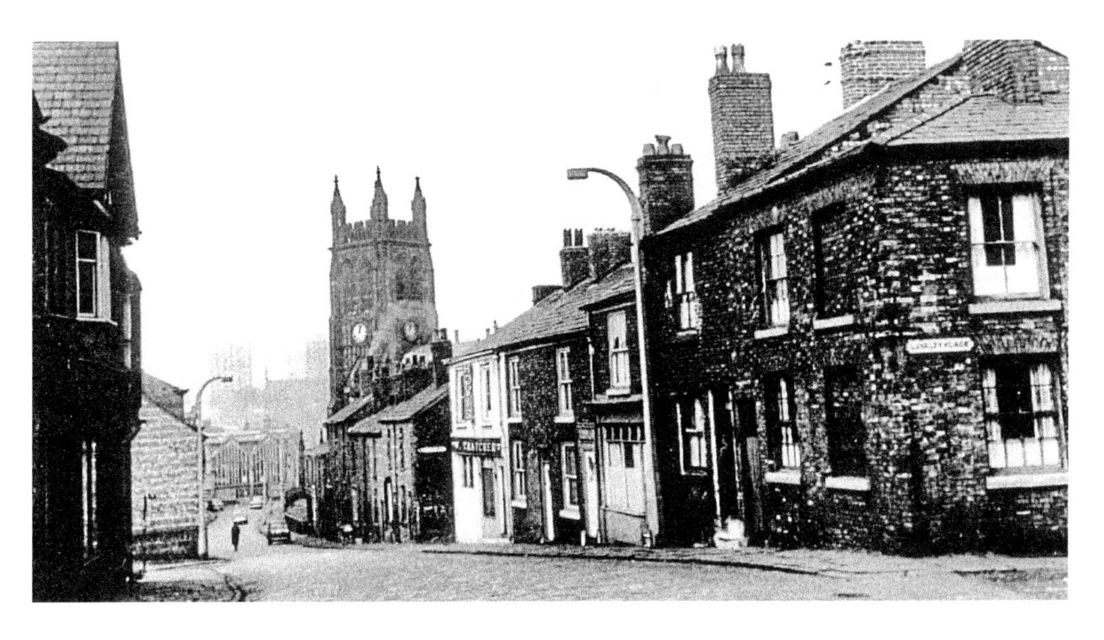

Loyalty Place

Near the front gate of the rectory, now called the Old Rectory, lies Loyalty Place, the scene of the infamous shooting of Constable Birch in 1819. Birch had arrested two radicals and was on his way back from reporting their arrests when he was accosted by three men. One, named McGhinnis, drew a pistol and fired a shot at the constable. Today there is no evidence of the drama, just the noise of a busy road. Birch's breastbone, complete with bullet, can be seen in the town museum.

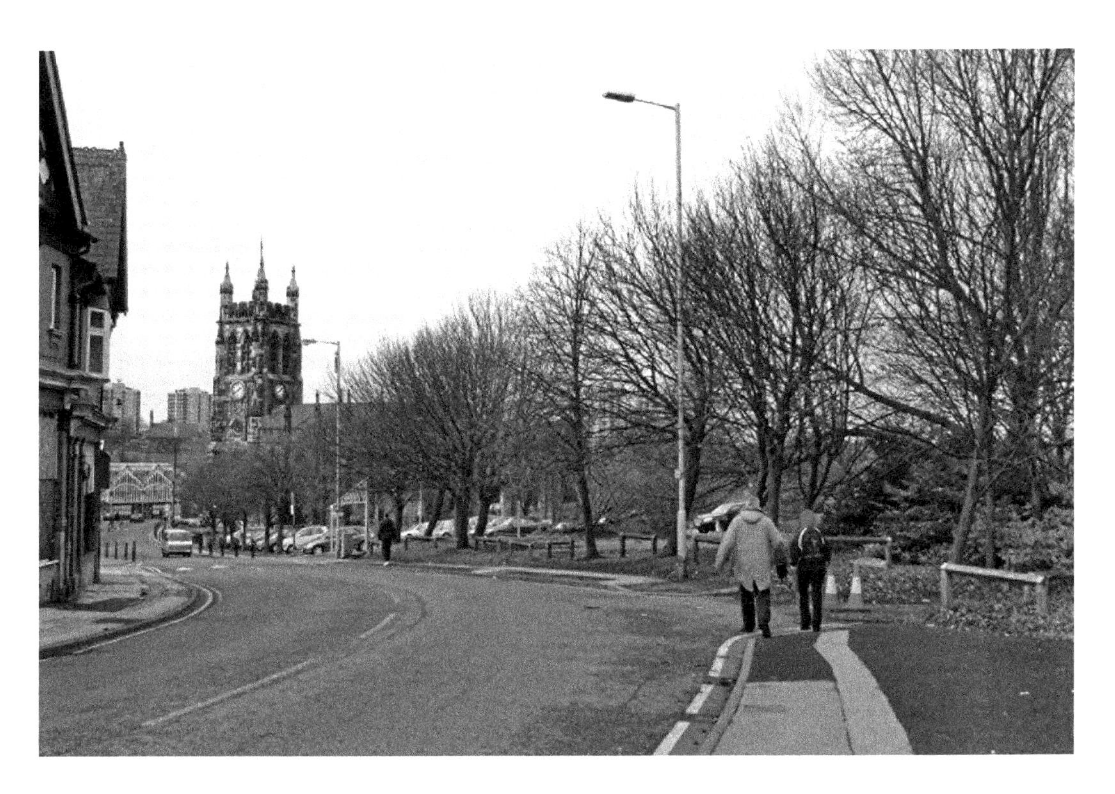

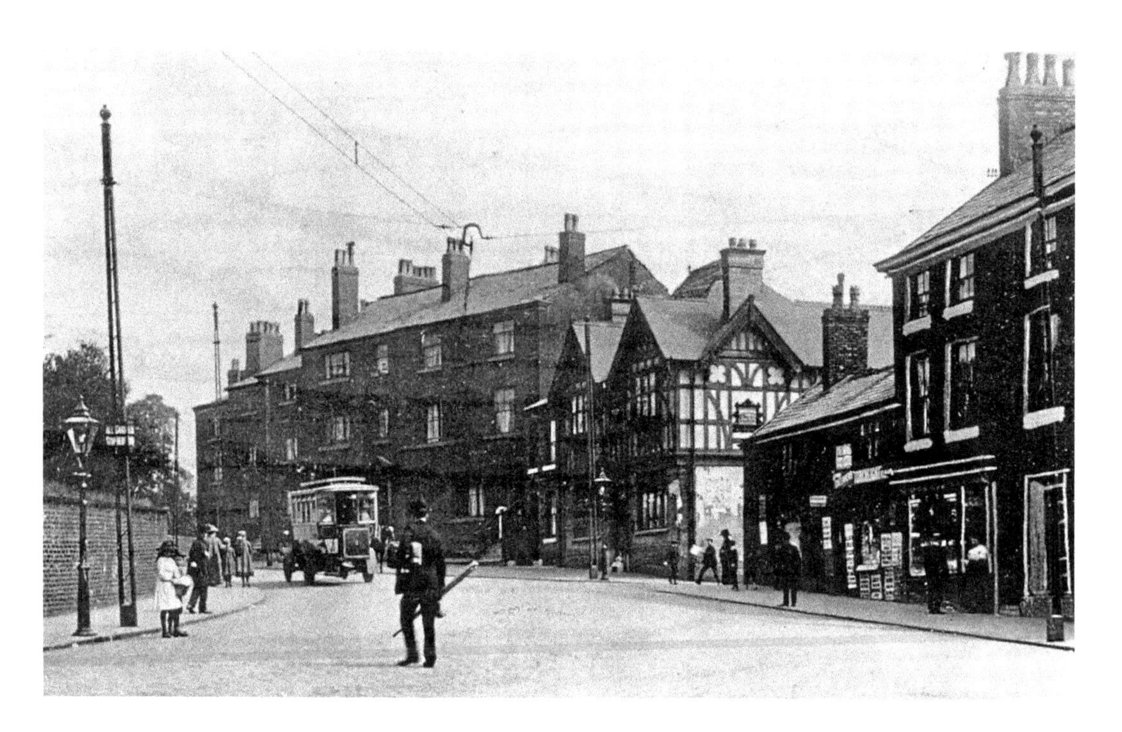

Trackless Tram

The newly opened trackless tram wends its way to Offerton on a peaceful summer's day before the carnage of 'the war to end war'. The scene has altered little over the years, apart from the replacement of the ornate gas lamp, the disappearance of the trolley post and wires, and modern traffic control. The Stockport trolleybus system was one of the first in the country and must have caused head scratching on the subject of what name to give the buses. The sign on the post reads 'All cars stop here' as though they were tramcars.

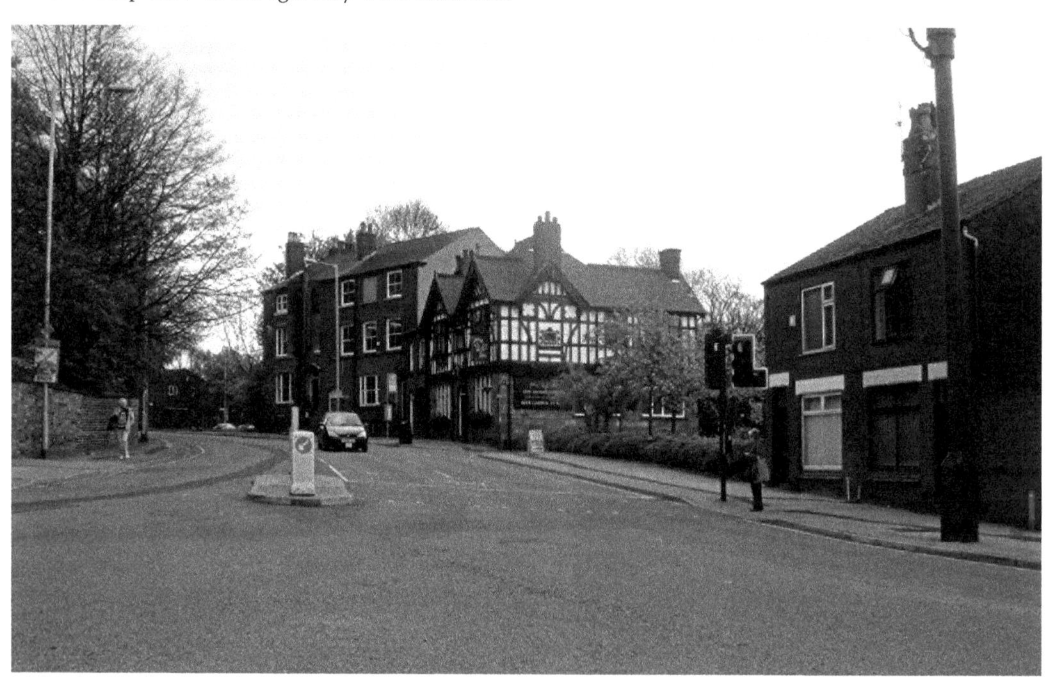

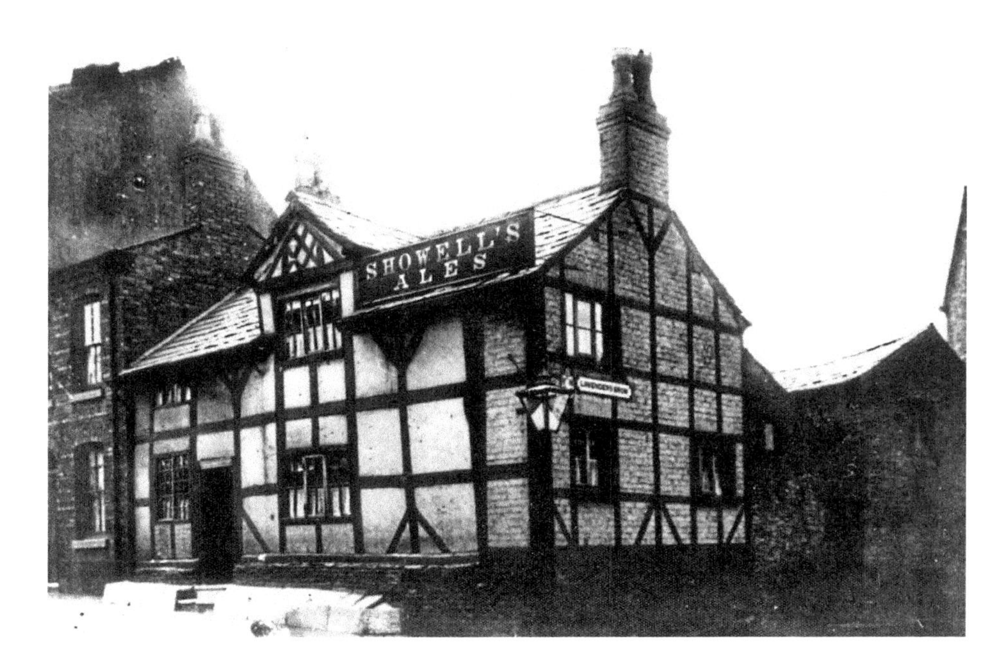

Thatched House

In 1792 this old timber-framed pub, the Thatched House, was the location of Dr James Briscall's dispensary for the sick, which was in the cellar. The dispensary later moved to Daw Bank, then, in 1833, to the magnificent Stockport Infirmary on Wellington Road. Showell's was one of the larger local breweries; its premises were next to Bell's Hempshaw Brook brewery. It must have taken confidence to hang a gas lamp from the corner of this rickety old pub. No wonder it was rebuilt in the early 1900s. Its new bulk overshadows the cottage next door.

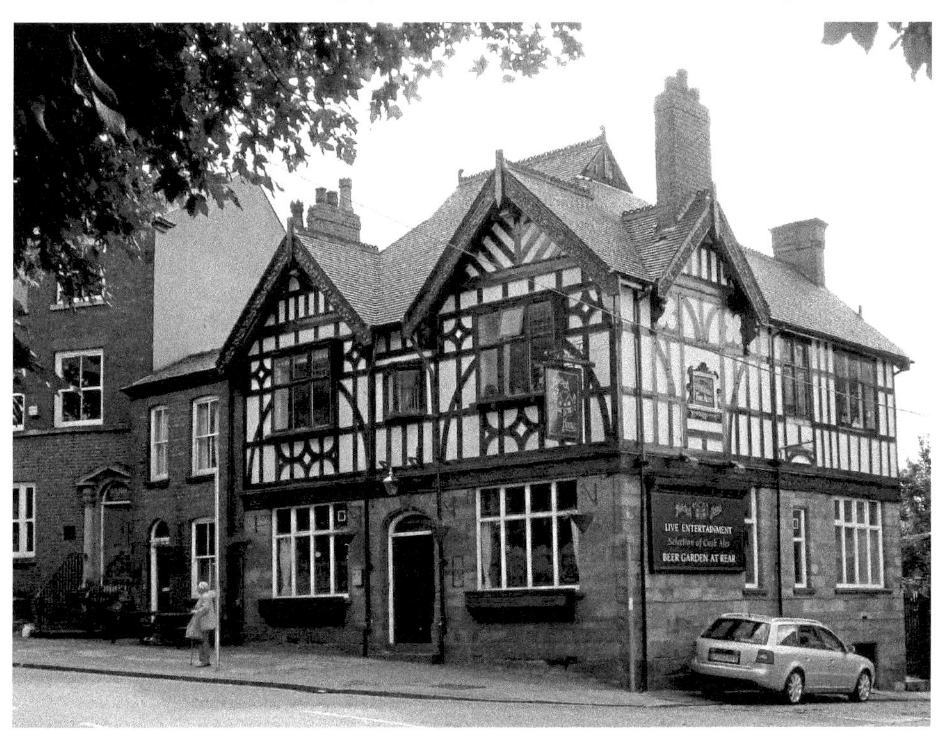

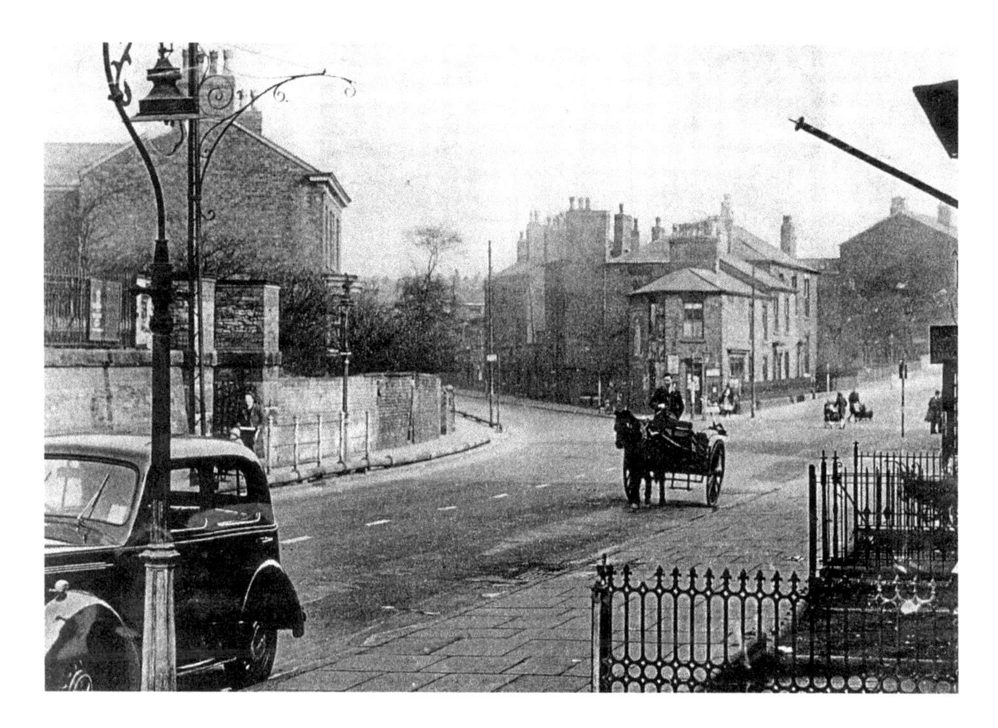

Hall Street

This picture dates to the Second World War. The emergency water pipe follows Turncroft Lane on the left, and some of the railings of the houses on the right have been taken for the war effort. The gate in the wall, now bricked up, went into St Mary's School, now a new housing estate. Behind Frank Hamnett, delivering milk by horse and cart, can be seen the old toll house for the Marple turnpike along Hall Street. Today protected by traffic lights, the new St Mary's Way pushes through towards the motorway.

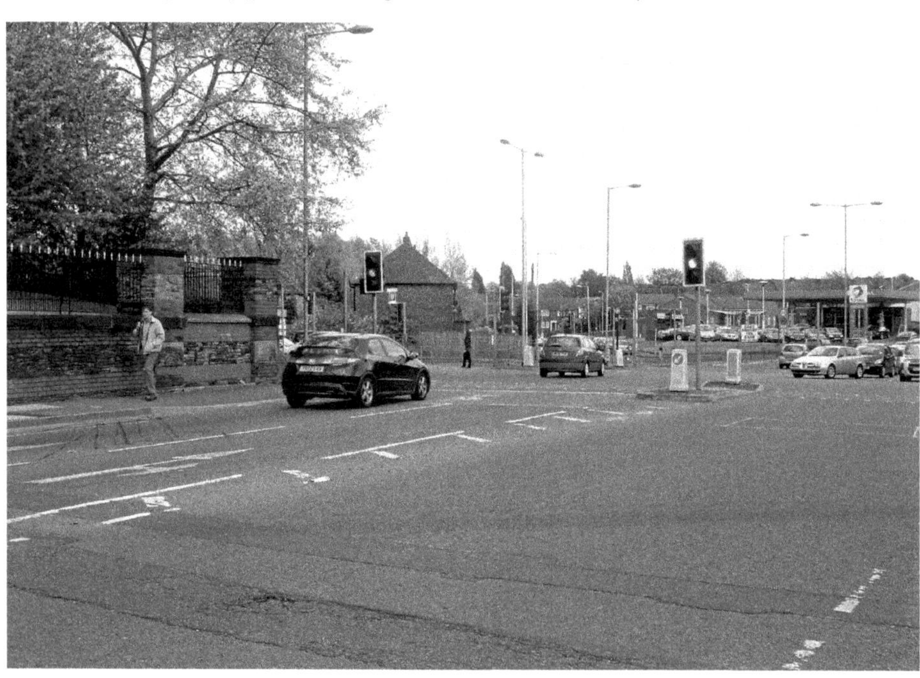

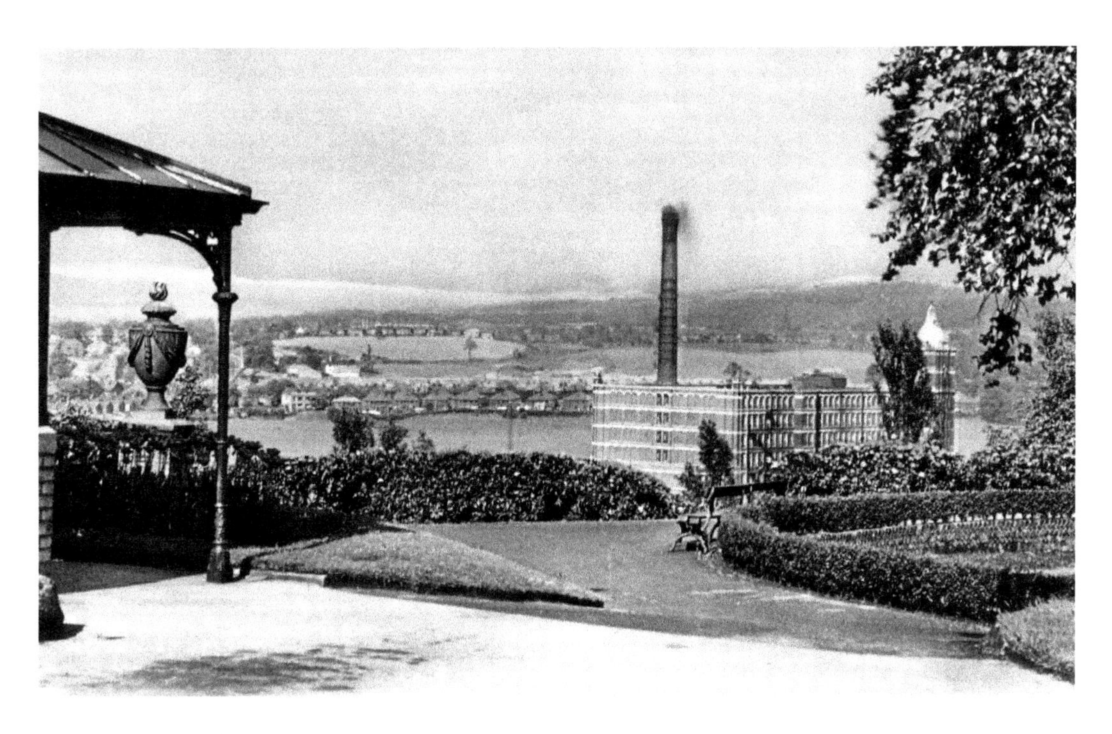

Vernon Park

In 1858, Lord Vernon gave a bequest to the town for a park, aptly called Vernon Park. From the museum and tearoom, fine views can be had over the Pennines. A little nearer, the new Pear Mill makes its presence felt. The pear-shaped dome on the roof conceals a water tank for fighting fires that is still evident in today's picture. The park recently benefited from a National Lottery grant and has been regenerated to again provide recreation for the town.

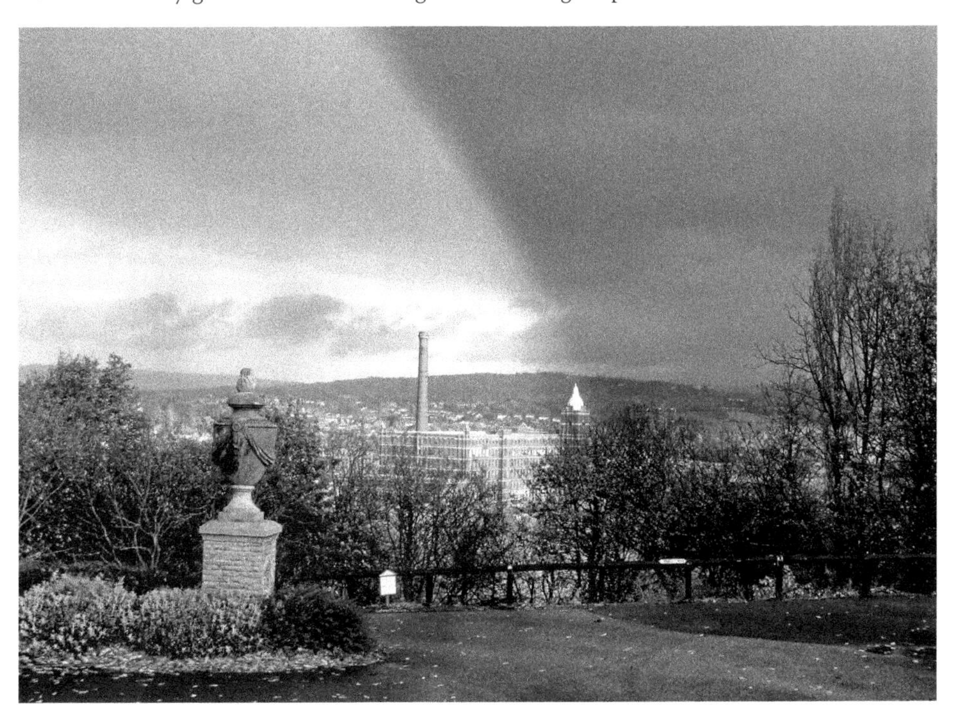

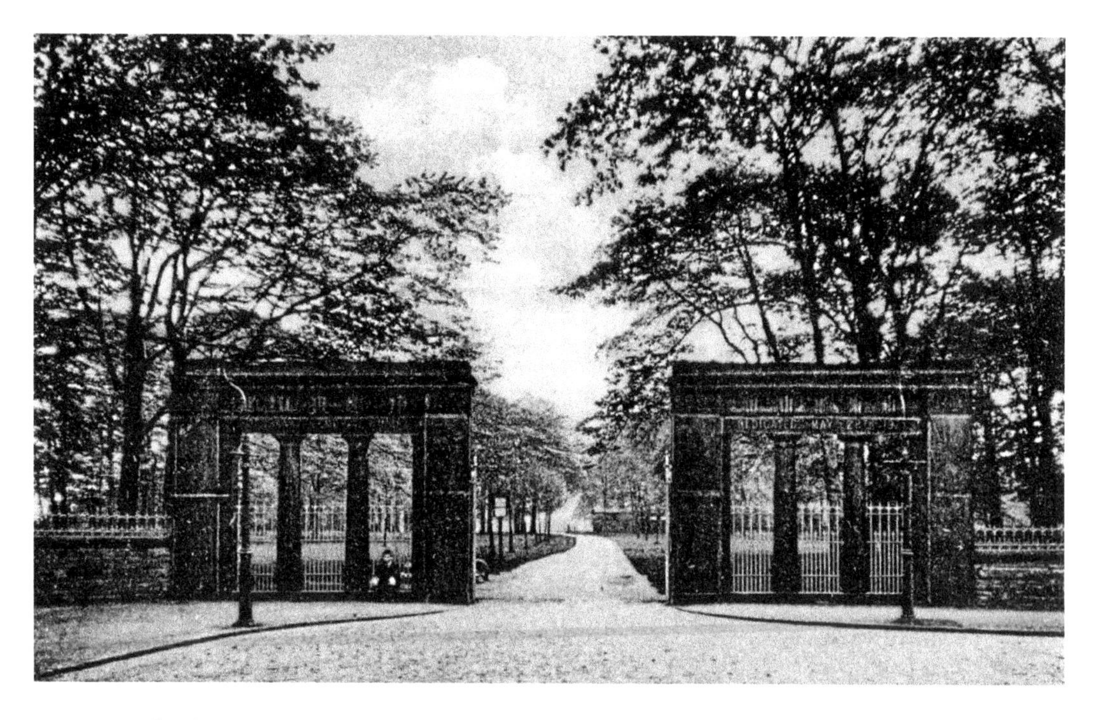

Woodbank Park

Alongside Vernon Park lies the estate of Woodbank Hall, which was built by the Stockport cotton magnate Peter Marsland. At the end of the First World War, the then-owner Sir Thomas Rowbotham, a former mayor of Stockport, bequeathed the house and park to the people of the town as a memorial to the sacrifices made in the war. At the entrance an imposing gateway was erected as a permanent reminder, but not so permanent in that a lorry managed to demolish half of the gate, as we can see. Recent regeneration, including new car parking facilities and landscaping, is changing things again.

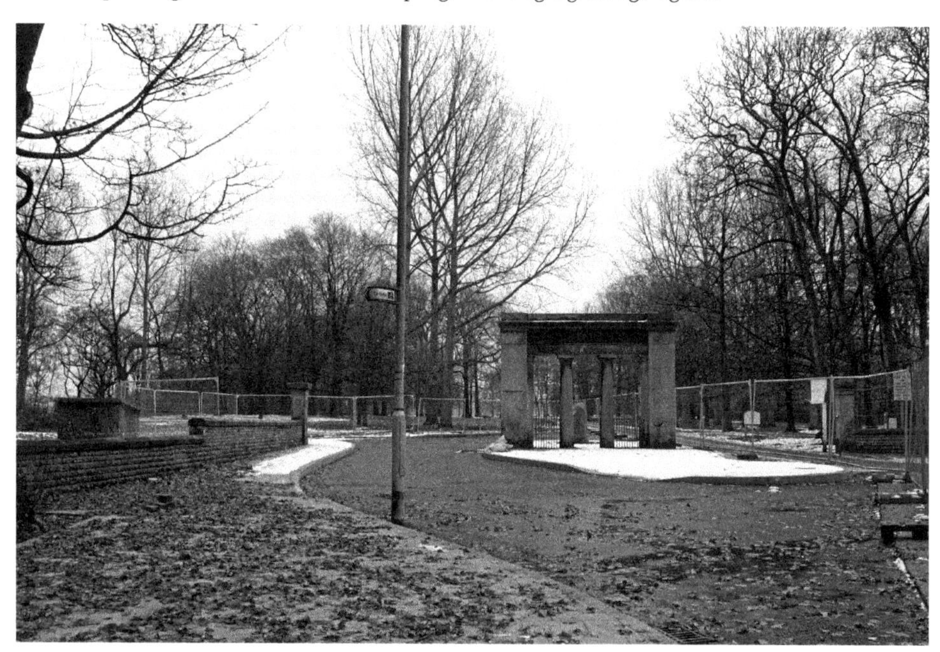

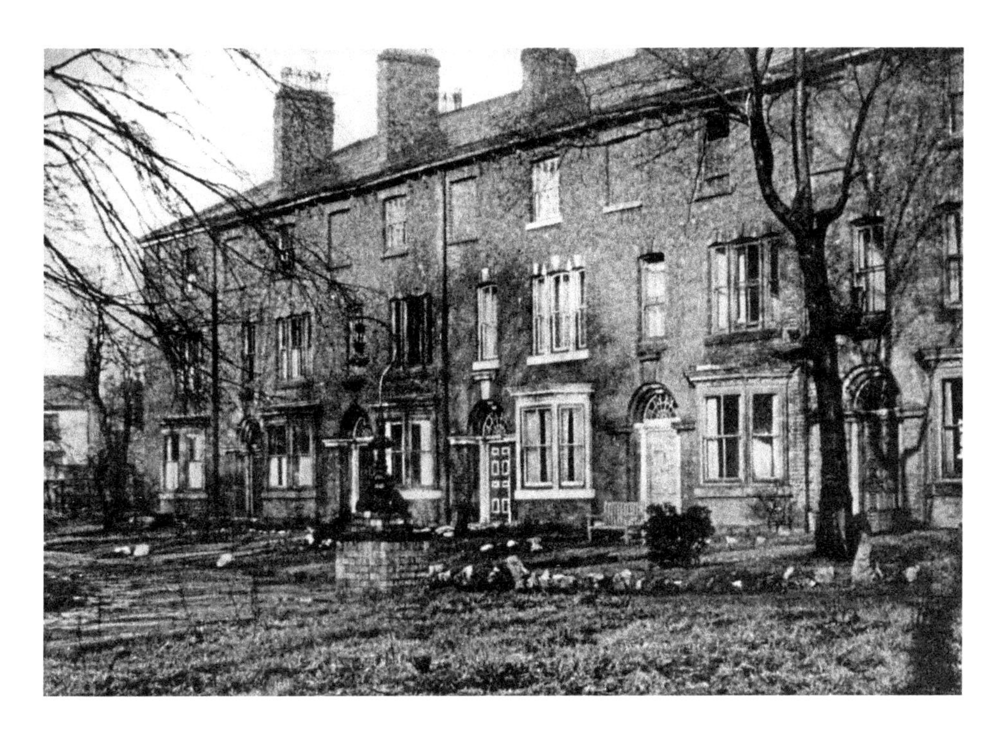

Victoria Park

During the Napoleonic Wars, any defence of Stockport was in the hands of a volunteer local militia or Yeomanry, but in 1818, possibly to counter political unrest, regular troops were based in Stockport. To house them the Government approved the construction of barracks on Hall Street, which were later known as Victoria Barracks, along with the pub across the road, which became the Queen Victoria. After demolition, Victorian houses were built on the site, some of which accommodated American officers during the Second World War. The name still reflects the area's history, but the houses have been replaced by flats.

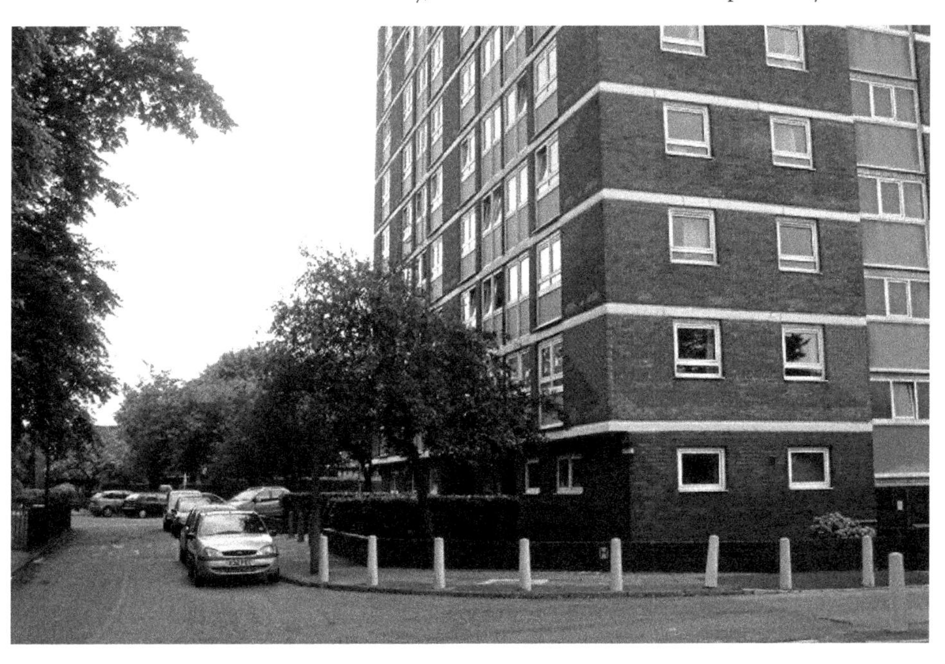

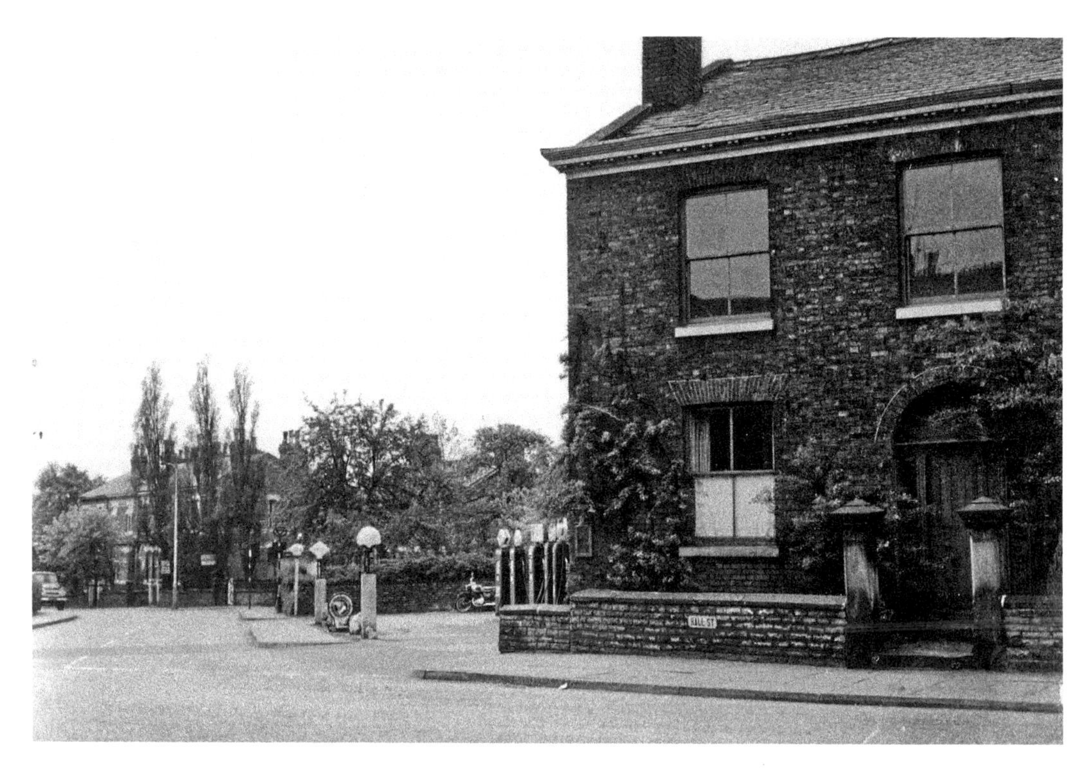

Banks Lane

The end of Hall Street makes a junction with Banks Lane, which has been, for many years, the site of a garage. In this 1960s photograph, the informality of this type of business is well shown with a solitary 'Cleveland Discol' sign as the only advertising evident. In those days an attendant would brave the uncovered pumps to sell petrol come rain or shine! Today, despite the adjoining garage owner's house being demolished, it still exists, not selling fuel but as a second-hand car dealership.

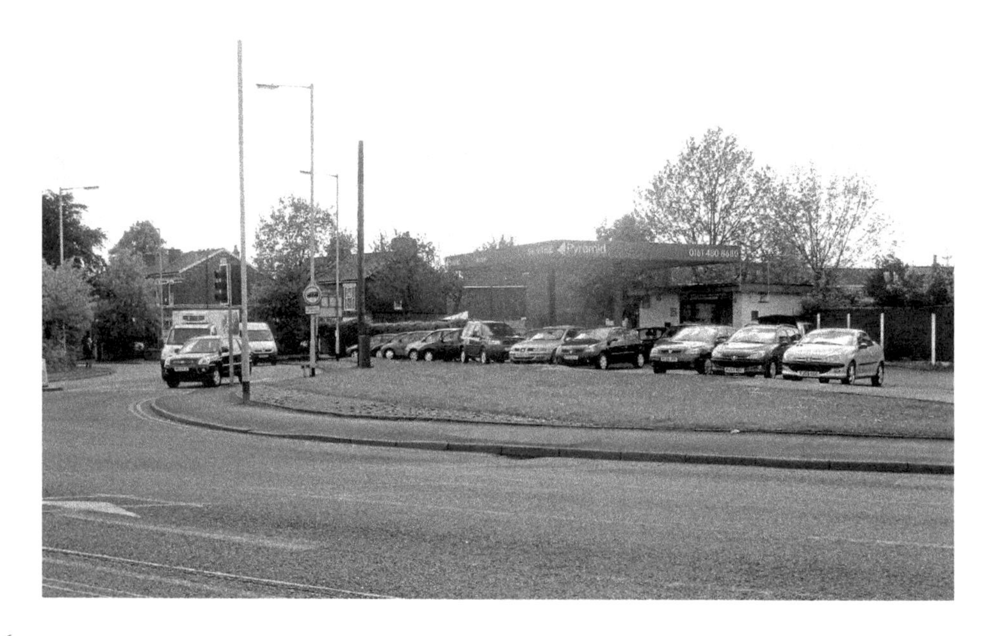

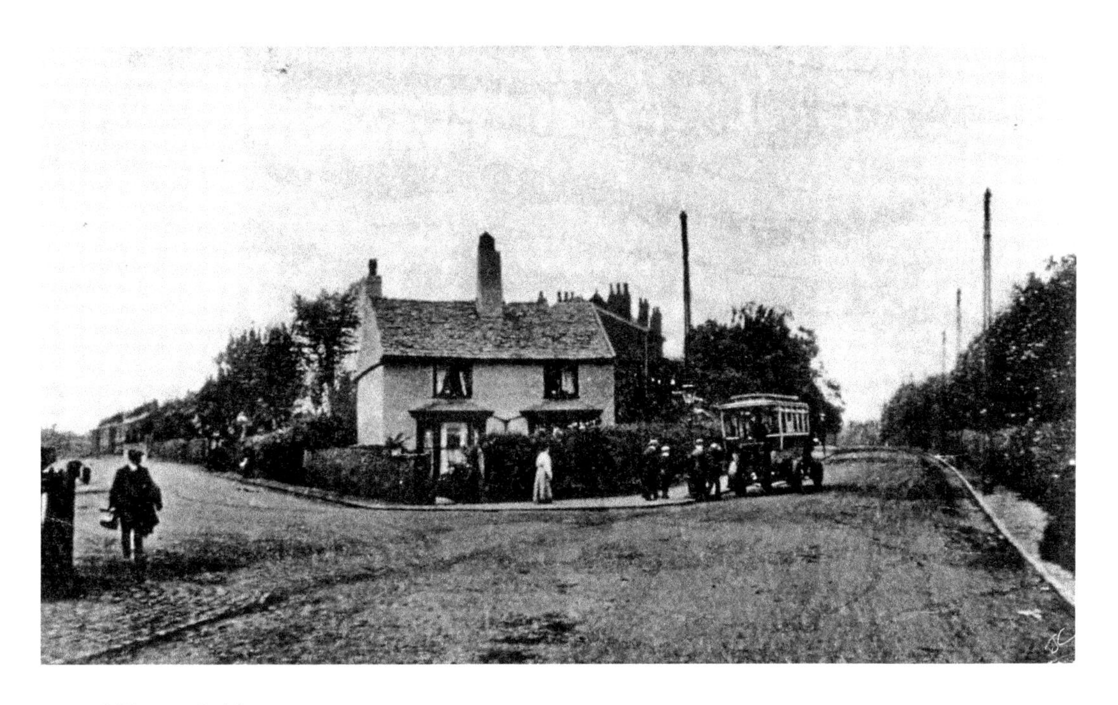

Offerton Fold

The trolleybus terminated at Offerton Fold; when the old photograph was taken this must have seemed like the beginning of the countryside. Where today's small green is located there was once an old country cottage, possibly a toll house, as the road on the right was the Marple turnpike, which opened in 1801. For many years this green has hosted a Christmas tree over the festive period. It is amazing just how much clutter is caused today by traffic management with bollards, signs, safety fencing and road markings.

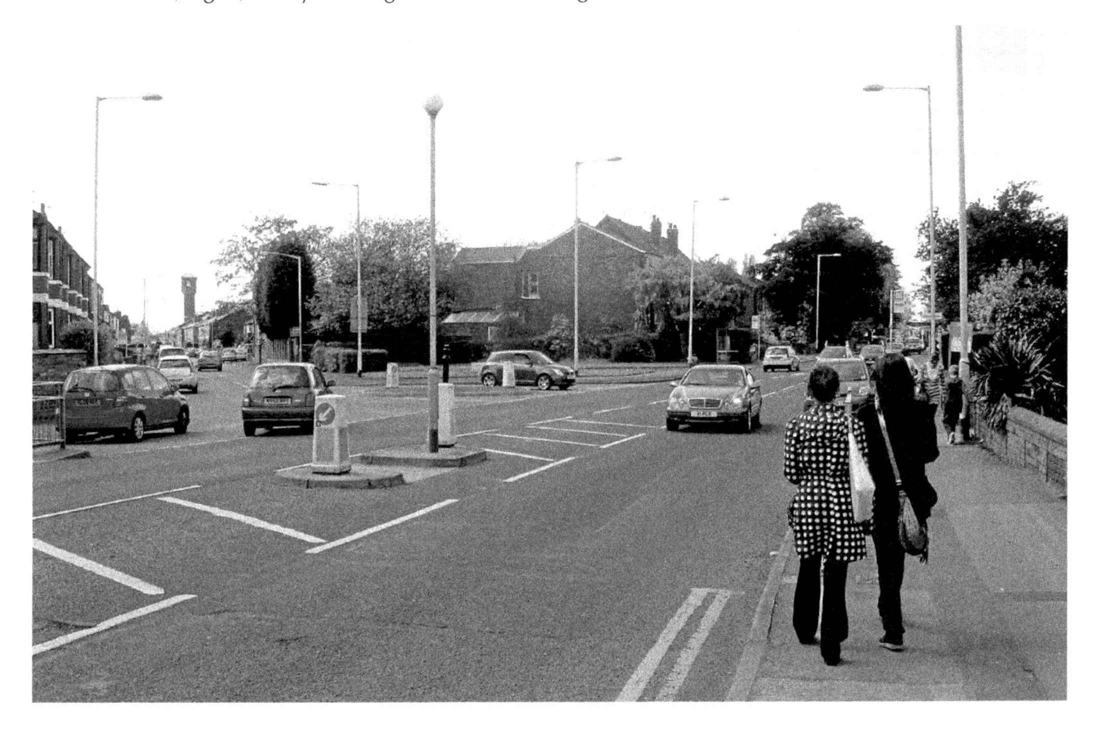

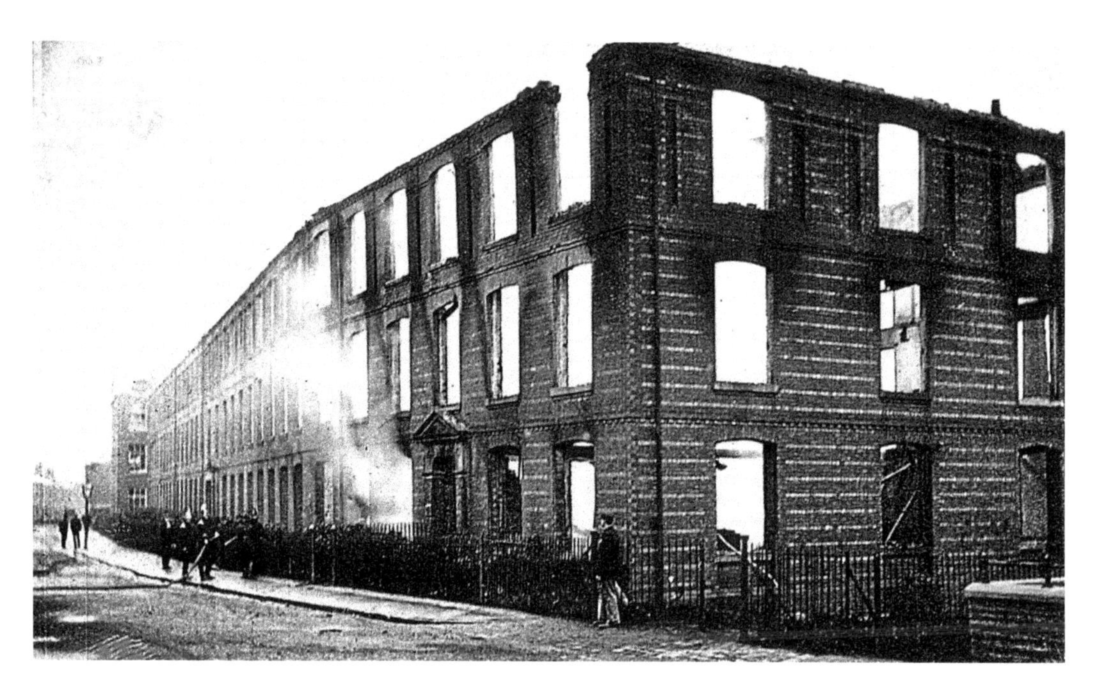

Battersby's Hat Works

Hatting and Stockport go hand in hand and Battersby's on Hempshaw Lane was one of the larger manufacturers. As we can see, disaster struck in 1906 when fire ravaged the factory, leaving just a fire-blackened shell. When the factory was rebuilt, the top floor was discarded. To reduce the risk of another fire, a tower supporting a water tank was added to supply a sprinkler system. The 'B' for Battersby, scripted in the brickwork, is a well-known landmark in the Offerton area.

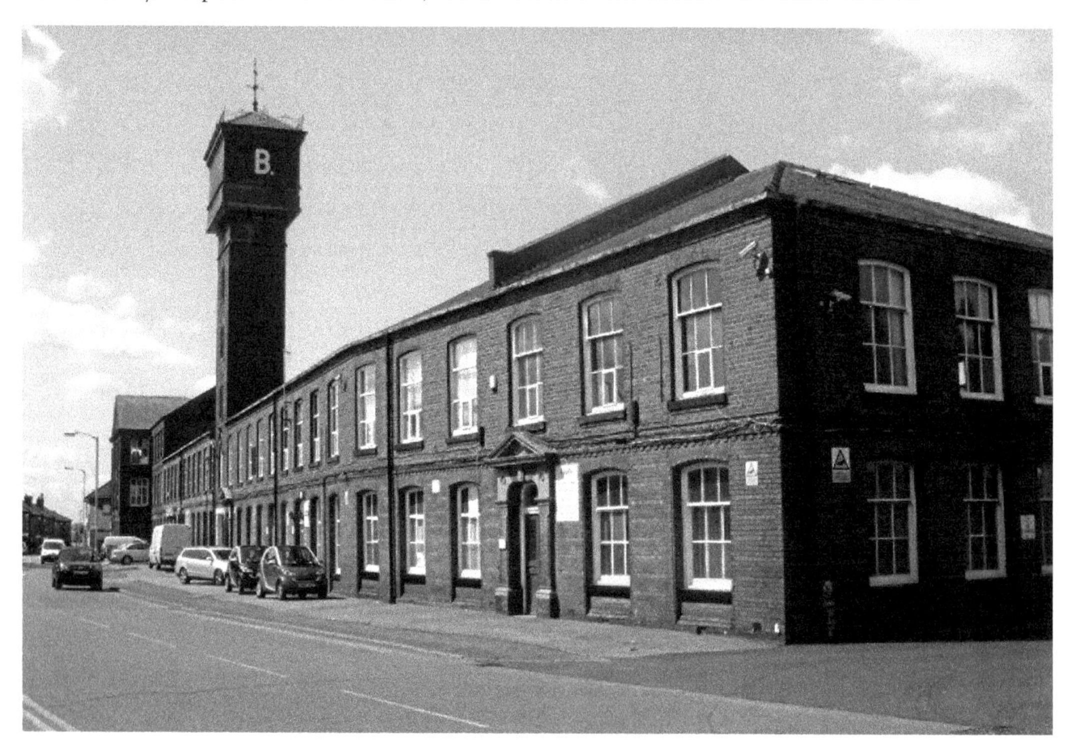

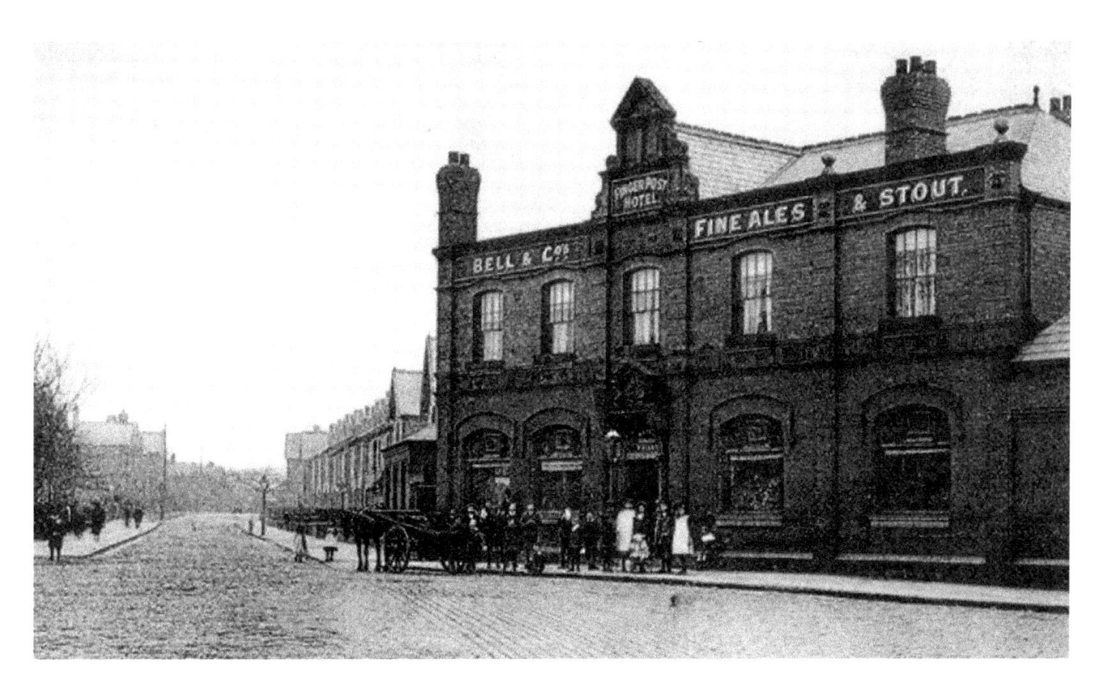

Finger Post Hotel
At the junction of Hempshaw Lane and Dialstone Lane stands the imposing Finger Post Hotel. In the earlier picture, a delivery by horse and cart, plus the presence of a camera, has brought out all the local children. Dating to about 1850, the hotel was taken over and rebuilt in 1892 by a local brewer, Bell & Co., whose brewery was down the road at Hempshaw Brook. Bell's succumbed to a takeover in 1949 by Robinson's, Stockport's last (and still operating) brewery. The Finger Post survives as a much-valued local pub.

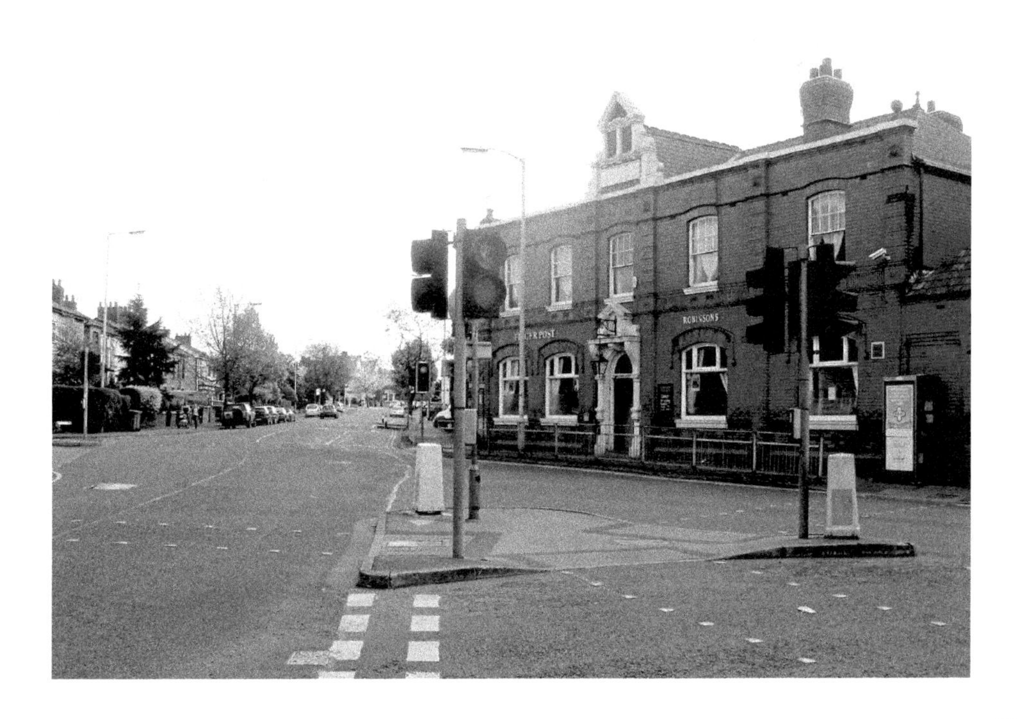

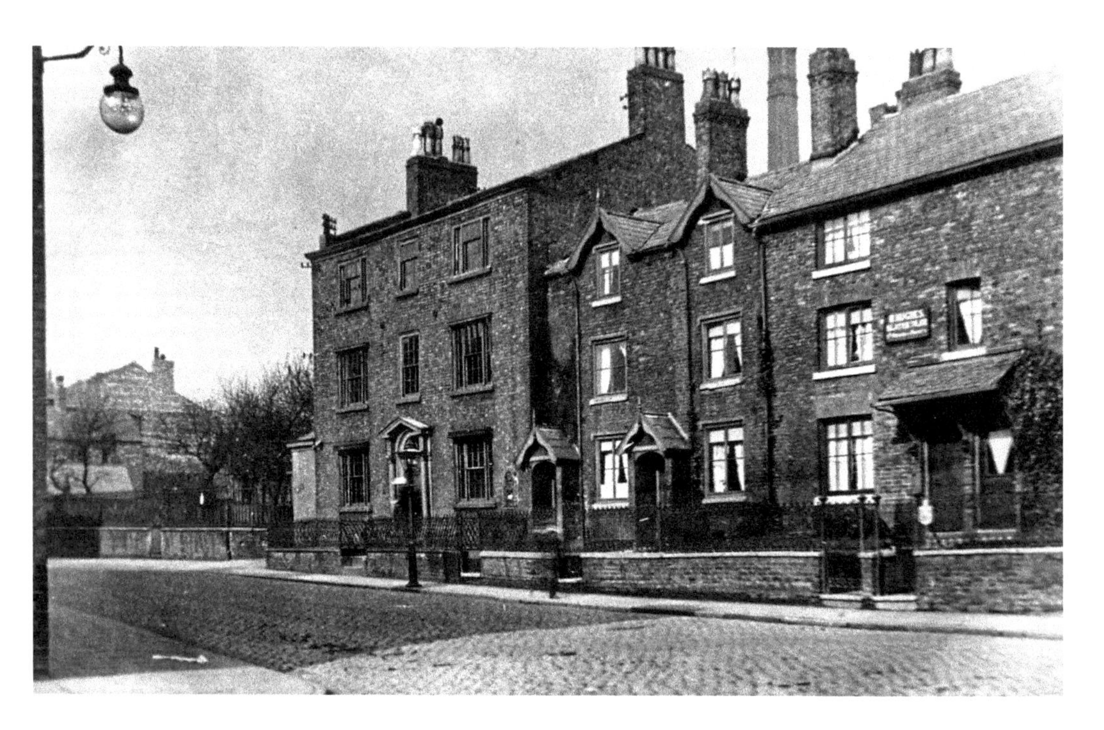

Oldknow's House

This house dates to about 1740, but its association with the cotton and hatting industries makes it special. Samuel Oldknow bought the house in 1784 and built his Higher Hillgate Mill, the first to power machinery by steam engine, alongside it. Oldknow left to develop Marple and, by the early 1800s, the owner was William Radcliffe from Mellor, the inventor of the 'dandyloom'. Later in that century the house became associated with the hatmaker Christys', whose offices were located in the building. Recently the house was restored by Miller Homes, but it is a pity about the modern lamp post.

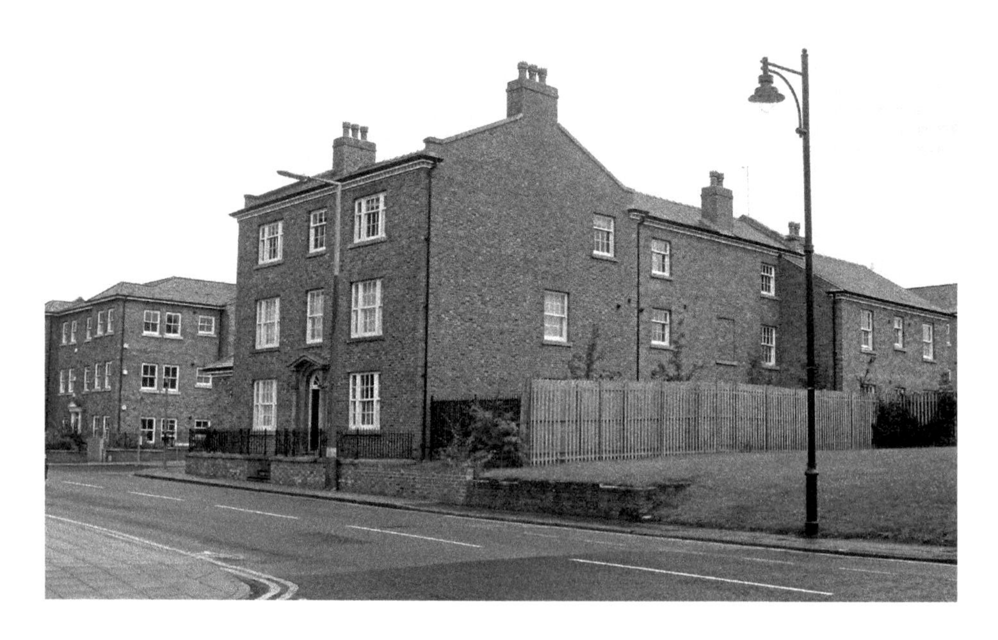

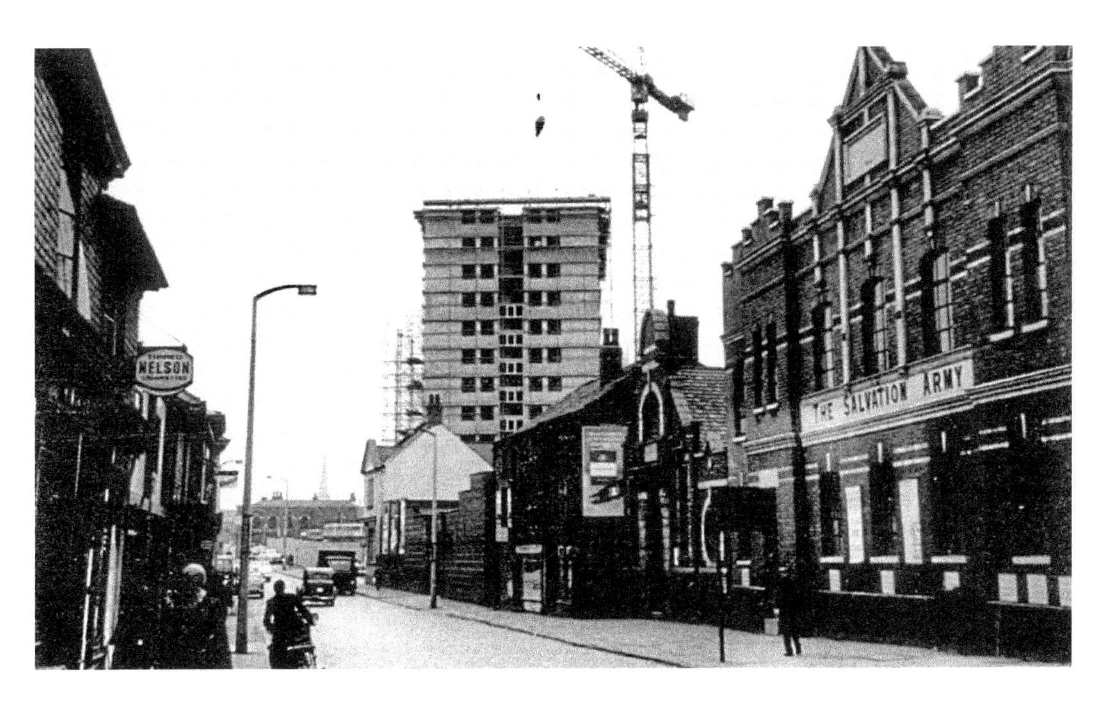

Citadel

The Salvationists came to Stockport in 1882 and very soon targeted the unruly Hillgate area, and not without reason. At the end of the nineteenth century, Hillgate hosted more pubs than the rest of the town. The Salvationists' headquarters in Stockport, the crenellated Citadel, was started in 1894 in their 'battlefield' and remained open for a hundred years. After an imaginative conversion by Johnnie Johnson Homes, it is now flats. Across the road, Tollbar Street identifies the site of one of the Manchester–Buxton turnpike tollgates of 1725, on Hillgate.

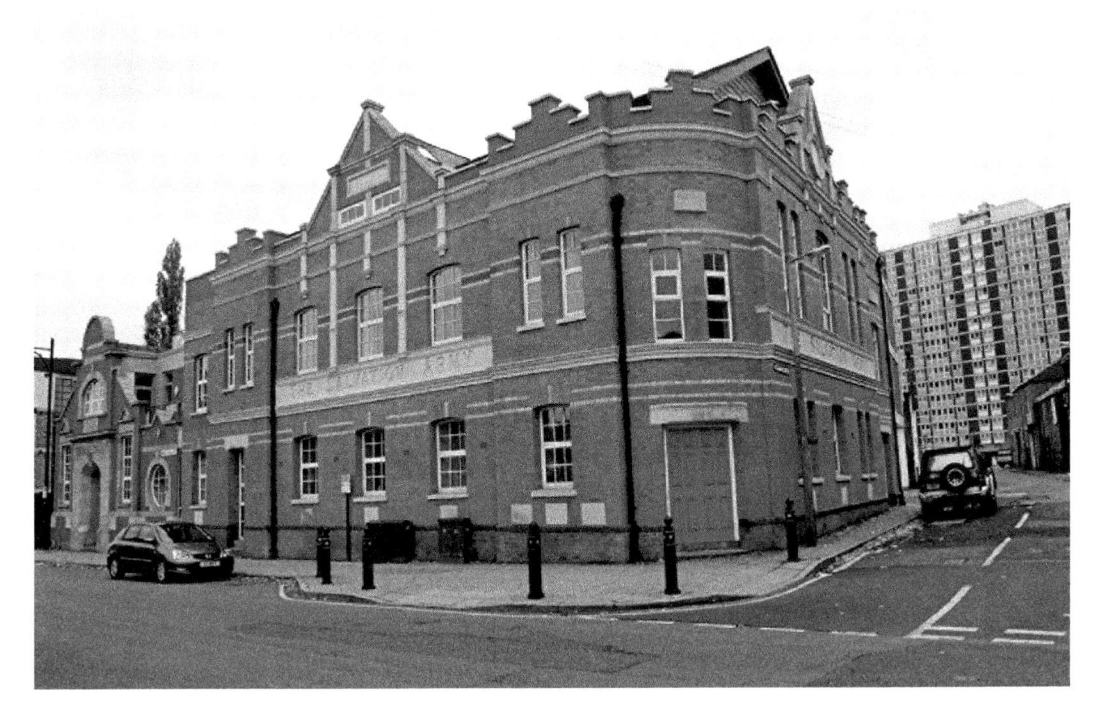

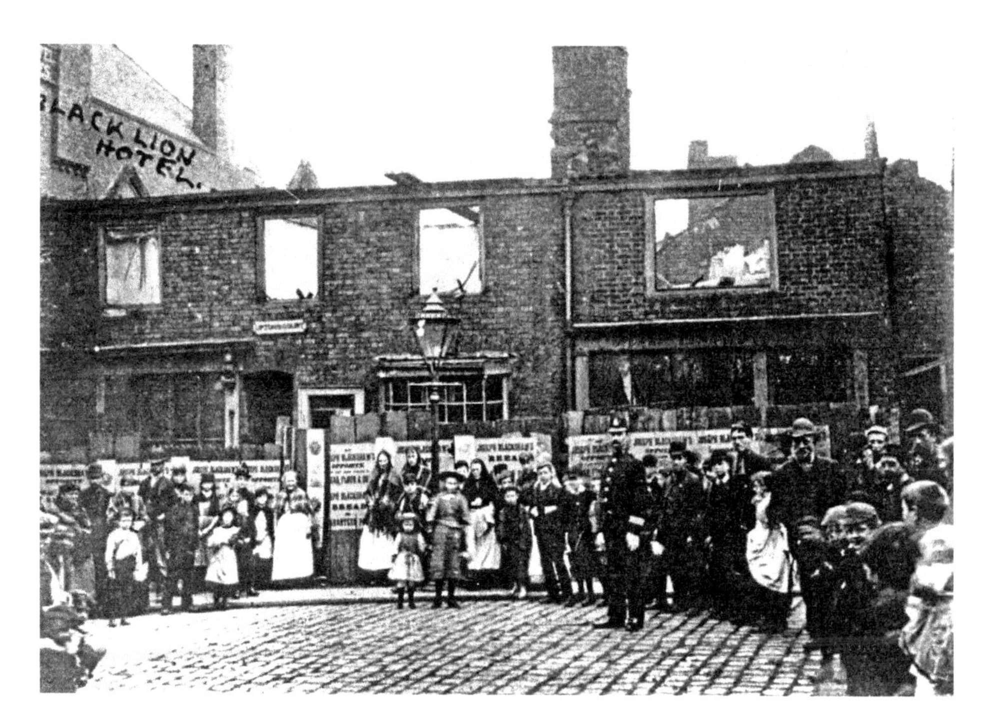

Middle Hillgate

The photographer recording the demolition of these old buildings, next to the Black Lion Hotel, seems to have attracted all and sundry! Was the authority of the moustached policeman needed for crowd control? Space evidently was required for three new shops next to the Black Lion Hotel and, as we can see, their pleasing Edwardian outline is still there today. The old photograph also reminds us of our changing town. The cobbled road, the cast-iron street name and the huge gas lamp with arms surely designed for boys to swing on have all disappeared.

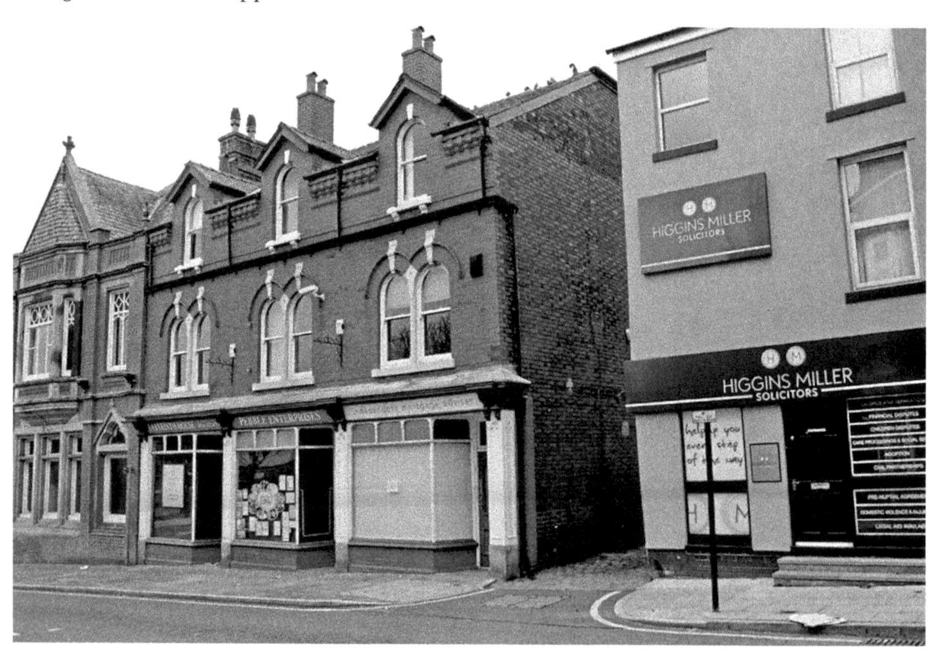

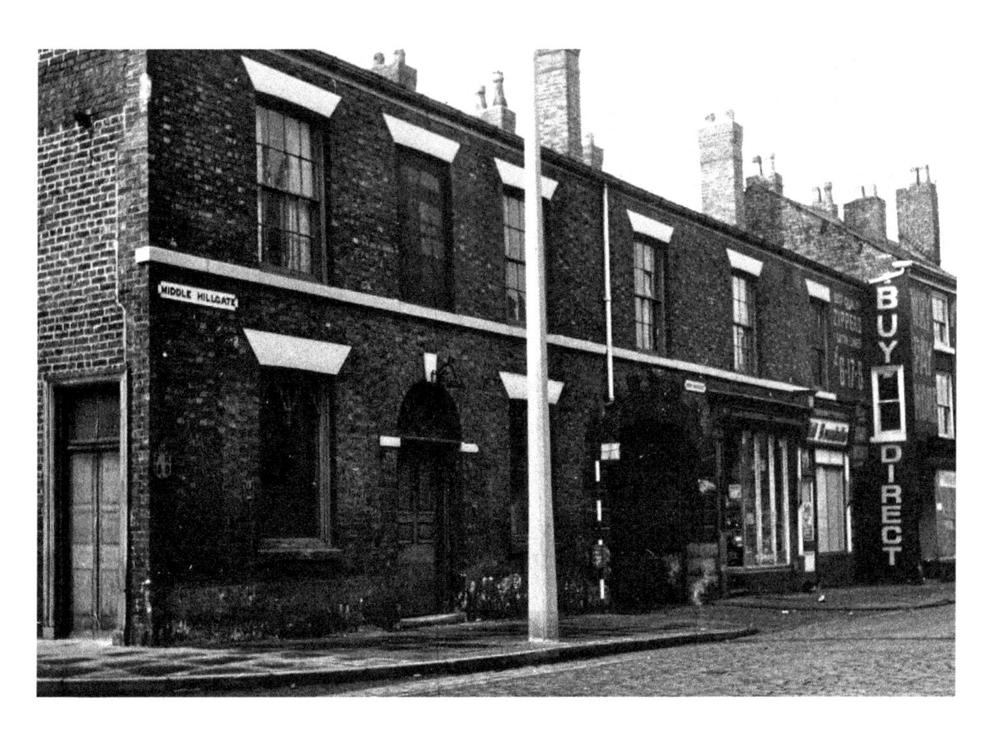

New Market

On the corner of Edward Street and Middle Hillgate through an arch of the former Old Admiral pub was the entrance to 'New Market'. This appeared to be an attempt by businessmen of the 1840s to challenge the manorial right of market by setting up a rival enterprise to the one in the Market Place. They failed, as they had no powers to run the market. Today the eagle-eyed pedestrian can see the 'New Market' street sign on the wall behind the tree; it was thoughtfully removed from the arch when the pub was demolished.

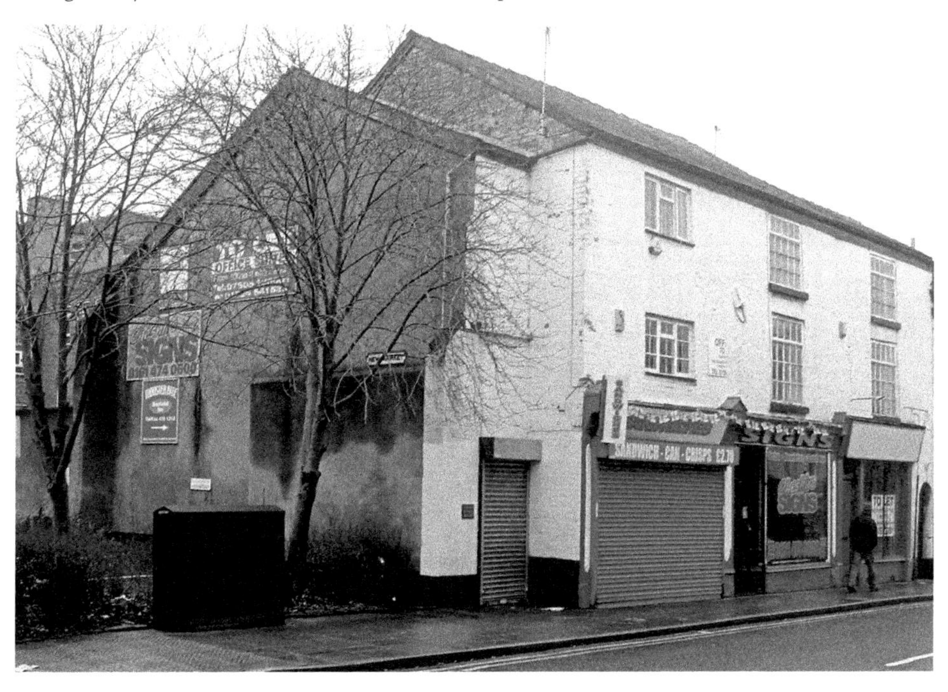

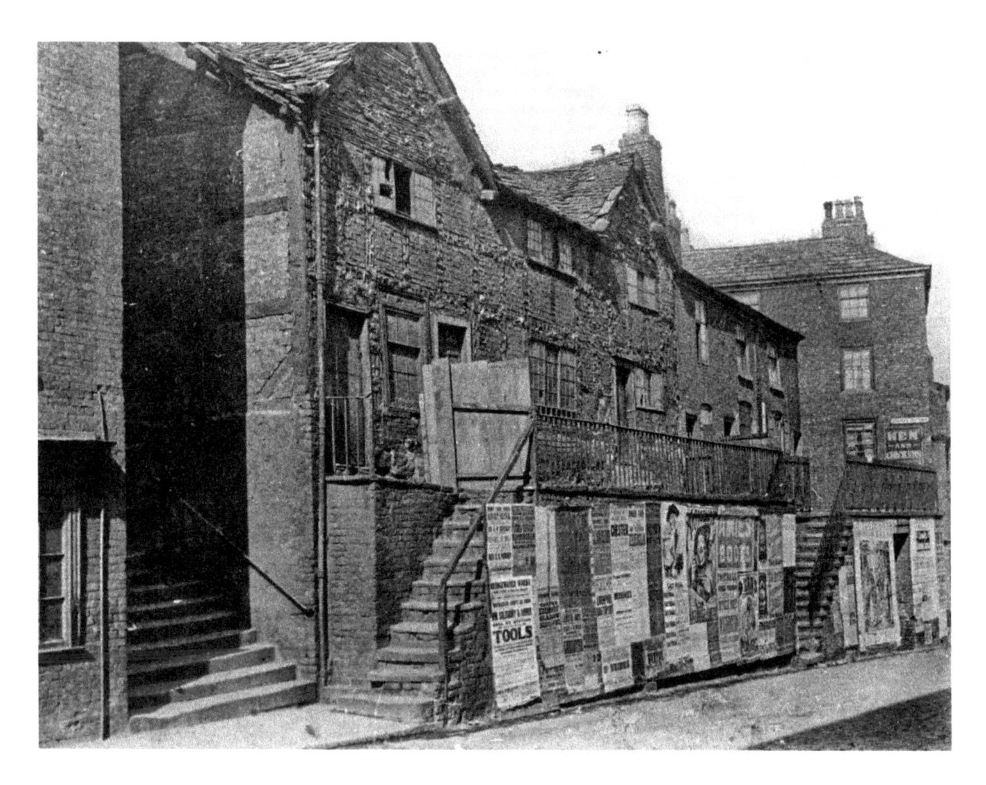

Covent Garden

This pleasant name belies the dreadful housing conditions in parts of the Hillgate area. This large, old, wood-framed, brick-infill house awaiting demolition must have at one time been very important. But by the nineteenth century its fortunes had faded. It had become home to numerous families, and included, behind the hoardings, some of Stockport's notorious cellar dwellings. Next door can be seen the Hen and Chickens pub; close by was a doss house in which tramps slept, not in a bed, but leaning against a thick rope stretched across the room.

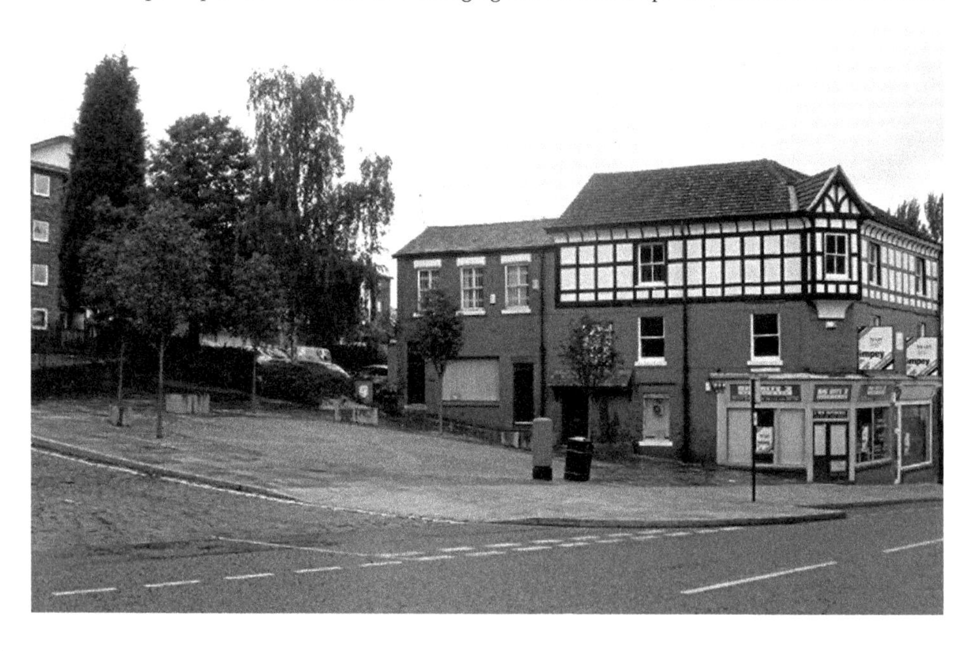

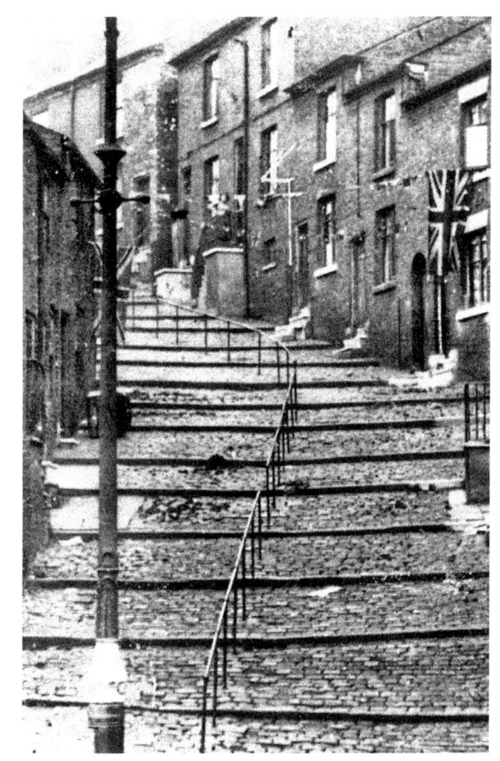

Crowther Street

Immortalised in L. S. Lowry's 1930 painting, Crowther Street is one of the many brows leading off Hillgate. Similar to a lot of property in the Hillgate area, despite a poor standard of housing, it engendered a high degree of community spirit. The old houses were demolished in the slum clearances, but another fantastic renewal was carried out in about 2005, which replicated the houses shown on Lowry's picture. The Lowry picture was bought by the council in 1935 and is displayed at the art gallery.

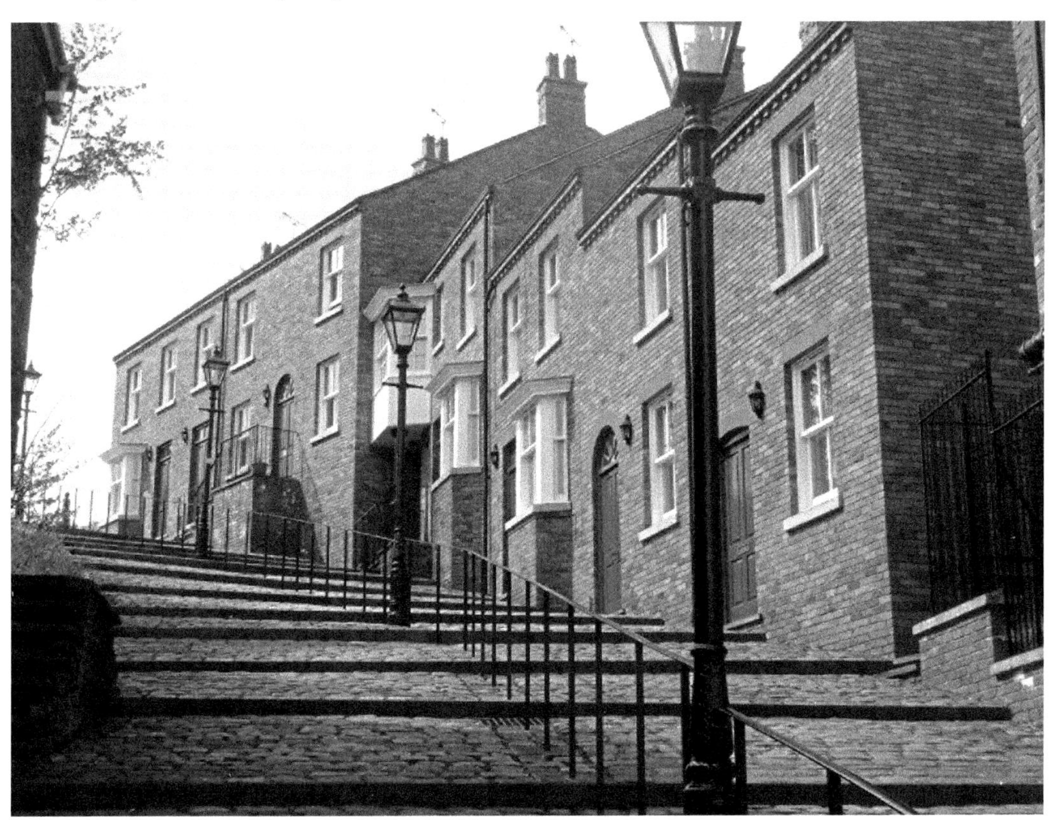

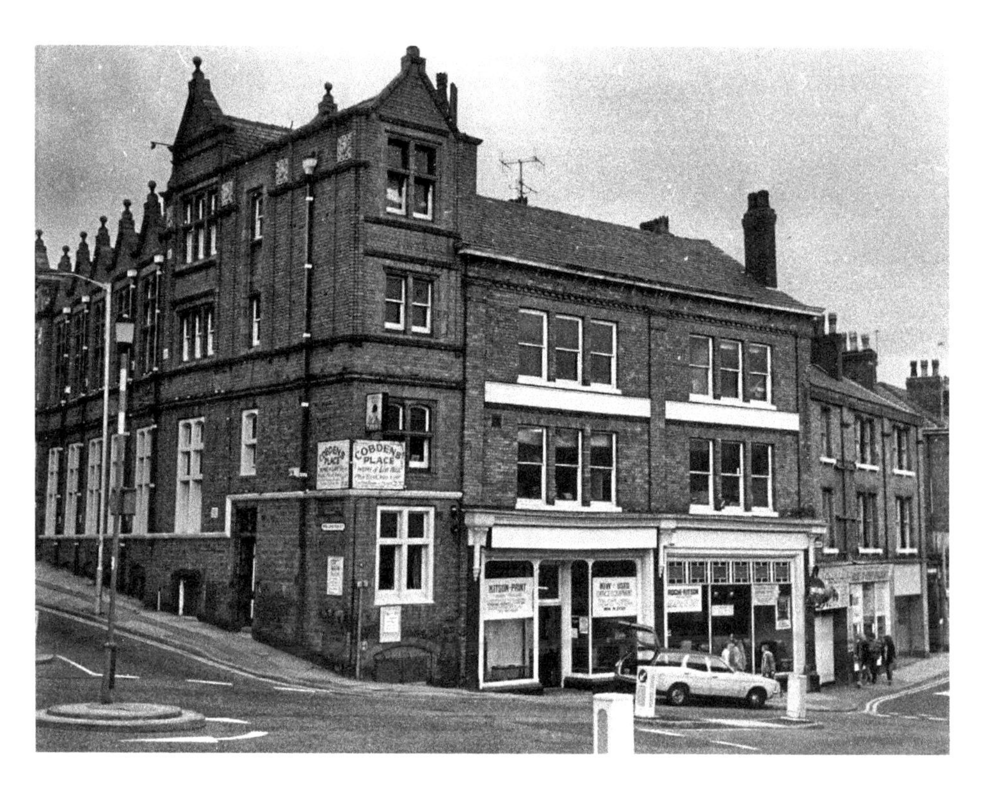

Reform Club

The 1830s was a great period of reform in the political and municipal life of this country and many reform clubs were founded to enable like-minded men to meet and discuss issues of the day. In the 1860s the Stockport Reform Club took over this site from the Mechanics' Institute and erected an imposing red-brick building. Changing times have not been kind to the old club. It became a night spot, then suffered years of neglect. Planned redevelopment into flats offers a change in fortune and the removal of the rooftop trees.

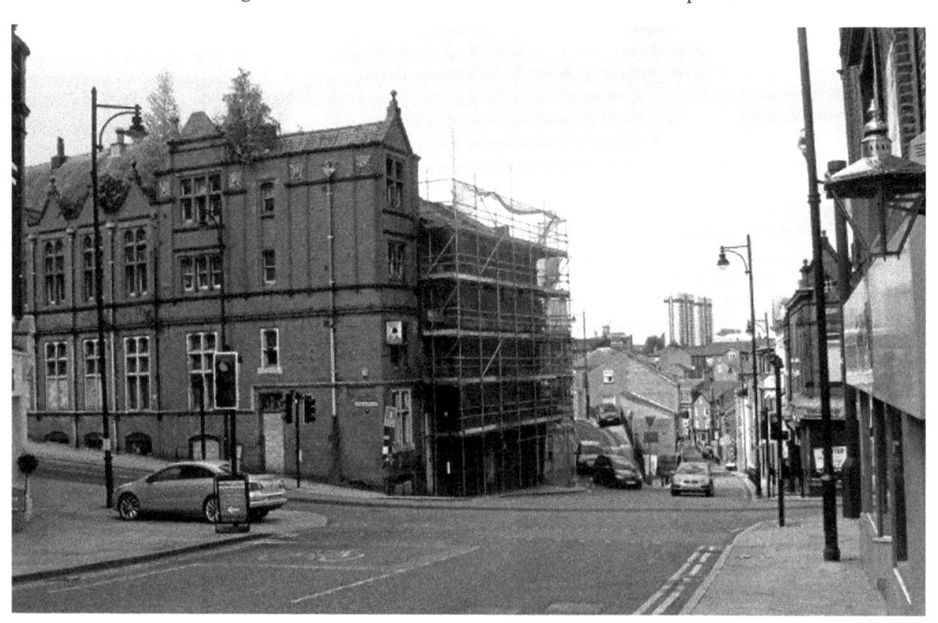

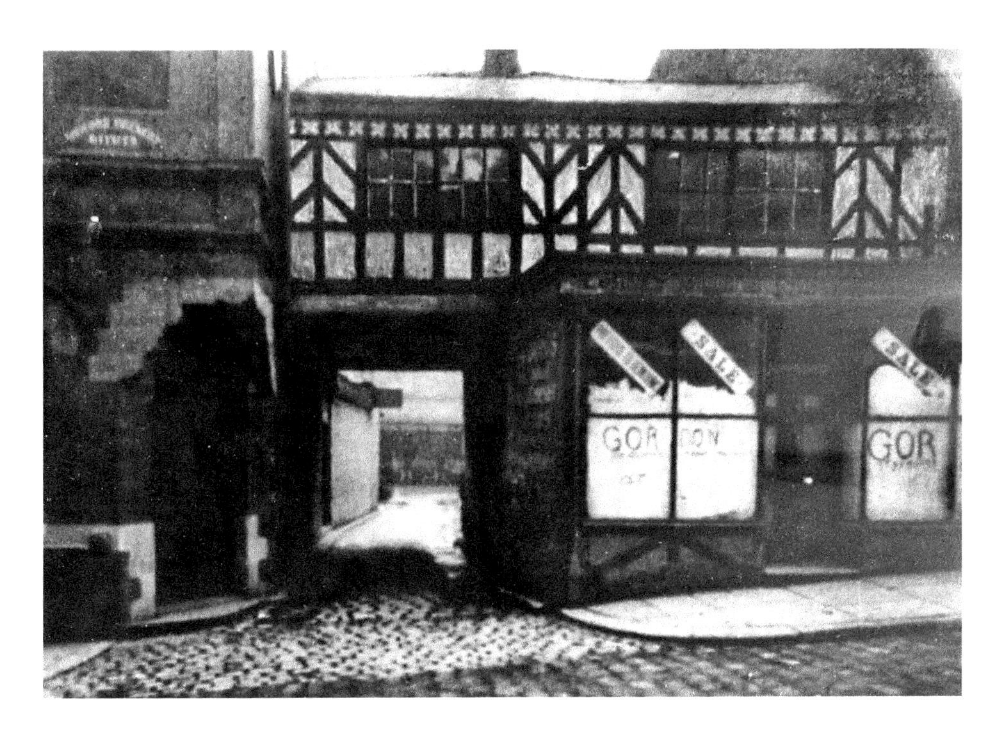

Robinson's Unicorn Brewery

In 1838, William Robinson bought the Unicorn Inn on Lower Hillgate. In 1865 the pub was taken over by his son, Frederic, who started brewing beer at the rear of the premises with such good effect that he was able to supply other pubs. The awkward entrance to the yard at the back was through a narrow opening under the black-and-white premises, but later property acquisition has allowed better access. The door on the corner survives, as does the name of the old inn.

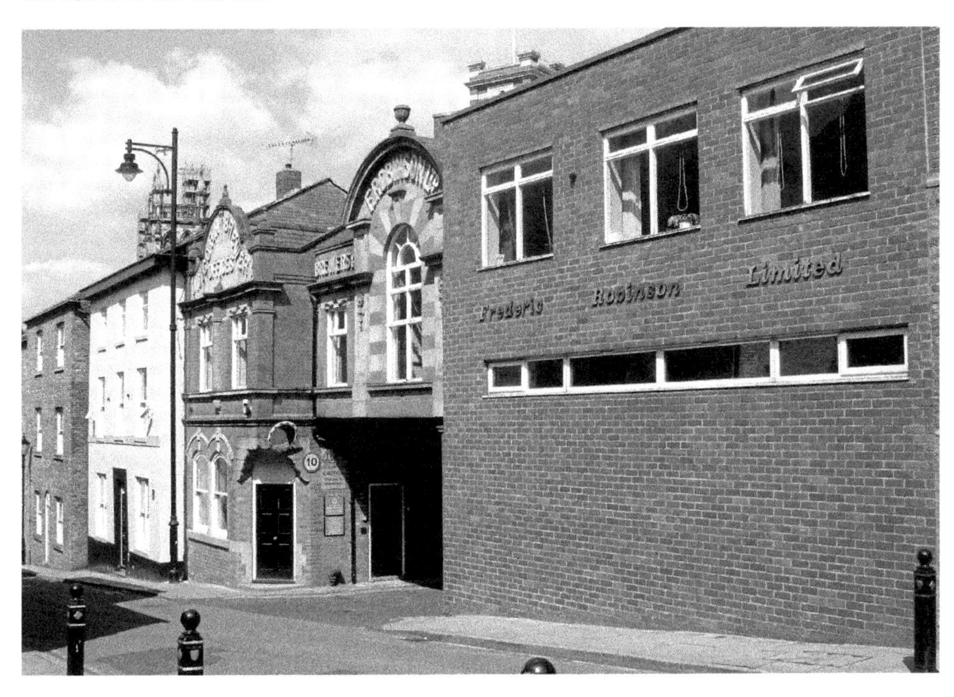

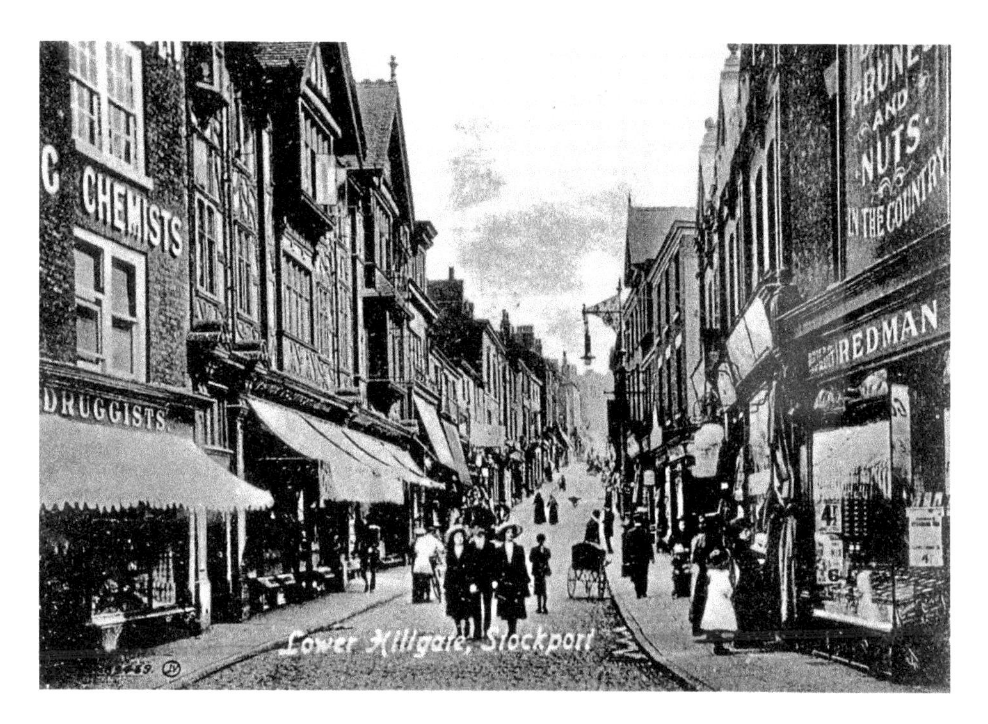

Lower Hillgate

In the more leisurely time before the First World War it was possible to shop along Lower Hillgate, the only traffic being a delivery handcart. Notice the shop window awnings; our shoppers pass the site of the old Bull and George Inn, whose replacement has a fashionable black-and-white frontage with a still-evident jettisoned window. Perhaps their next call for purchases will be Redman's, the grocer's, a well-known town establishment, or one of the many other retailers on this once-busy shopping street.

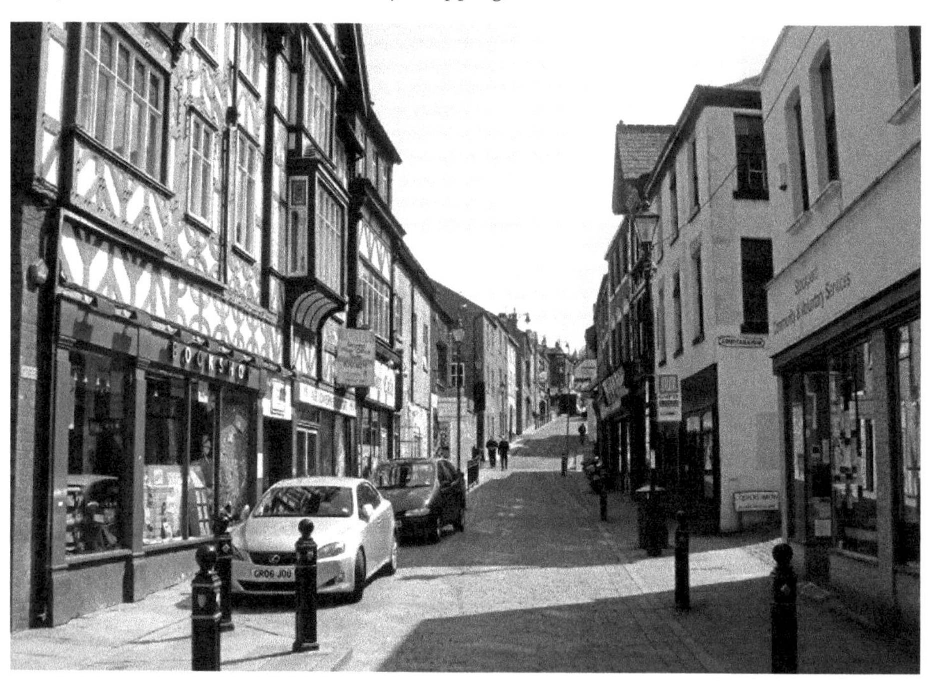

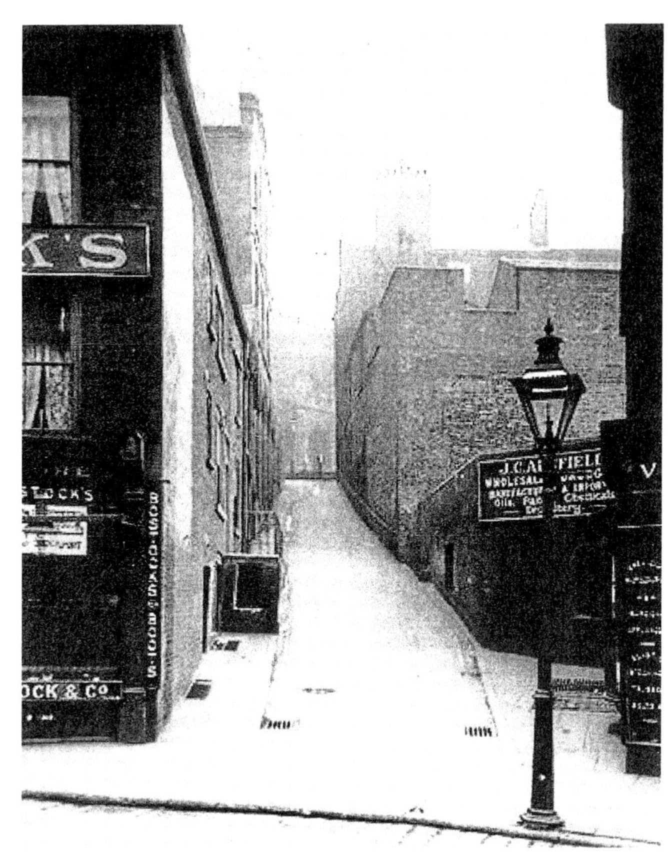

Rostron Brow
One of the famous brows leading up to the market, Rostron Brow, formerly Rosen Bank until its unfortunate decline in the 1800s, was an exclusive place to live. Near the top, the Hare and Hounds pub opened in the 1830s. The music hall at the rear of its premises was the notorious Dust Hole ale house. Regeneration has again made the brow a pleasant entrance to the market; adjacent properties were converted into flats. The first tobacco factory in Stockport, at the bottom left corner, has become a trendy boutique.

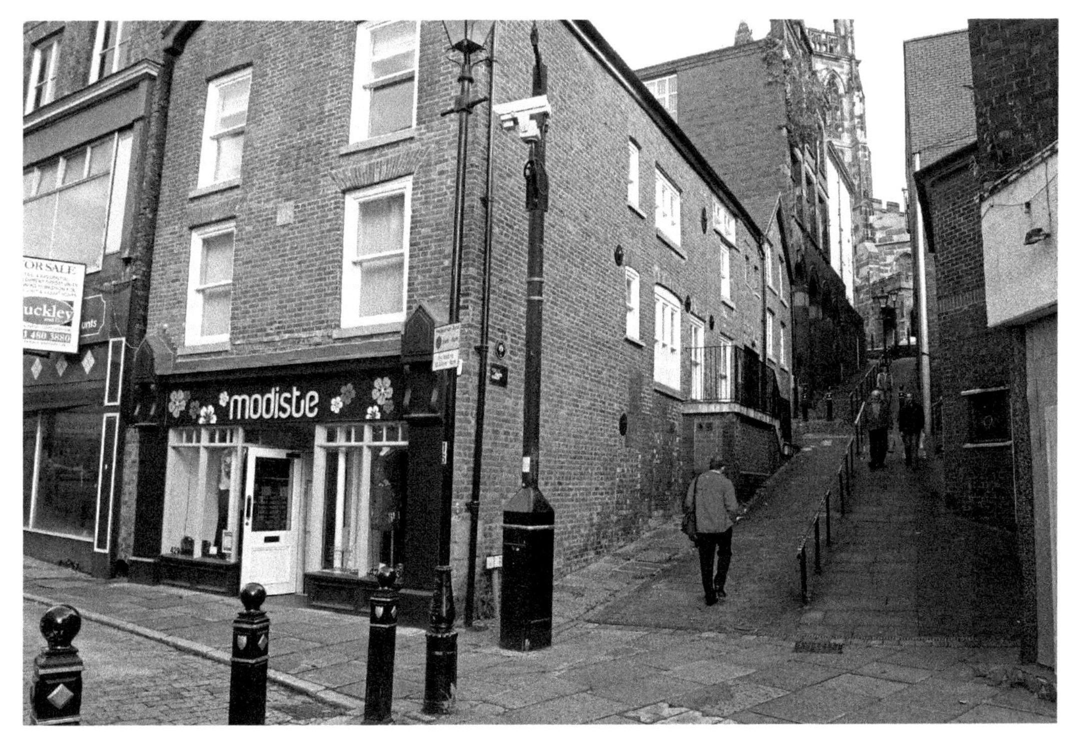

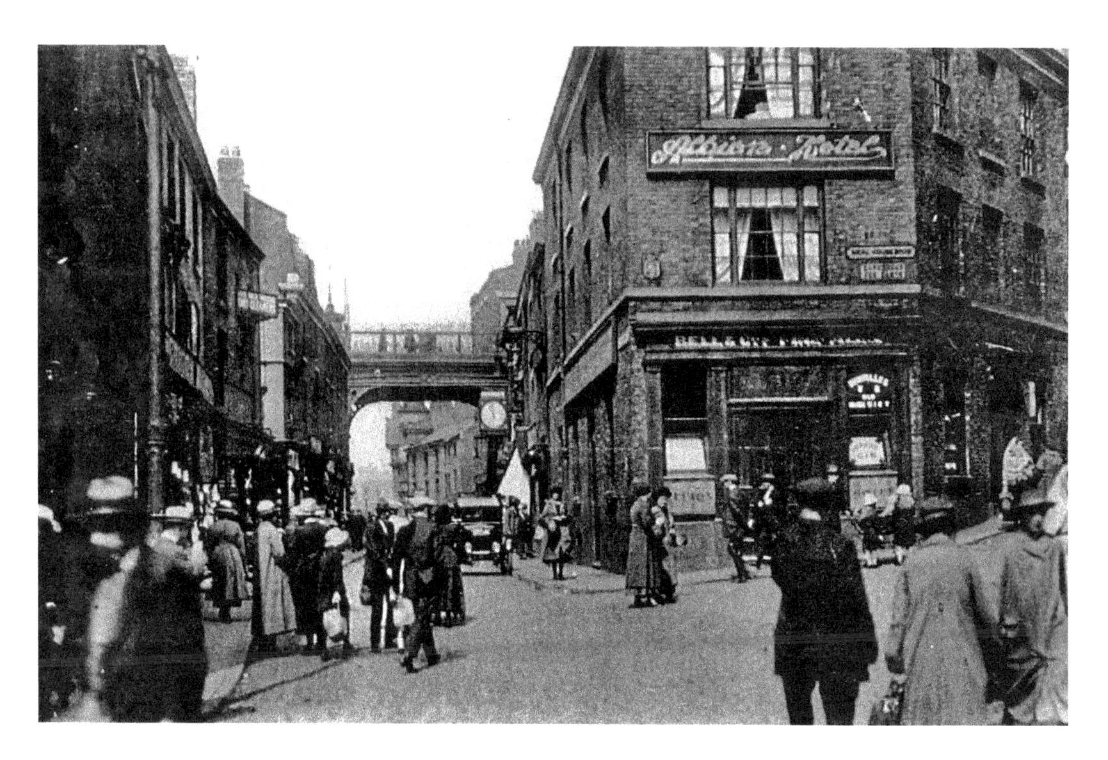

Little Underbank and Mealhouse Brow

Located below Castle Hill are the Underbanks. In this picture Mealhouse Brow, on the right, climbs up the hill to the market. North, towards Great Underbank, a lone car threads its way through the busy shoppers and reminds us that until 1826 this was the main road to London. The Albion Hotel, called the Rising Sun Inn in 1784, witnessed Jonathan Thatcher riding his saddled cow into town to avoid paying horse tax. Today, despite some modern intrusions, the charm of the narrow medieval street remains.

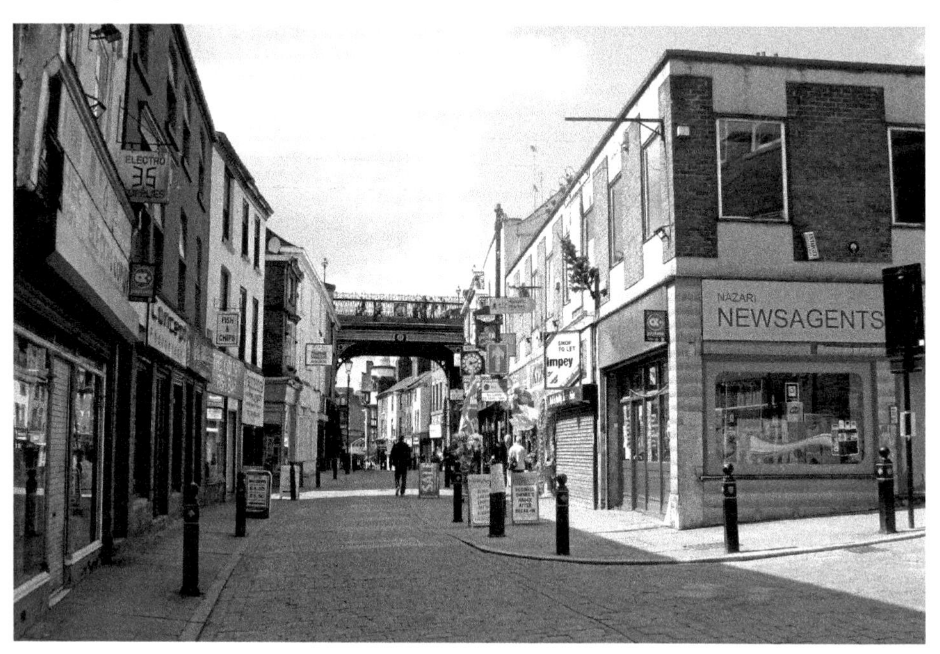

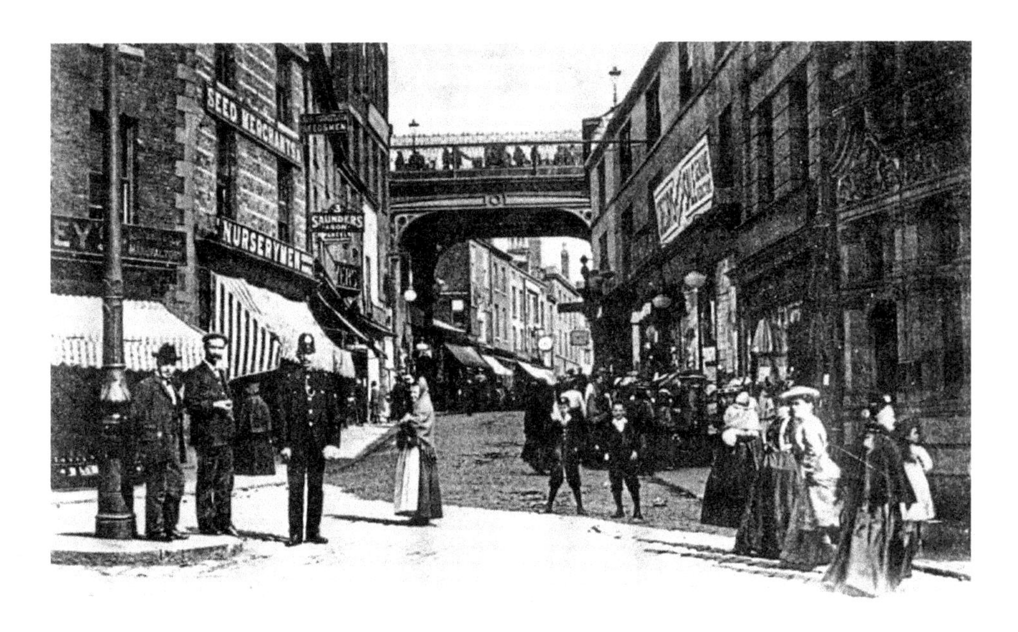

Little Underbank from Great Underbank

These photographs show Little Underbank again, but looking south. The St Petersgate Bridge is an unusual urban feature and its prominent height reflects the hilly nature of Stockport. Beyond the bridge, the dial of Winter's clock stands out. Today it has animated figures chiming the hours, much to the delight of the children who for generations have watched from the bridge. The sale banner of our Victorian ancestors certainly seems to have attracted a larger crowd than the competing pavement sandwich boards of today.

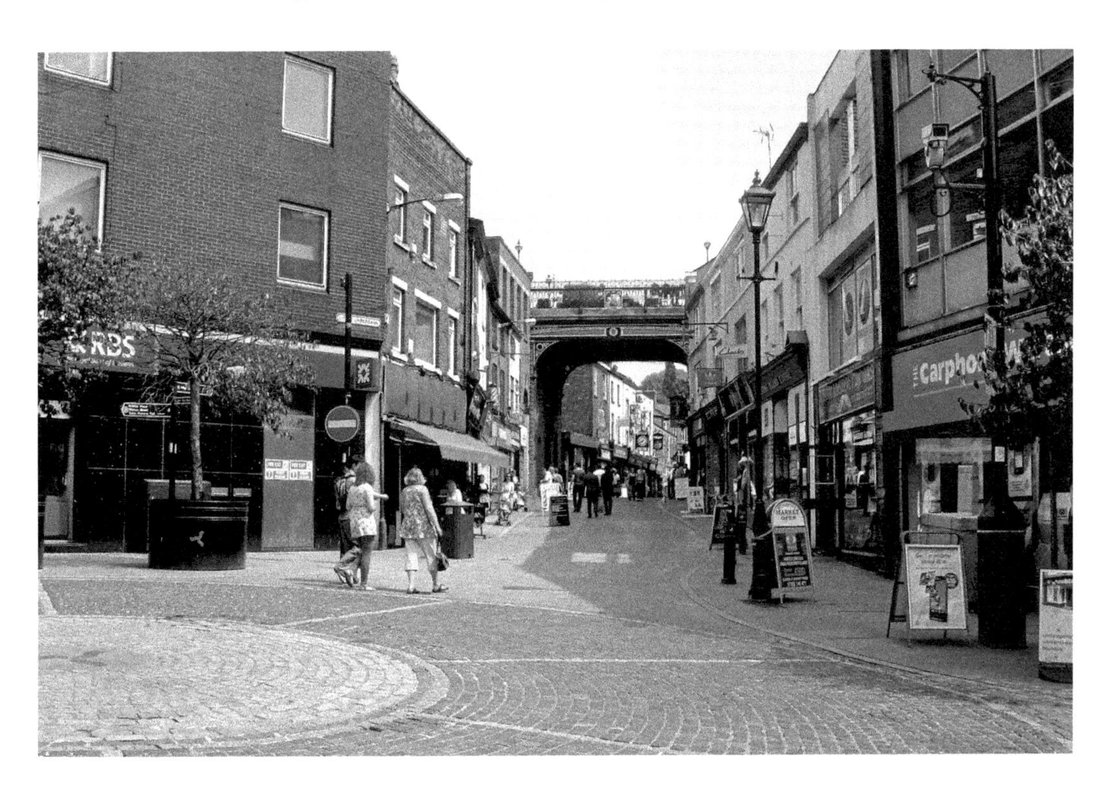

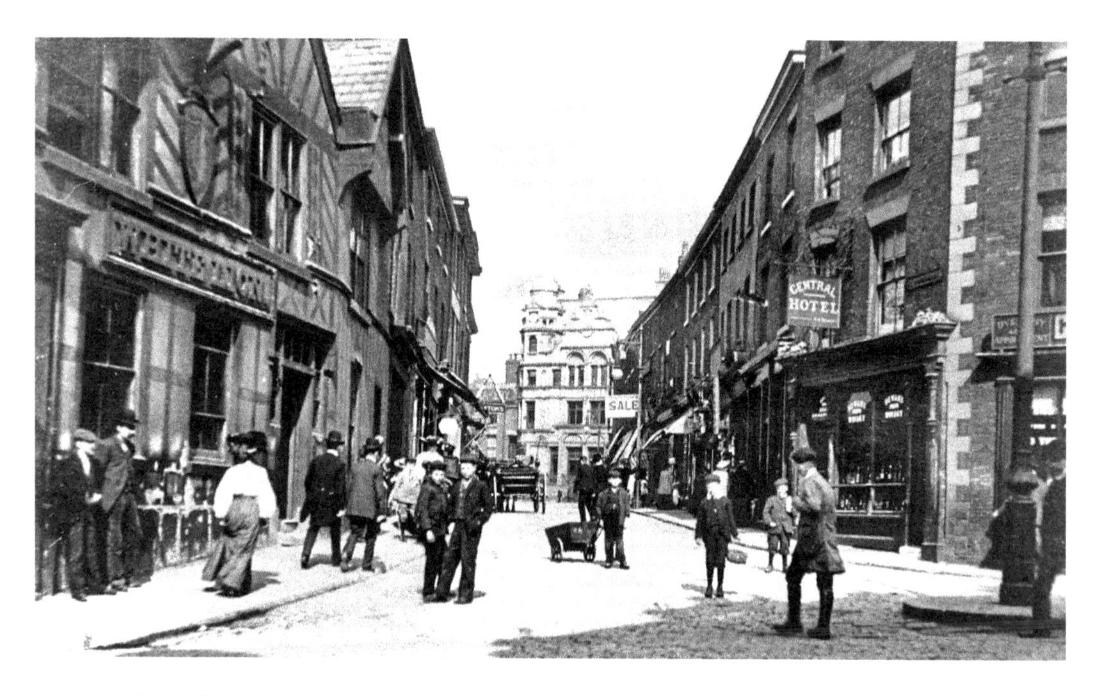

Great Underbank
Here seen from Lancashire Bridge, Great Underbank was from medieval times the most important road in Stockport, with traffic to the south and west travelling over it. On the right is the aptly named Central Hotel, while across the road two customers for the White Lion seem to be waiting for opening time. Or are they watching the street urchin with his hand cart? At the end of the road, at Bridge Street, the new county bank fills the skyline as it still does, although not now as a bank.

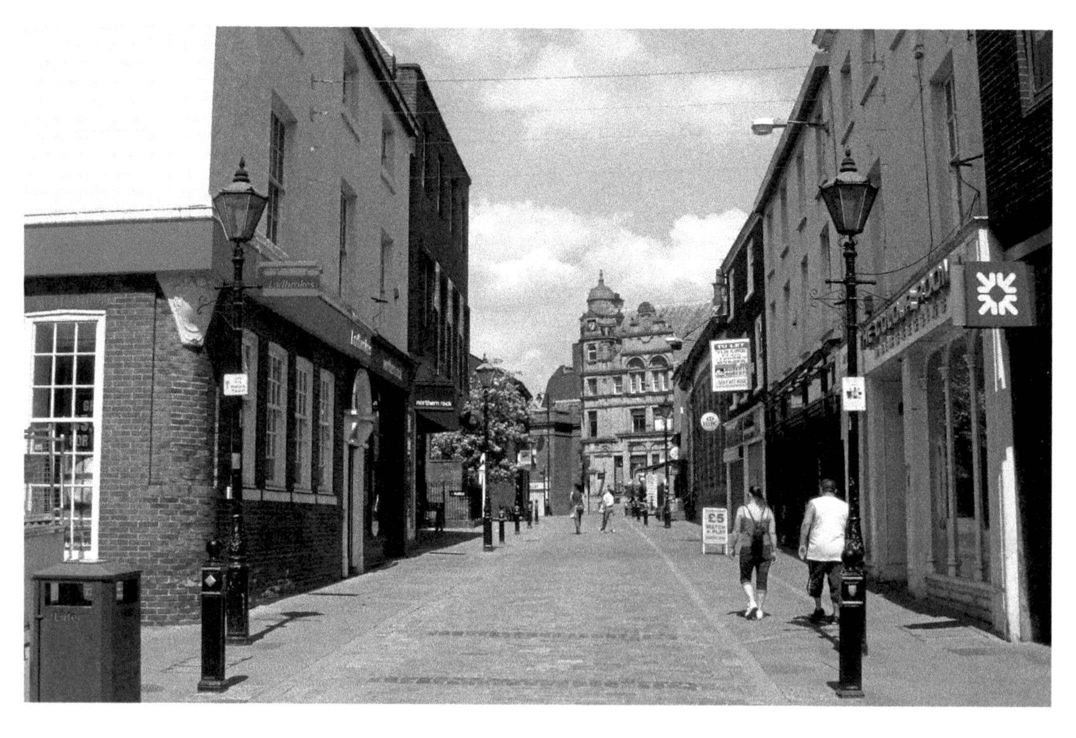

Underbank Hall

Stockport was unrivalled as a market town and commerce centre for many years, and most of the local gentry owned, as well as their country seat, a town house to support their activities. The fifteenth-century Underbank Hall was the town house of the Ardernes of Bredbury, but was sold in 1824 and became the first successful bank in Stockport. Behind the original frontage lies a magnificent banking hall, opened in 1915; this enables the hall to continue functioning as one of the main banks in the town.

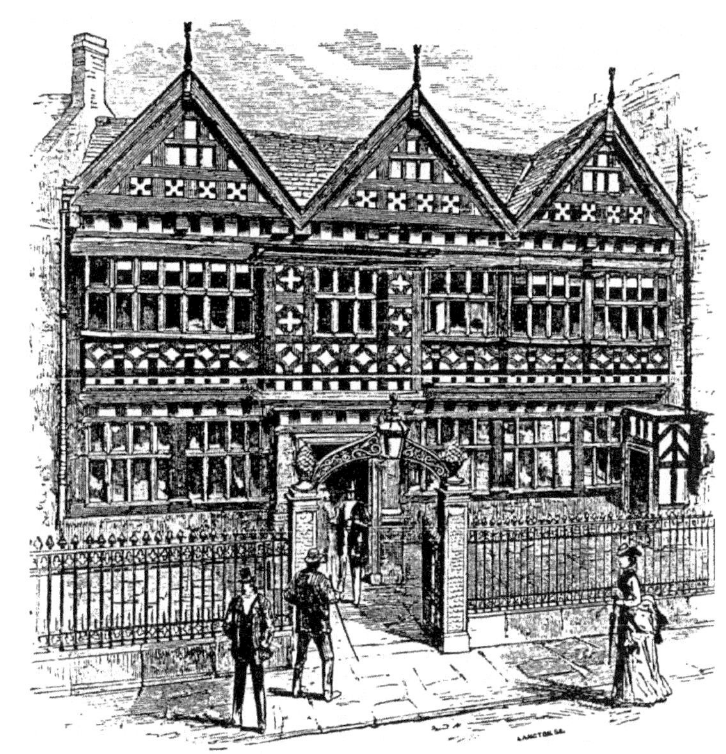

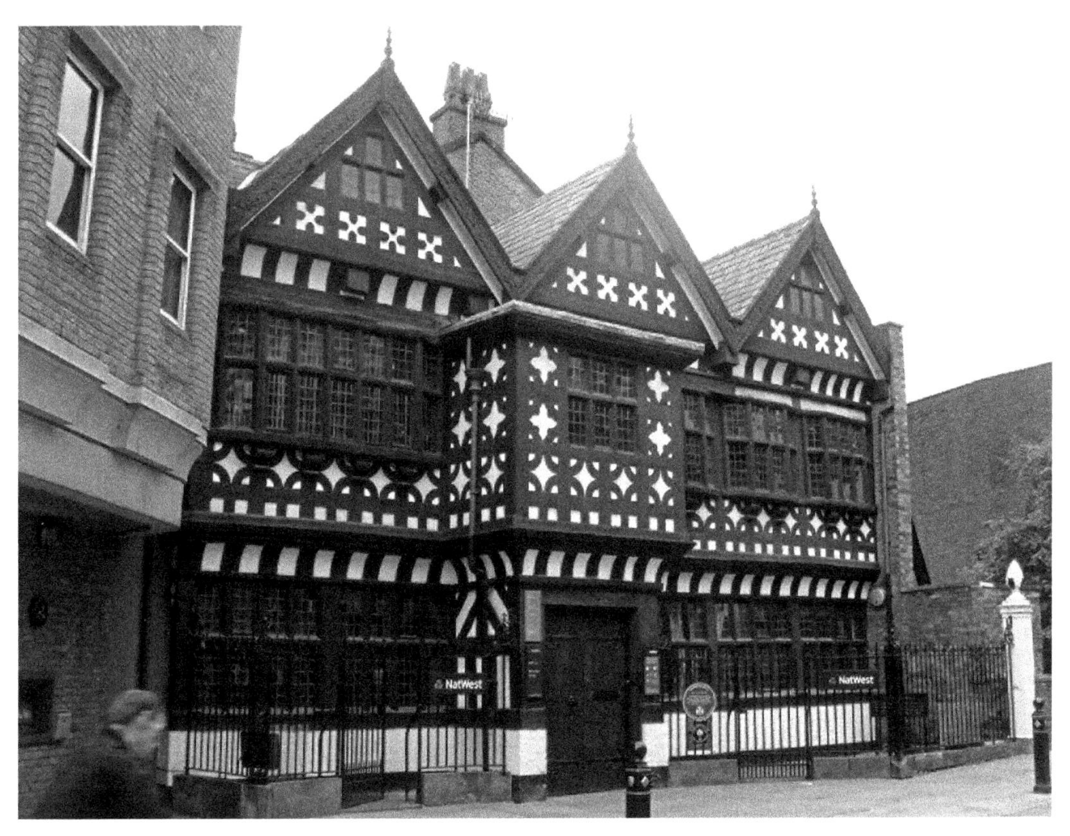

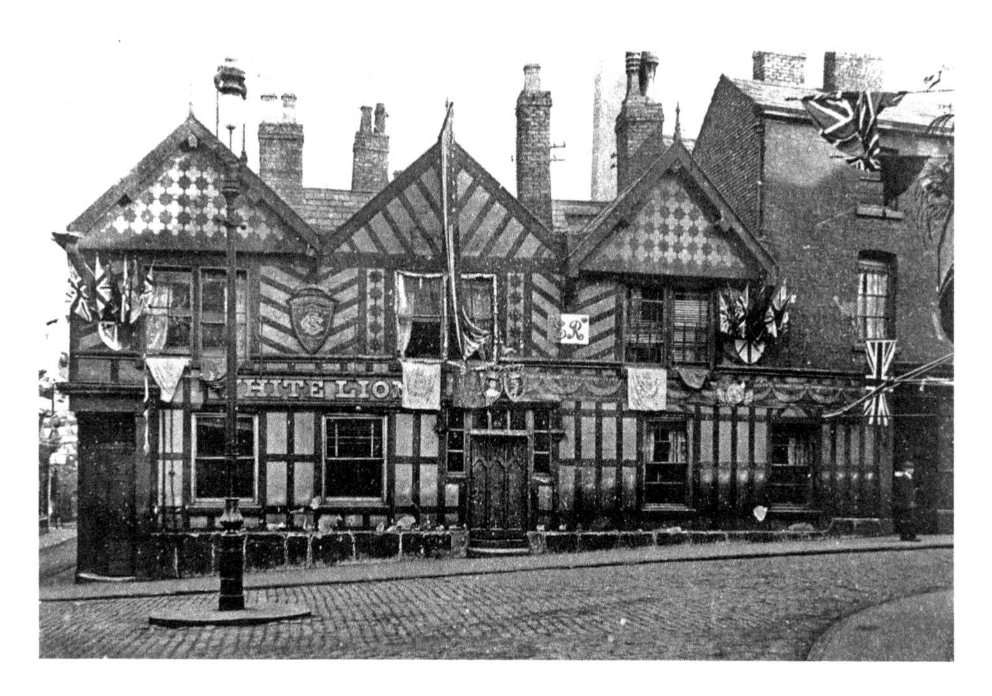

The White Lion

Possibly the oldest hostelry in Stockport and an important coaching inn, the White Lion was well positioned on the road to London. The photograph shows it decorated for King Edward VII's coronation in 1902. Upon the arrival of newspapers during the Napoleonic Wars, the landlord would fire a cannon, summoning townspeople to hear the latest news read out. Infamously it was the scene, in 1831, of one of the last 'wife sellings' in the country when William Clayton sold his spouse for five shillings! Rebuilt in the grand style in 1904, behind the old inn, it struggles to find its niche in the modern town.

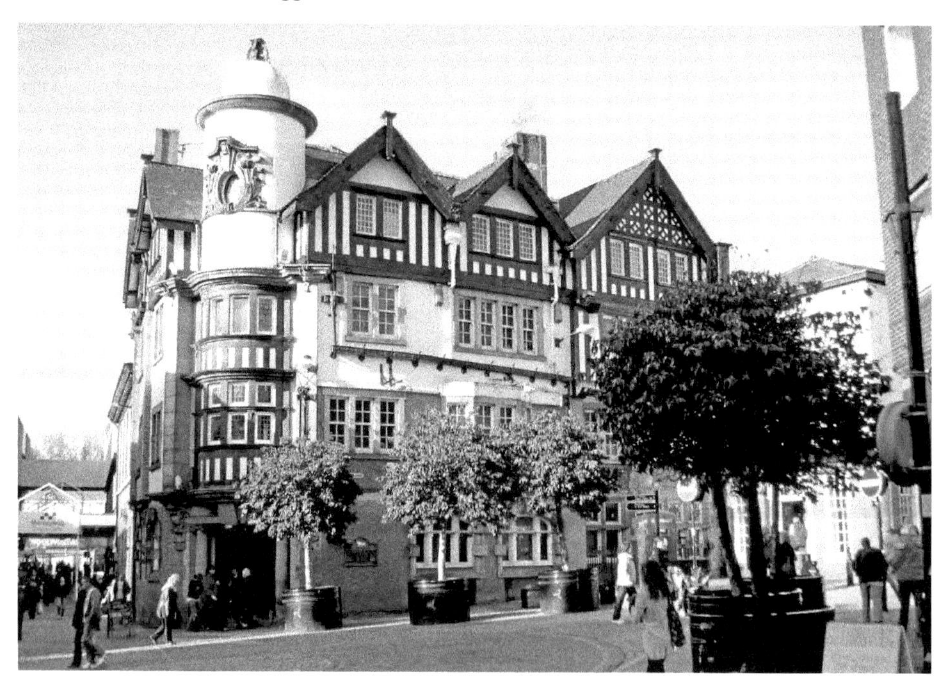

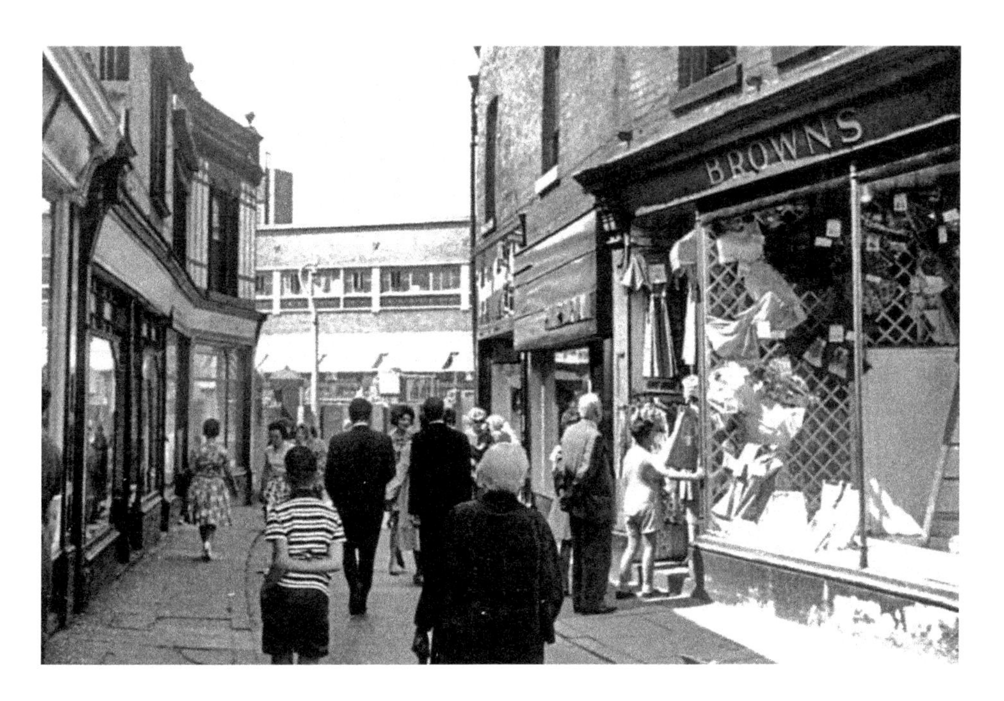

Union Road

Up until the Merseyway development, Stockport was a town divided by a river. One of the few crossing points was Union Road and its footbridge. Today it is a pedestrianised area. The old Vernon Bridge itself was of lattice construction and children looking through the girders were fascinated or horrified to see rats on the riverbank. Today it provides an entrance to the Merseyway Shopping Centre. The river has been discreetly covered, the bridge's name changed to a less descriptive Deanery Way.

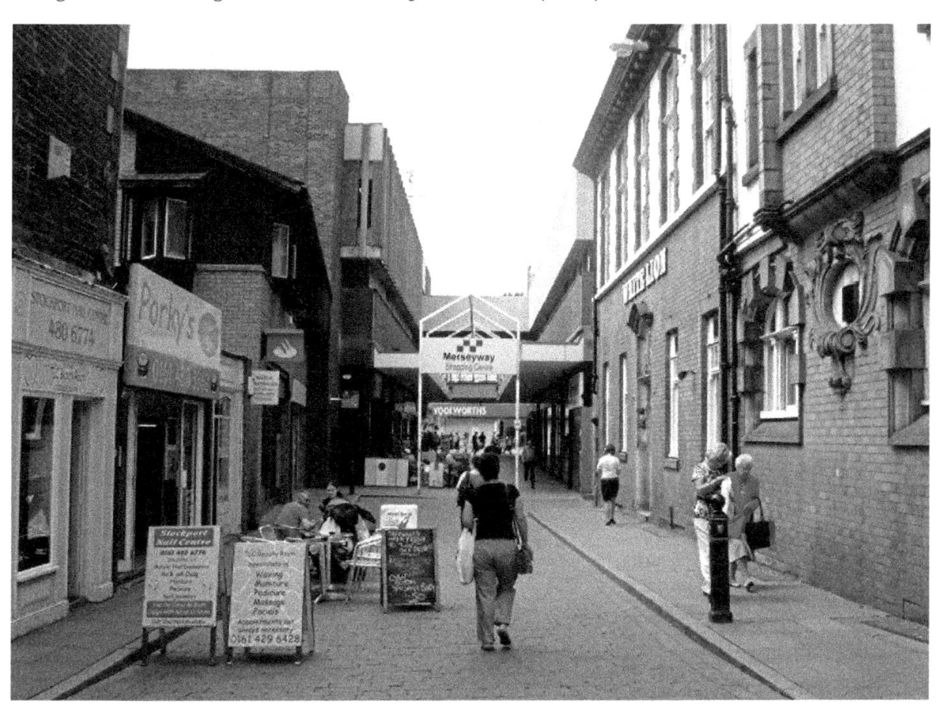

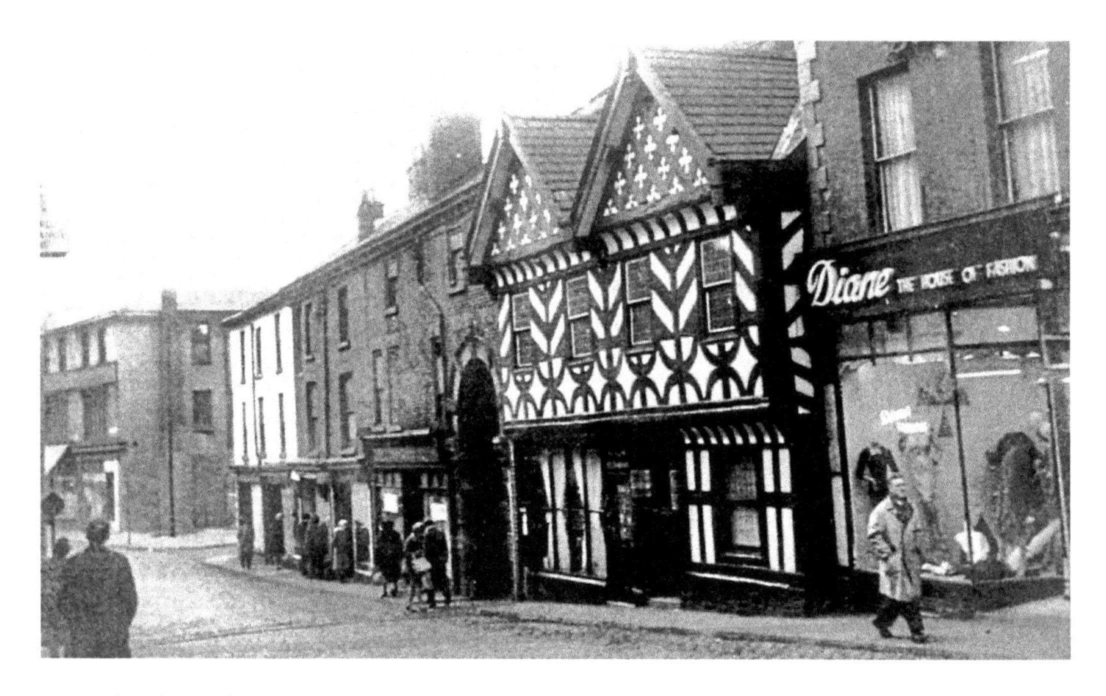

The Three Shires

Like Underbank Hall, the Three Shires was originally a town house, in this instance owned by the Leghs of Adlington. Its earliest deeds date back to 1657 but there is little doubt that the black-and-white building, only the second to survive in the town, was built much earlier. The house was sold and converted into a shop with the insertion of windows in 1824 and has had many tenants since, mainly food-and-drink providers. Today it sits rather sadly next to the Merseyway Precinct and behind a mass of traffic-control measures.

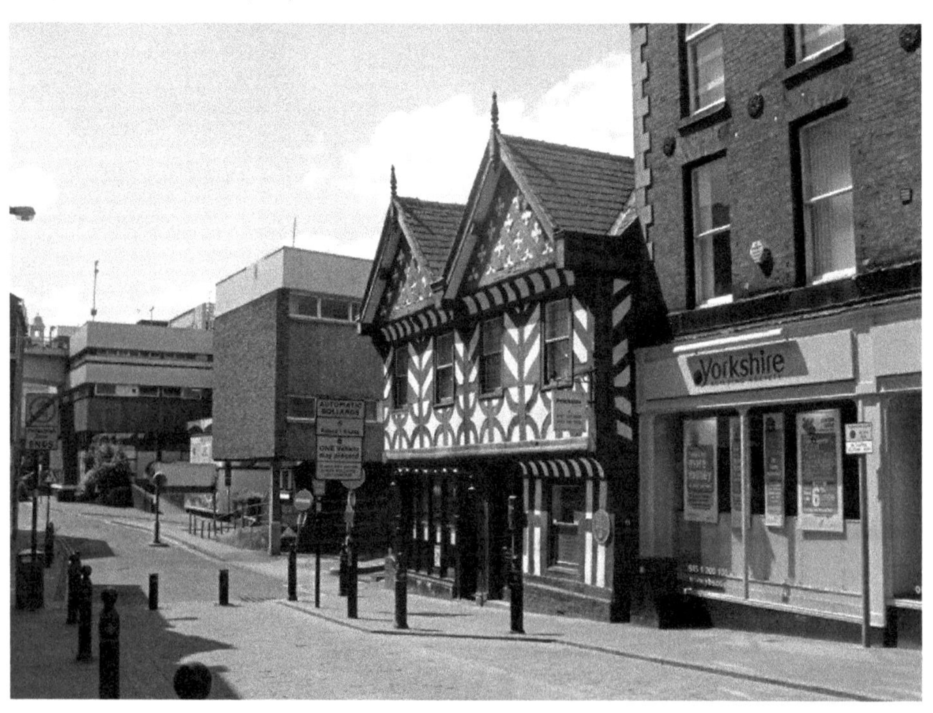

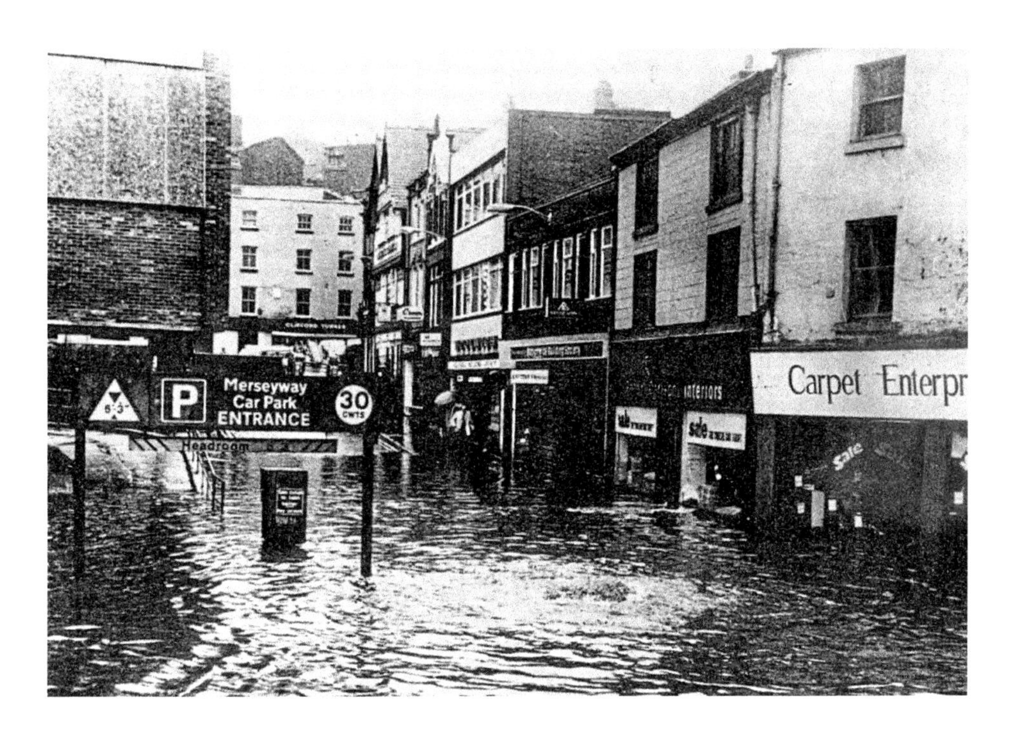

Tin Brook

It may come as a surprise to many Stopfordians to find that there is another 'underground' river in the town, the Tin Brook. Culverted down Hillgate, it crosses Great Underbank beneath the road, unnoticed – that is, until it floods, as seen here in the early 1970s. In medieval times, the road crossed the brook by a ford, later replaced by a narrow bridge. The cyclist in the picture below would have been getting his feet wet. How things change. Who today knows what '30 cwts' is?

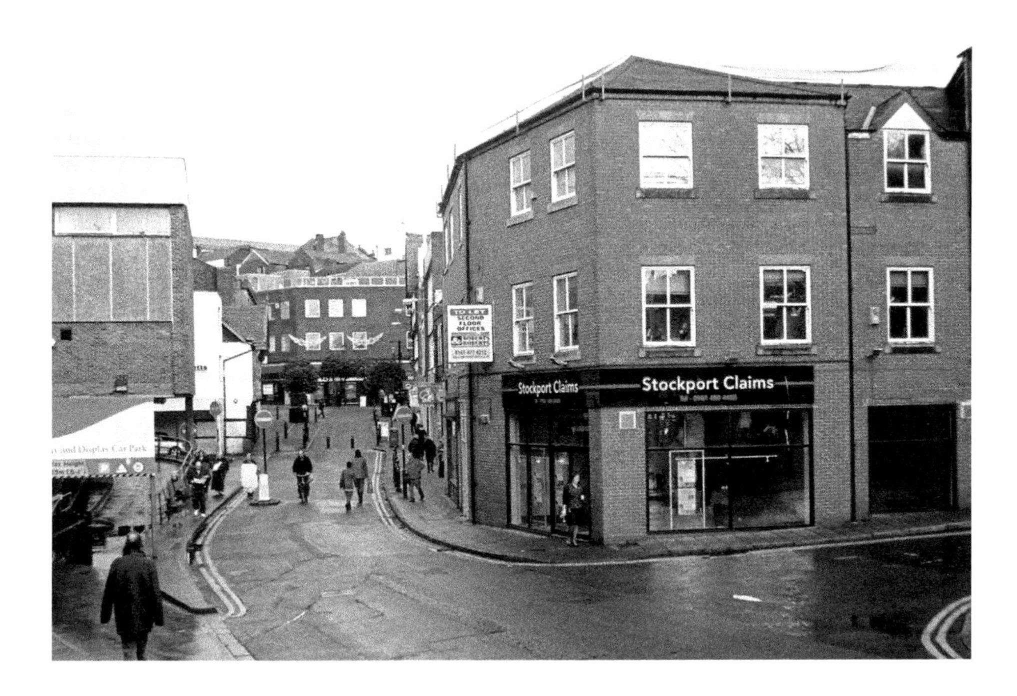

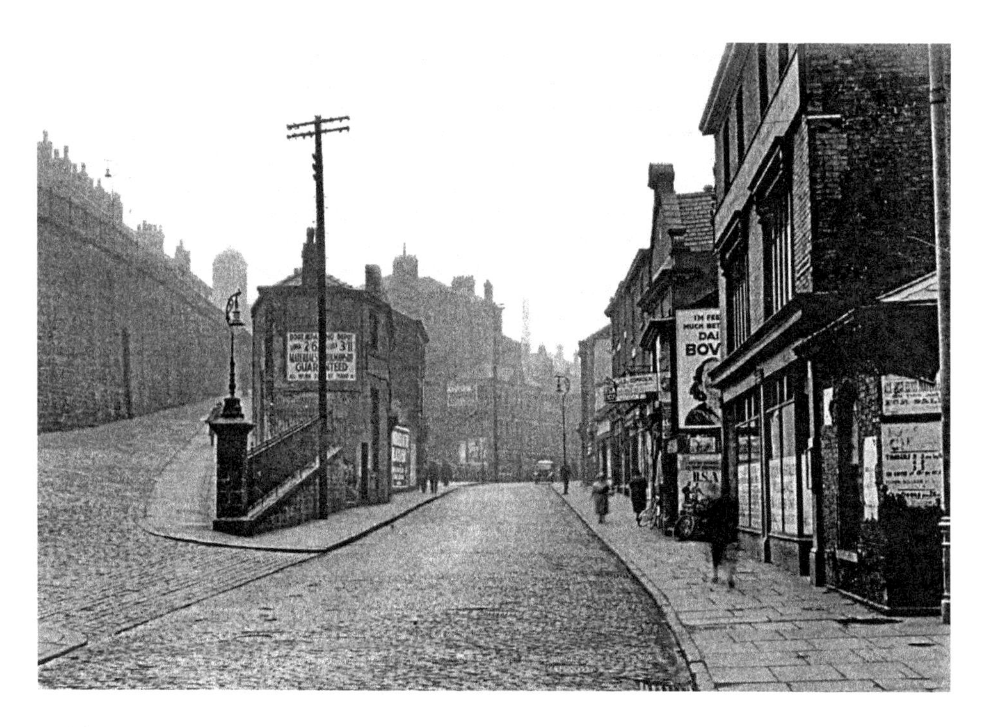

Pickford's Brow

Some scenes of Stockport show little change but others, like this view of Pickford's Brow, are completely different. An early landlord of Chestergate's White Hart Hotel – as seen in the centre of the picture but long-since demolished – gave his name to this brow. Now the access bridge to the precinct car park shadows the road as well as one of Stockport's superb attractions – the Air Raid Shelter Museum. Past the entrance, against the wall, you walk into the largest purpose-built Second World War shelter in the country, which was capable of housing over 7,000 people.

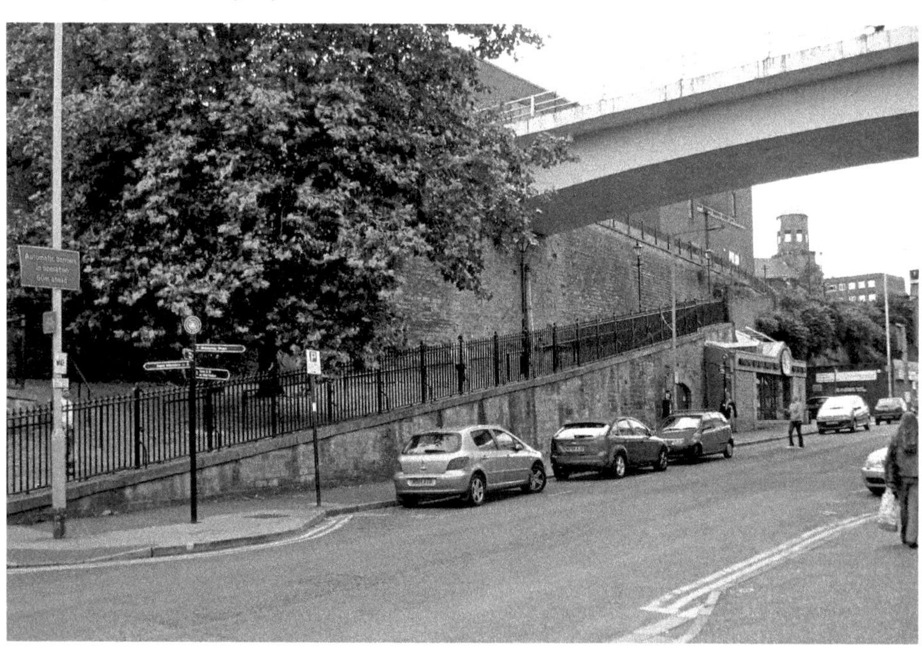

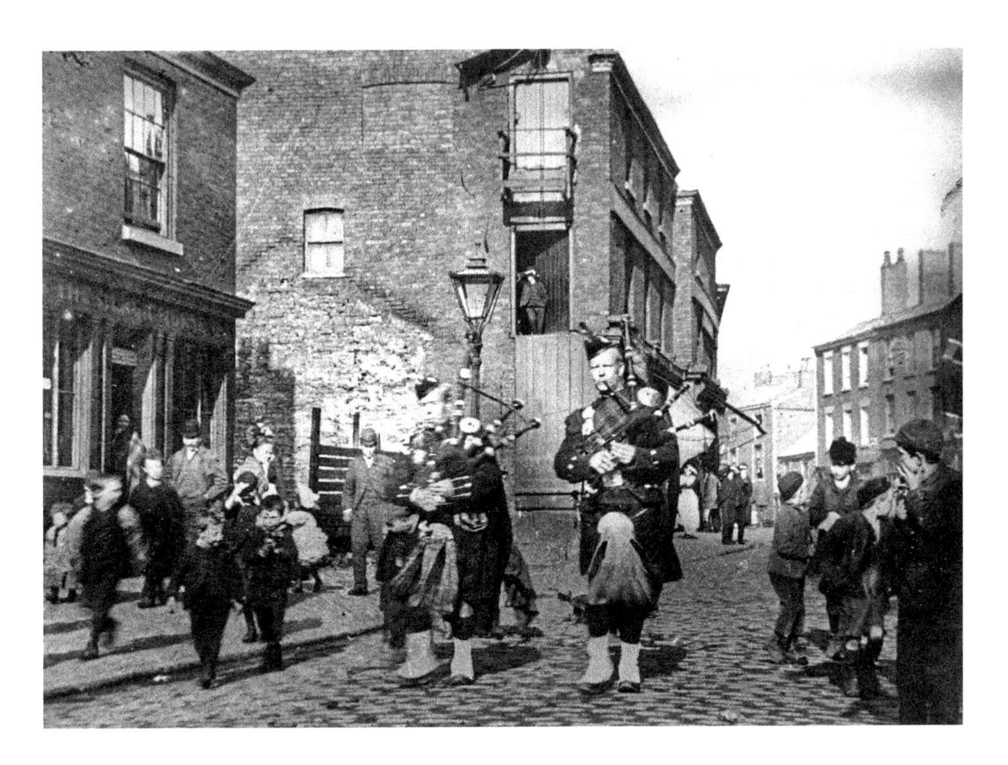

Chestergate

Why Scottish pipers are marching through Stockport is a mystery. Perhaps they are soldiers stationed here. They seem to have attracted the youngsters of the town as well as a precarious onlooker in the doorway on the side of the mill. Chestergate was the main road west from Lancashire Bridge and has seen great change; every property in the black-and-white photograph has been demolished. This includes the Black Horse pub on the left and the mill next door, which made way for the new Co-operative store in 1926.

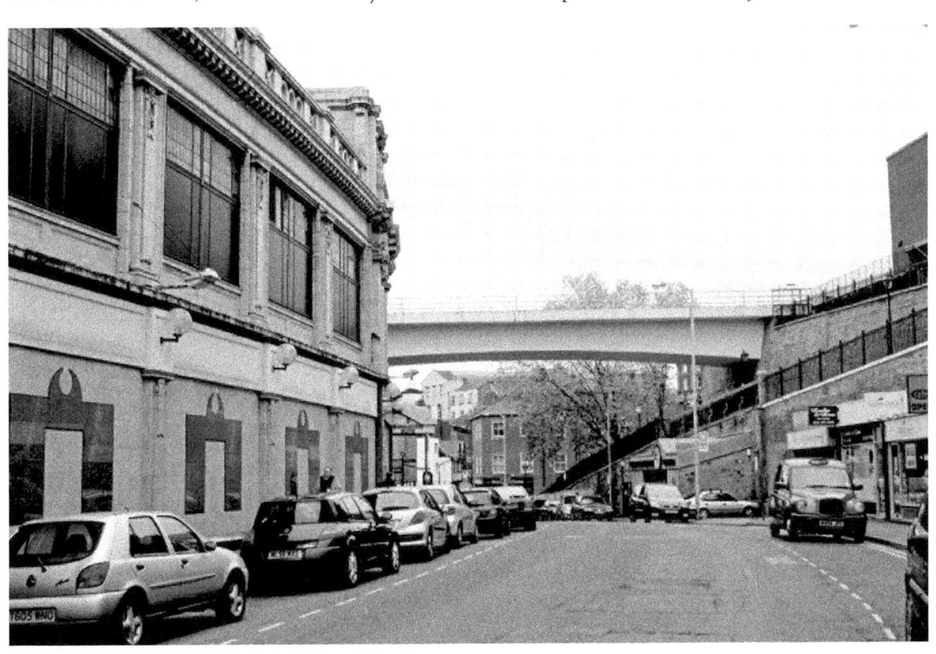

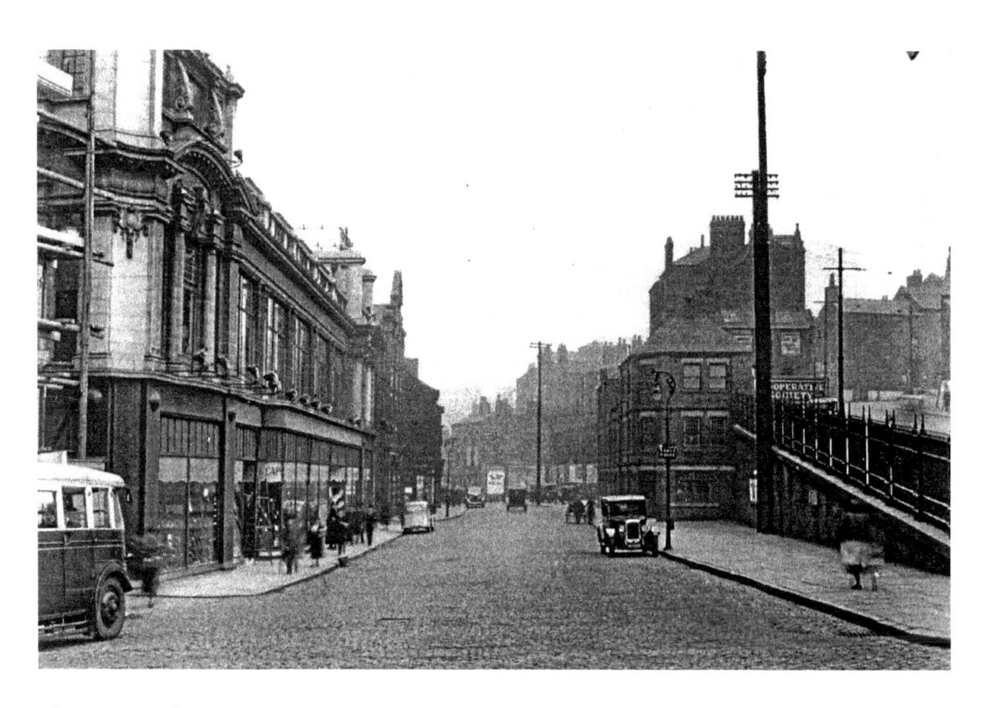

Chestergate from Mersey Square

Before Merseyway was opened in 1940, Chestergate was the main road westwards towards Cheadle. In our photograph from the 1930s a single-deck bus leaves Mersey Square and makes its way towards Great Underbank, past the Co-operative store. Facing Mersey Square, a single taxi waits for a fare. Today, eighty years later, it is still possible to pick up a cab. What have disappeared are the massive telegraph posts, which used to carry wires all over the town. Now everything is neatly underground.

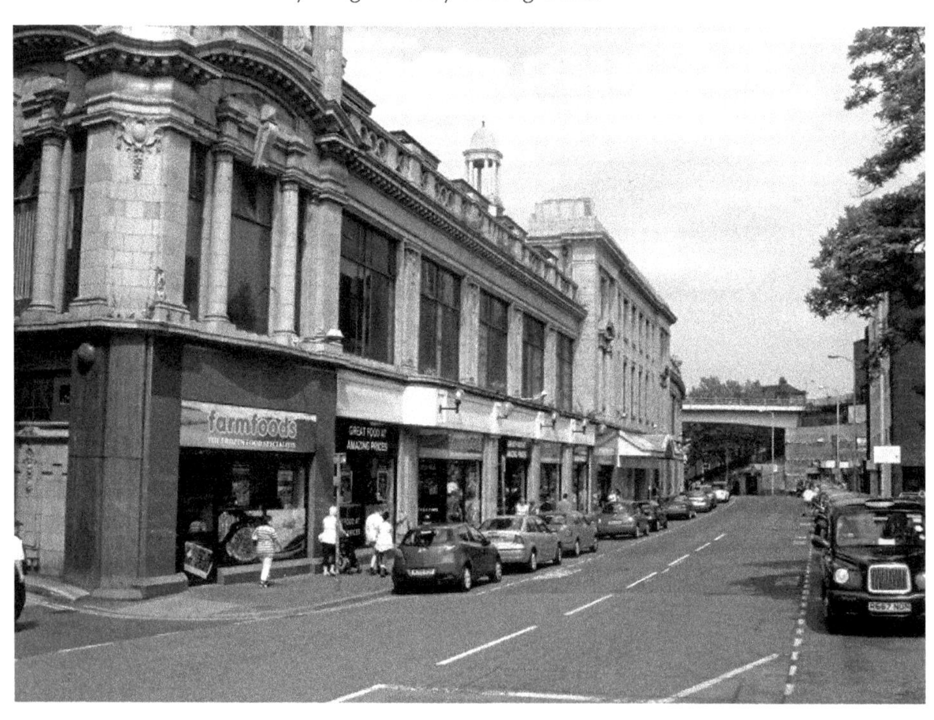

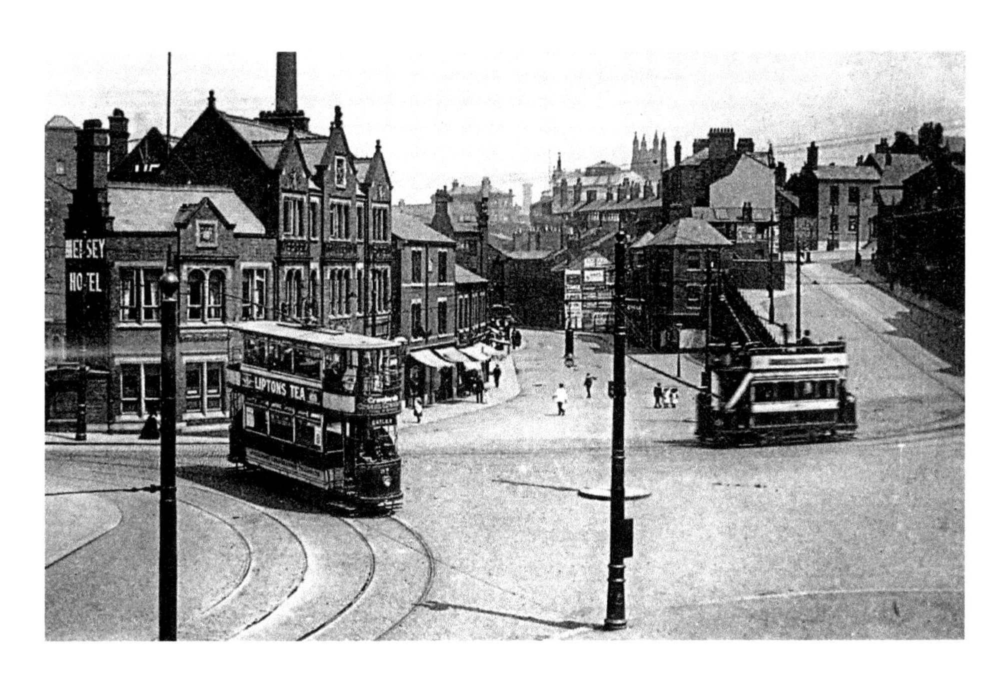

Chestergate and Rock Row

It is about 1910 and a Stockport tram swings past the Mersey Hotel on its journey to Gatley while an open-topped Manchester tram prepares to grind its way up Rock Row to St Peter's Square. Rock Row had poor housing and many Irish immigrants were forced to live there. It was the scene of the riots in 1852 when a mob of unemployed Stockport cotton workers attacked the Irish homes. So great have been the changes in Stockport's town centre, only the imposing Mersey Hotel survives to be seen in the modern photograph.

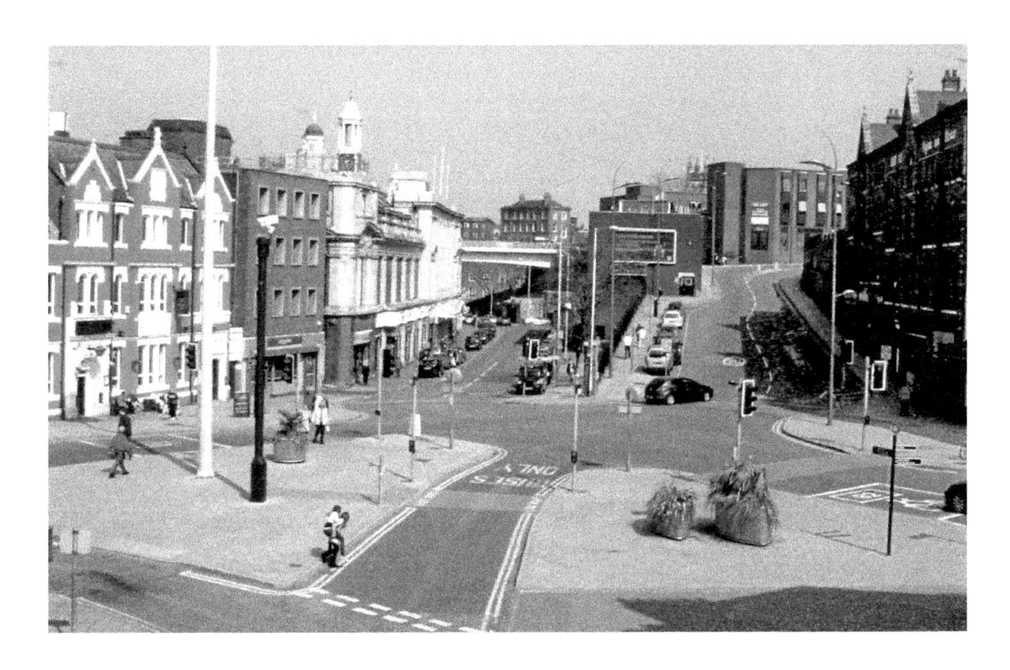

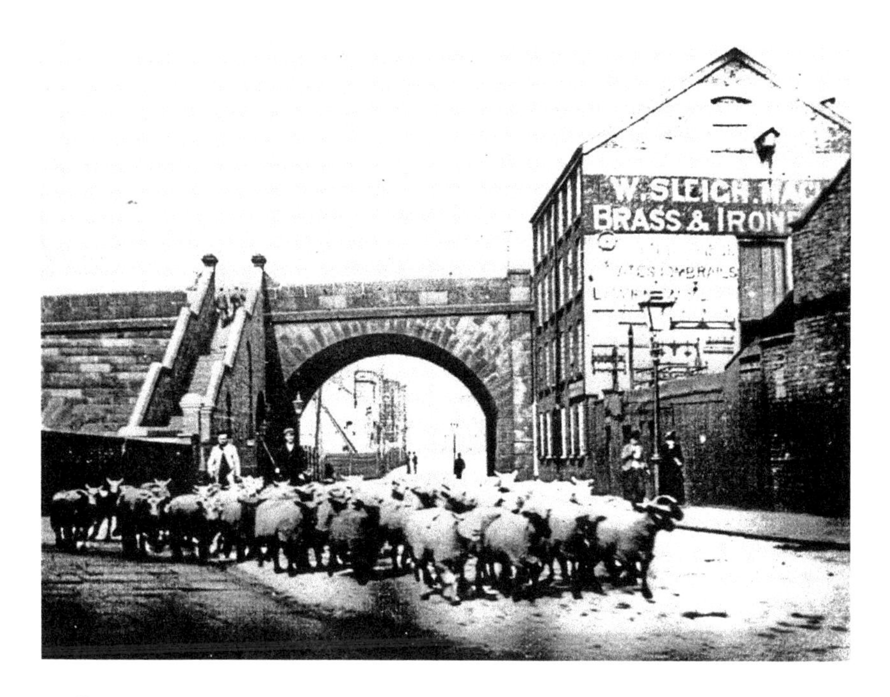

Wellington Viaduct

It was a common sight, before the benefits of refrigeration, to see animals being driven into our towns to provide fresh meat. In this photograph, taken in the 1890s, a flock of sheep have just passed under the Wellington viaduct and are heading along Chestergate towards Brinksway, overlooked by two shepherds. The same journey today would take you under the thundering traffic of the A6 and into the bus station. On the wall of the steps is a plaque erected to commemorate Howard Beckwith, Stockport's fire chief, who died near here in an accident in 1926.

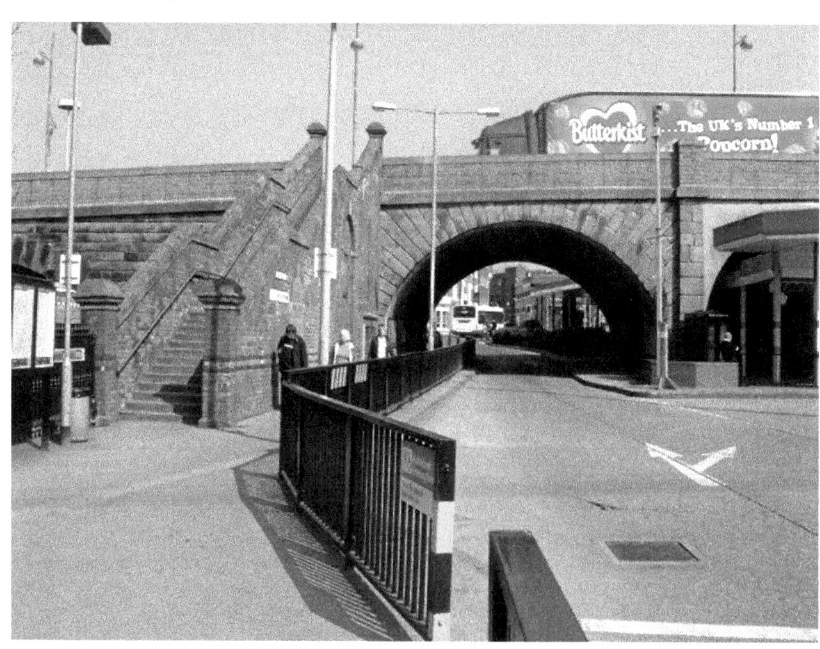

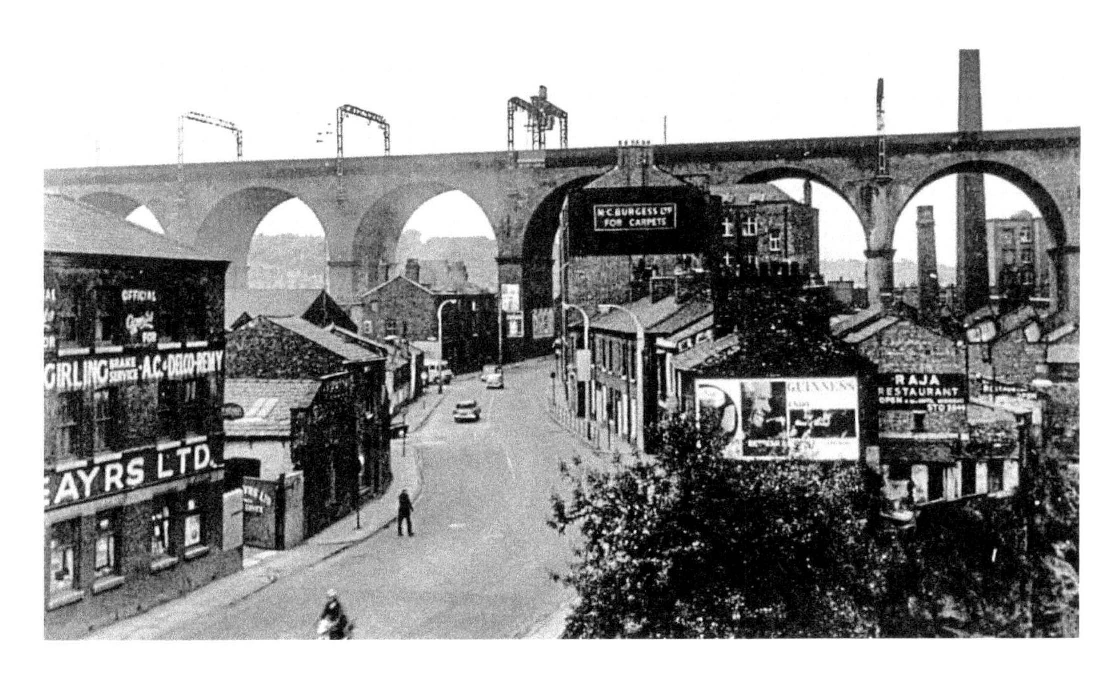

Bus Station

Looking from Wellington Road, we can see Chestergate making its way towards Brinksway and passing under the magnificent viaduct, the largest brick structure in Europe, which was completed in 1840 and took only twenty-two months to build. In this 1960s photograph, by the riverbank, note Raja's, one of the first Indian restaurants in the town. In the modern photograph, apart from the viaduct, it is difficult to see any of the old buildings due to the new bus station and the tree-lined riverbanks.

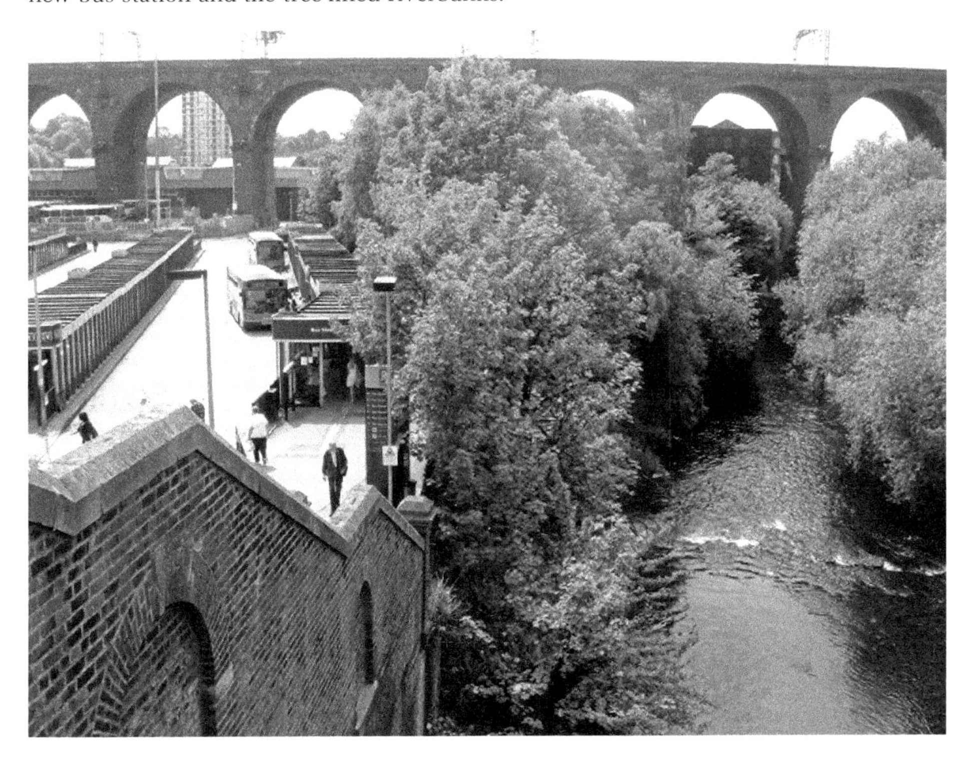

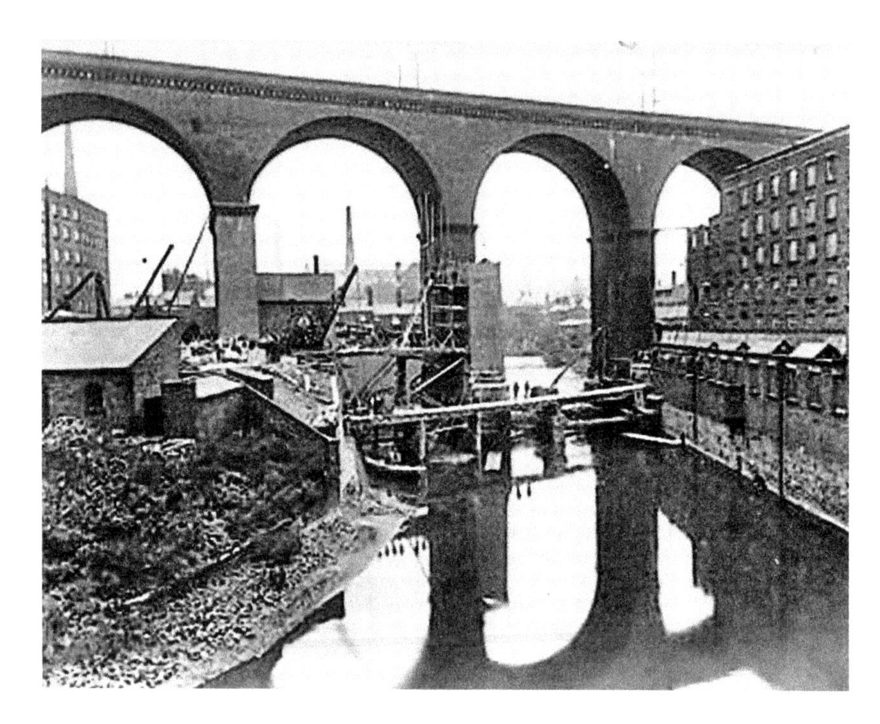

Weir Mill

By the 1880s the two-track viaduct was becoming a bottleneck, so widening was necessary. However, the area was now more built up. The greatest problem was Weir Mill, right under the works. The only solution, as we can see here, was to demolish the top floor to construct the arch above, then to rebuild it. On today's photograph the widened section can clearly be seen. Weir Mill, as its name suggests, was originally water-powered and was one of Stockport's earliest cotton mills. It opened before 1800.

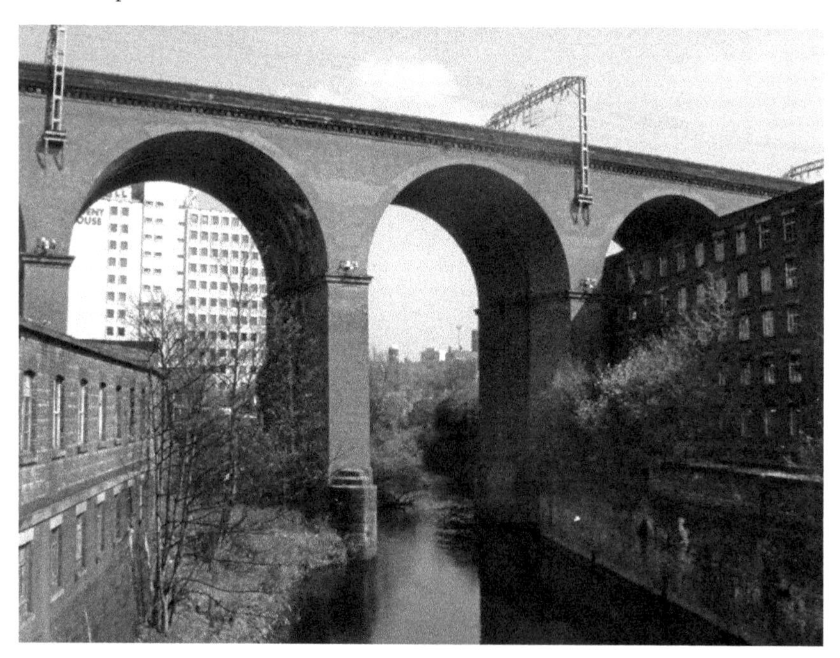

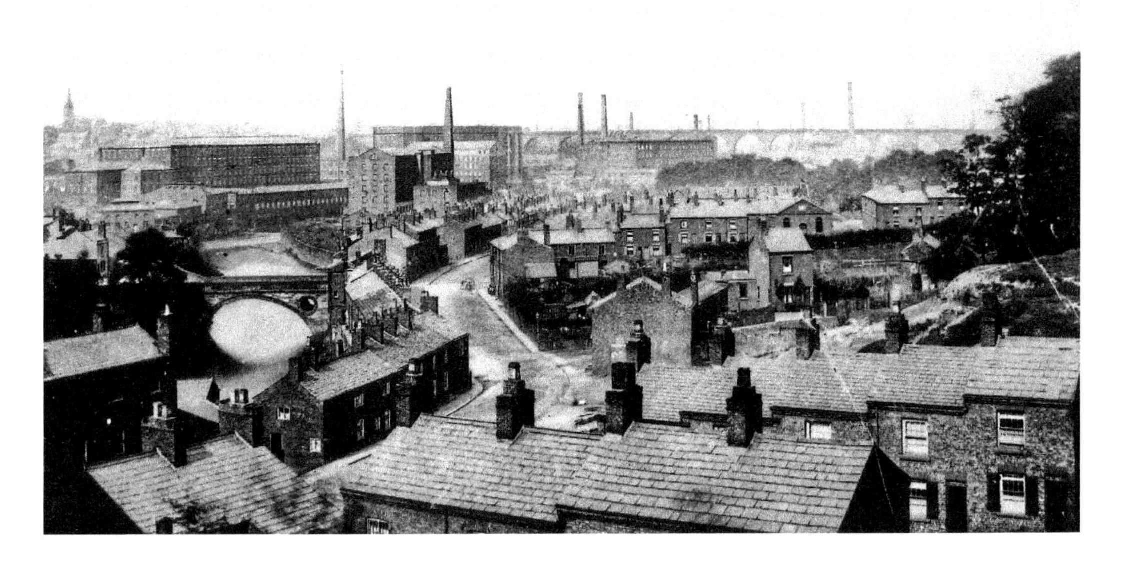

Brinksway Bridge

This wonderful panoramic view towards Stockport from Lark Hill emphasises the dominance of cotton in the town, with mill after mill stretching into the distance. Spanning the River Mersey is the Brinksway or Woolpack Bridge, once the site of a cross-river ferry boat. The old bridge still spans the Mersey, but only for pedestrians. The road to the M60 required a new girder bridge that can be seen behind the old arch. All around, the mills have disappeared, replaced by uninspiring industrial units giving a completely different aspect to the view.

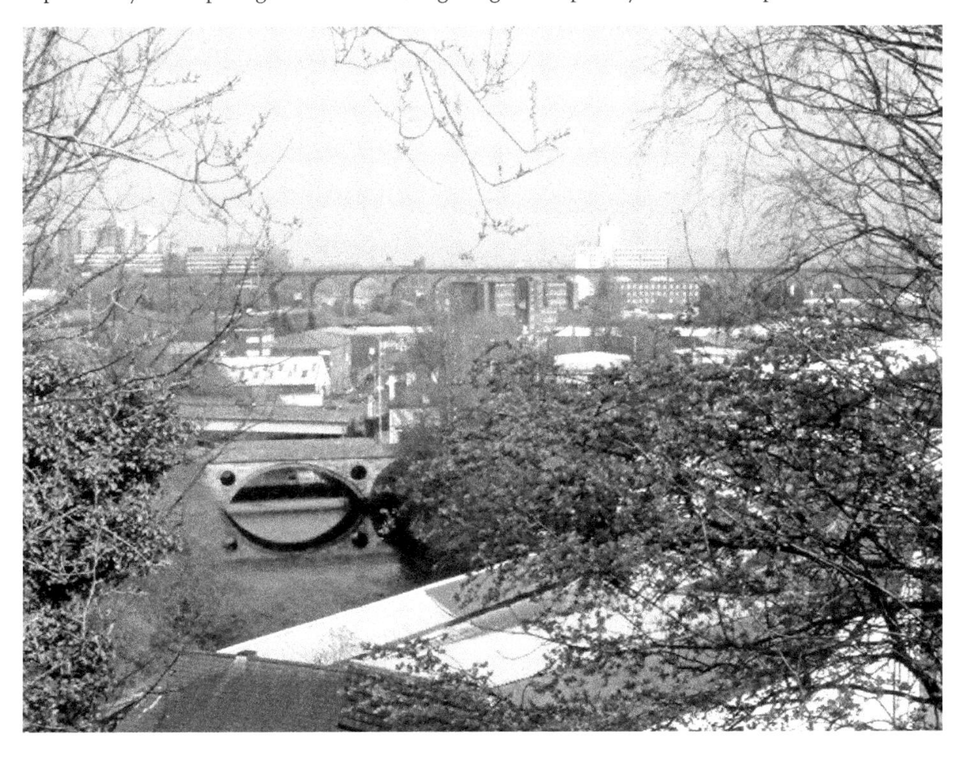

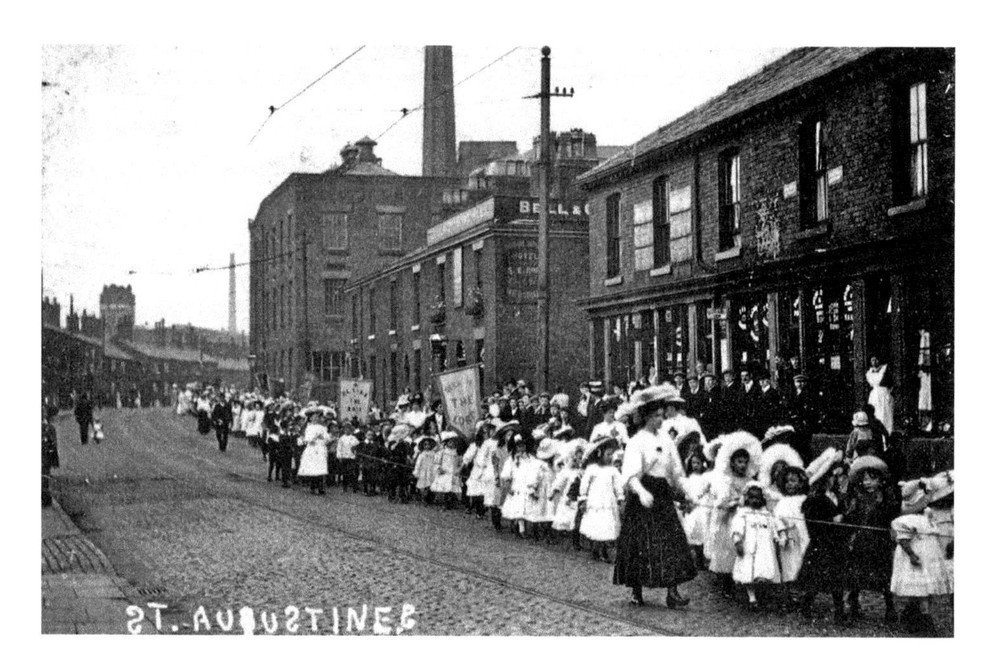

Whit Walk on Brinksway Road

It's about 1910 and a Whit Sunday parade of children makes its way along Brinksway Road towards St Augustine's church. The walks were a northern tradition and every effort was made for the children to wear a special outfit or dress – and, since it was Stockport, a new hat. Later there would be lemonade and cakes with games in nearby Hollywood Park, a welcome relief from the mundane life of that time. Change has been so great that everything on our old picture has gone, even the cobbled road, replaced with modern housing and green spaces.

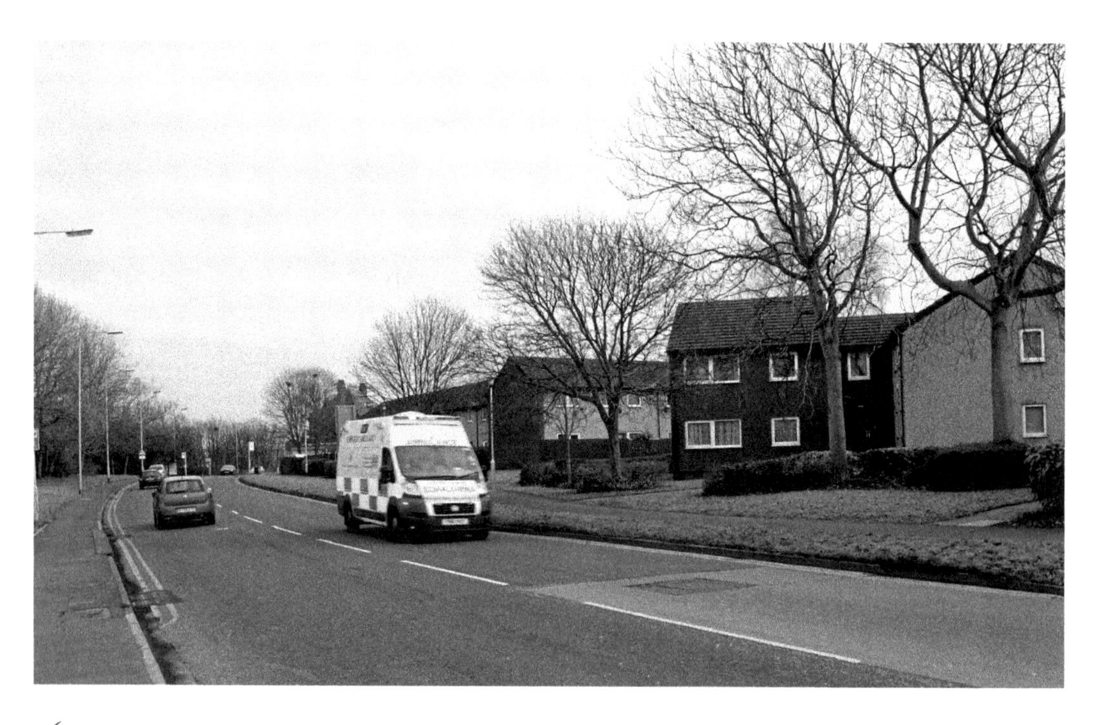

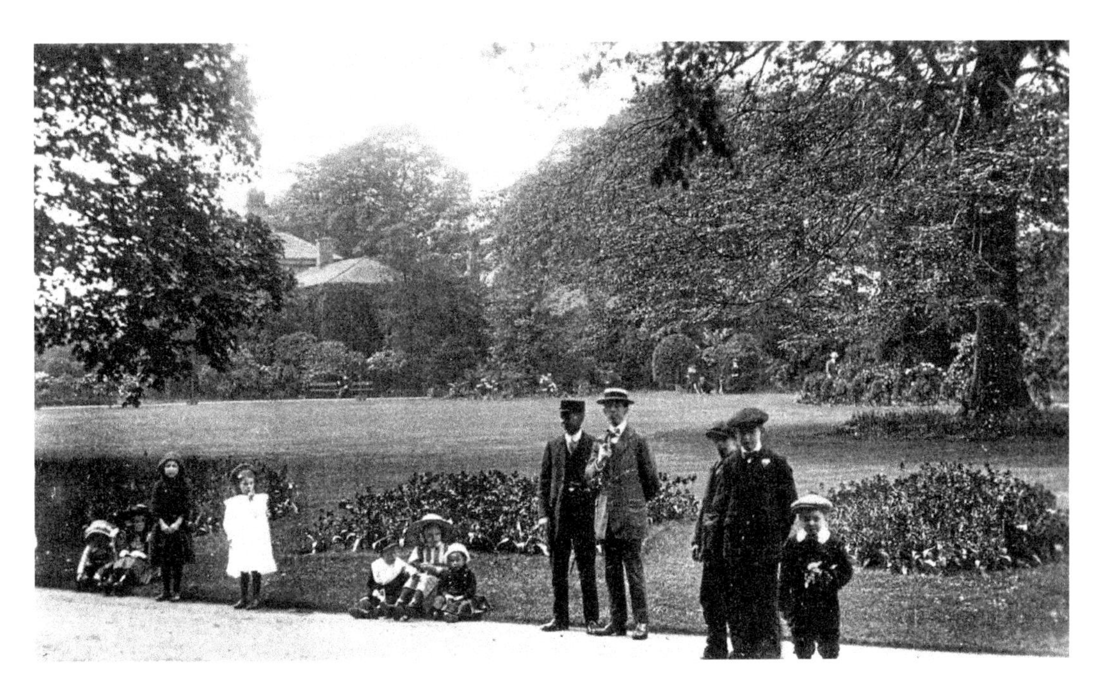

Alexandra Park

There are three parks in Edgeley; Alexandra Park can be considered the most traditional. Once the grounds of Edgeley House, the home of the Sykes family, it was bought and landscaped by the Stockport Corporation at a cost of £8,000 and opened to the public in 1908. Near the Parks Department depot can still be found some of the courtyard paving of the original house stables of 1795. The park is still very much appreciated by the local people as it provides play areas for children, bowling greens, and somewhere to go for a stroll.

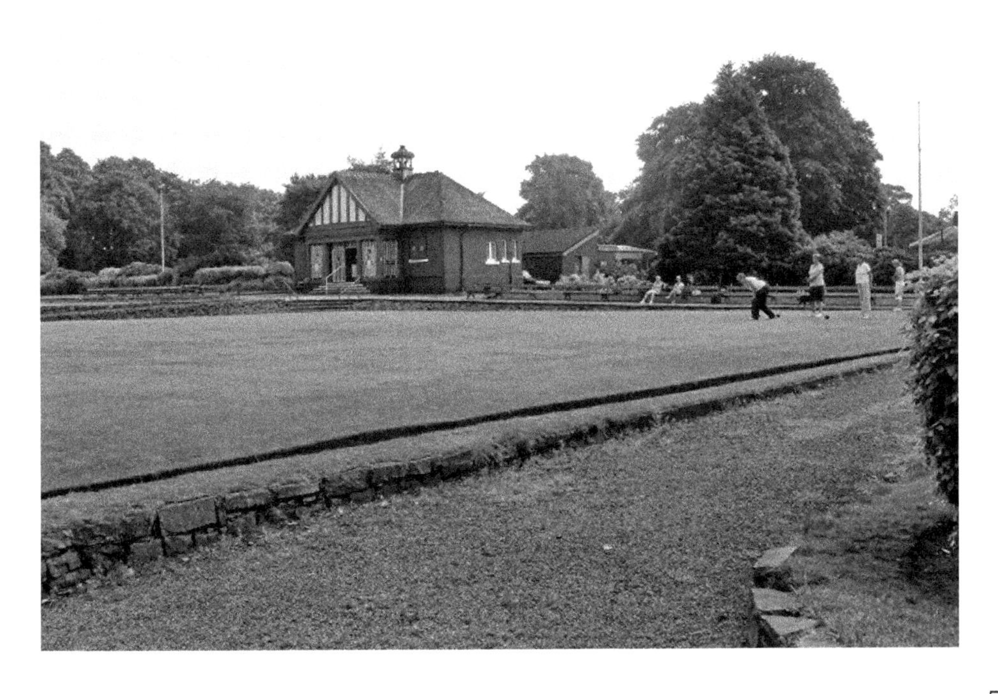

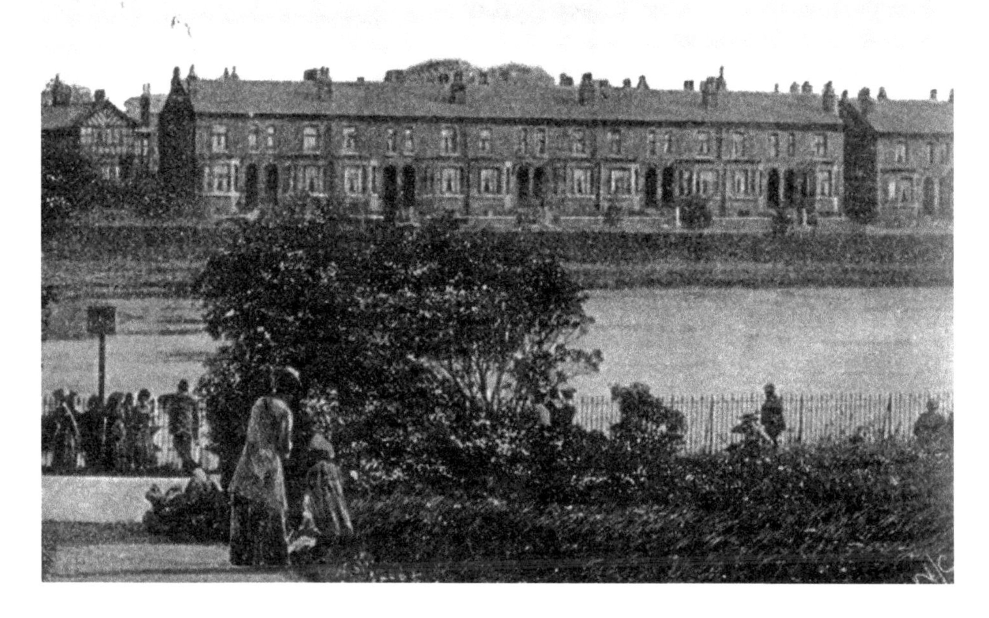

Sykes' Reservoirs

The Sykes family, mentioned on the previous page, can be traced back to William Sykes, who set up a bleachworks in Edgeley in 1792. Bleaching was part of the finishing process of cotton manufacture and required large amounts of water, hence the need for the reservoirs. The two pictures reflect little change to this tranquil part of Stockport, but in 1867 there was great excitement. Stockport Sunday School had paid for a lifeboat and, to much cheering, the boat was pulled from the school by the pupils and trial-launched on the reservoirs.

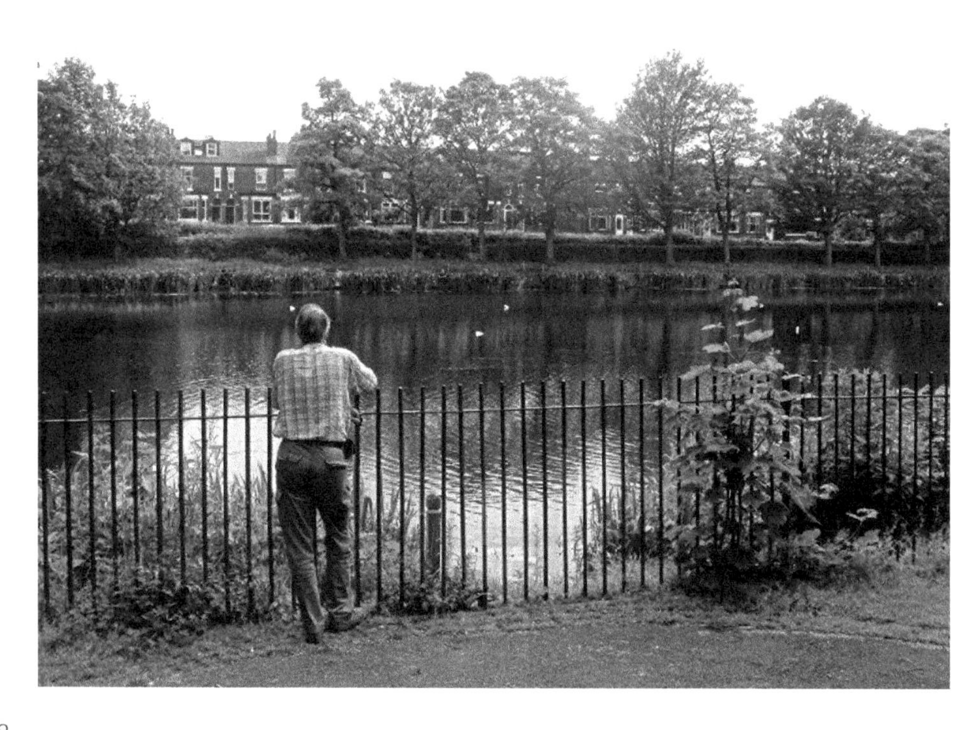

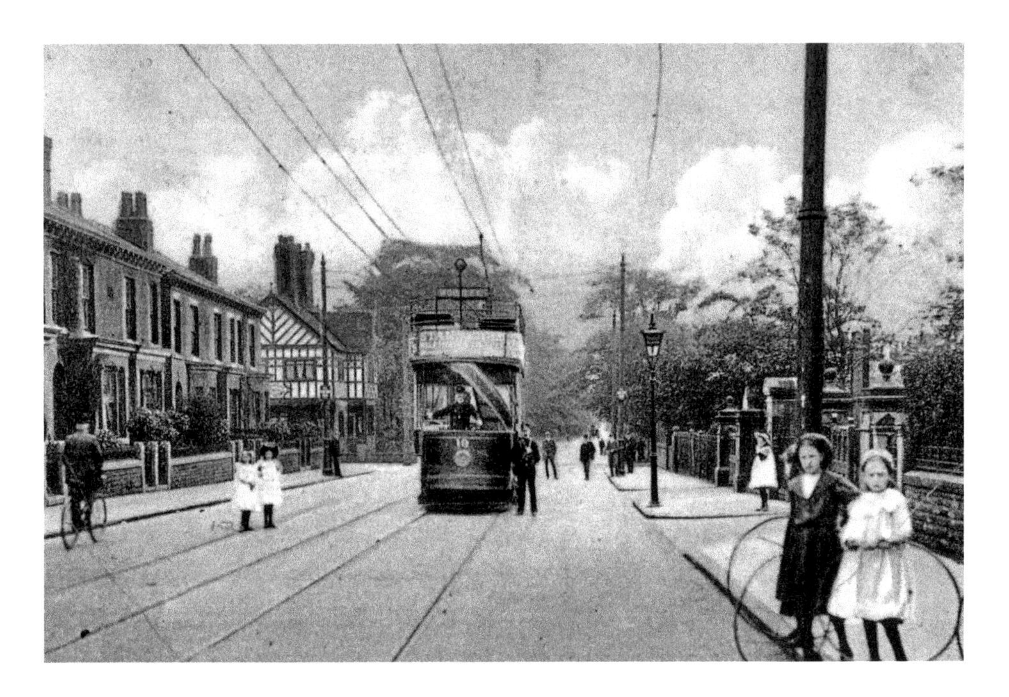

Dale Street

In the early 1900s a tram waits to depart from the Dale Street terminus for Woodley. All have stopped to stare at the camera except the gentleman on the bicycle, who is watching where he is going and avoiding the treacherous tramlines. The innocence of the time is reflected in the girls: two stand in the road and the pair with iron hoops are mesmerised by the shutter. The black-and-white building, Edgeley Cottage, stands out in both pictures, but change is minimal except for the graffiti of modern road markings.

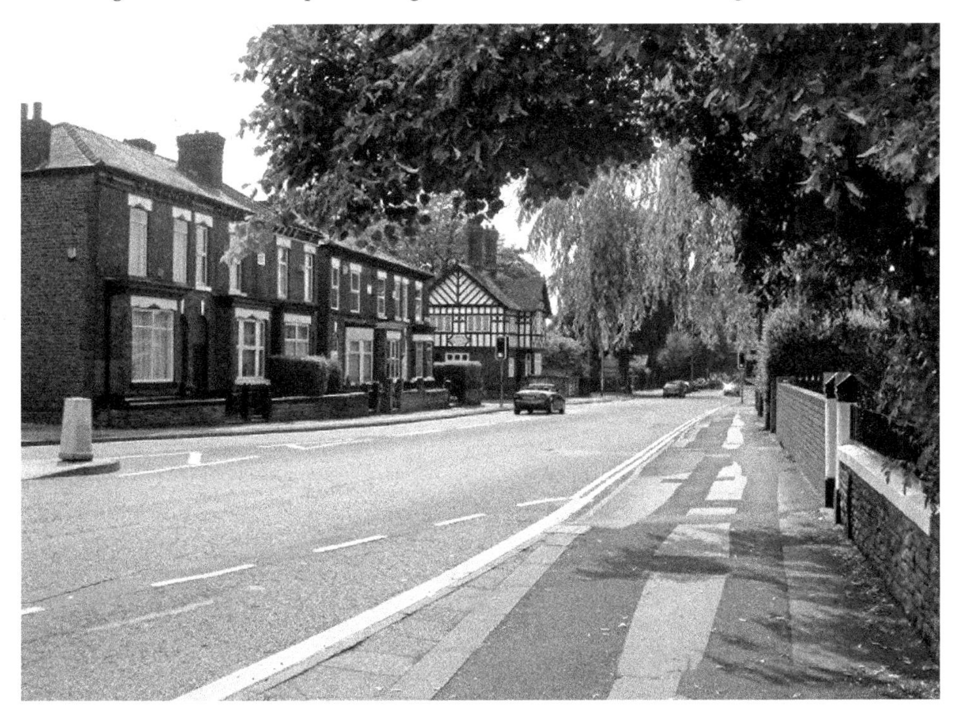

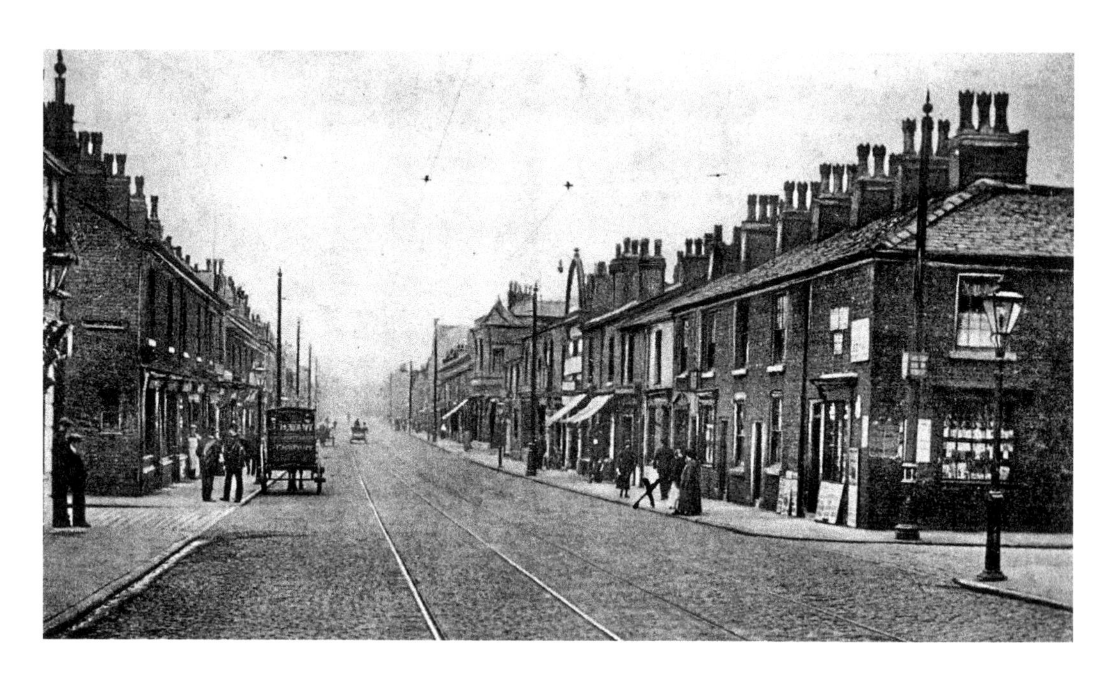

Castle Street

Looking towards the Armoury, again in the 1900s, this old photograph highlights the new road of Castle Street, part of the Stockport–Warrington turnpike of 1820. In our picture, the local 'bobby' appears to be talking to the postman while, across the side road, there is evidence of that well-known pastime, leaning on a lamp post. In the distance an early car keeps to the tramlines to reduce the effect of the bone-shaking cobbles. Little has altered over the years apart from the removal of chimneys and the addition of green bins. There is even a lamp post to lean against.

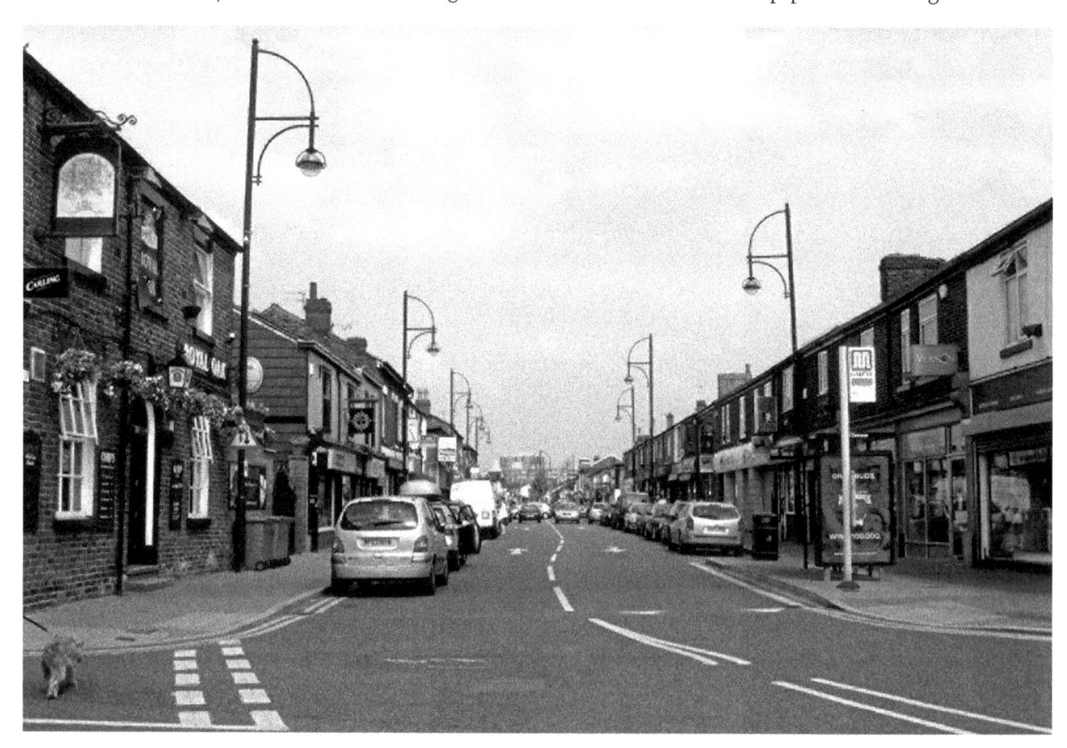

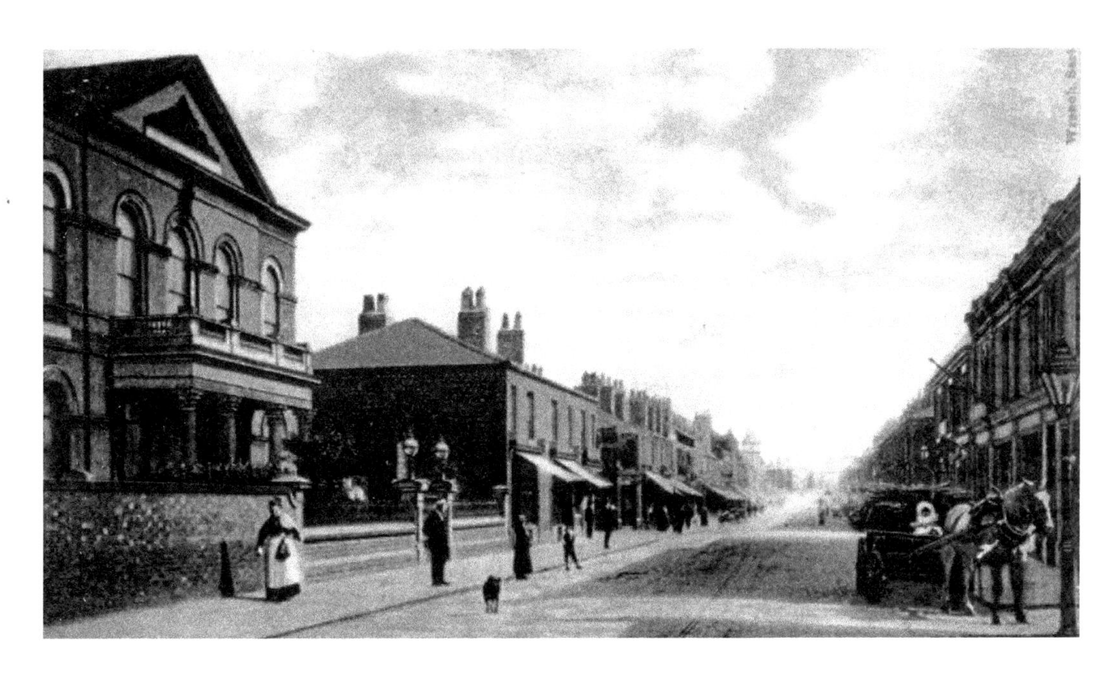

Methodist Chapel

This very early coloured photograph of the 1890s, taken further along Castle Street, shows the Edgeley Wesleyan Chapel opened in 1872; it was later closed to make way for a supermarket, only the developers got more than they bargained for when cast-iron coffins were unearthed that defied all attempts to open them. Rumour has it that they were reburied under the pavement between the shops, unbeknown to shoppers. A new Mercian Way now takes traffic past Castle Street, most of which is pedestrianised, making shopping less stressful.

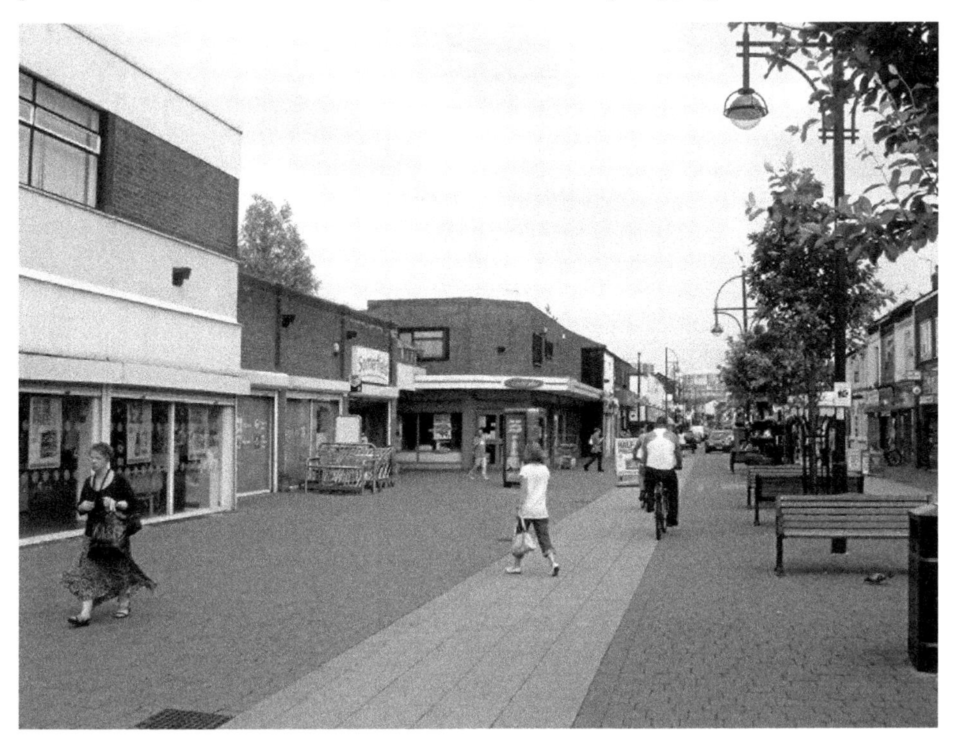

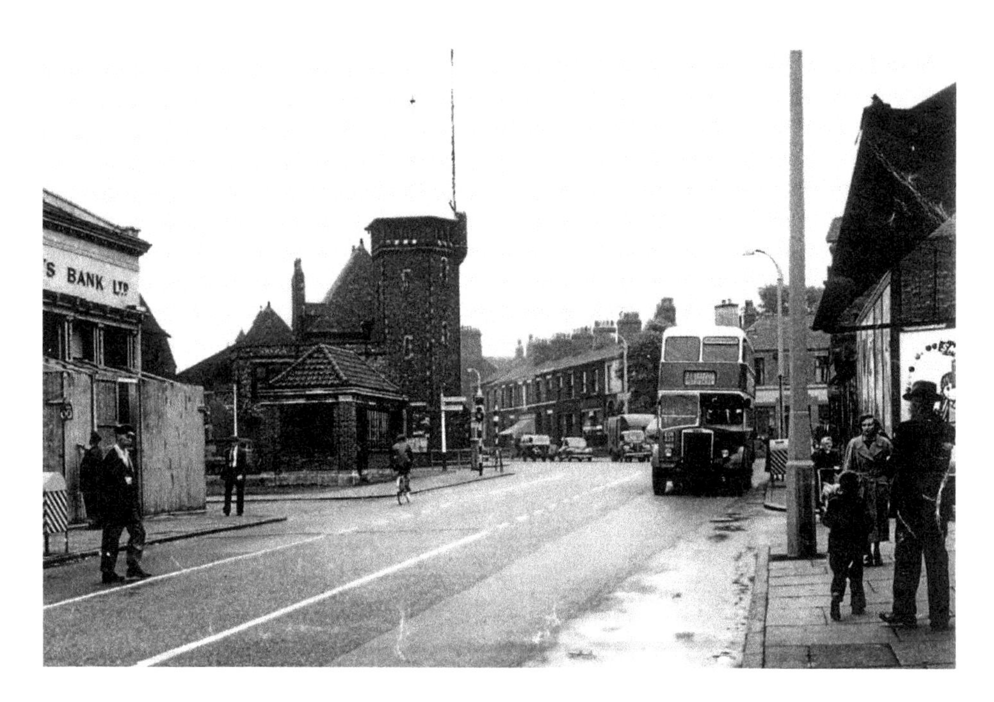

Armoury

Because of a French invasion scare, the Armoury, with its distinctive tower, was built in 1862 to house the Rifle Volunteers. Despite the lack of an invasion it still remains one of the main military establishments in the town. In the 1950s photograph, strolling across the road in front of an Altrincham bus is a young railway fireman. Given his clean shirt, he appears to be on his way to start his shift at Edgeley engine shed. The road here crossed over a railway tunnel, which was replaced by a bridge in 1958, with a roundabout above that you can still see today.

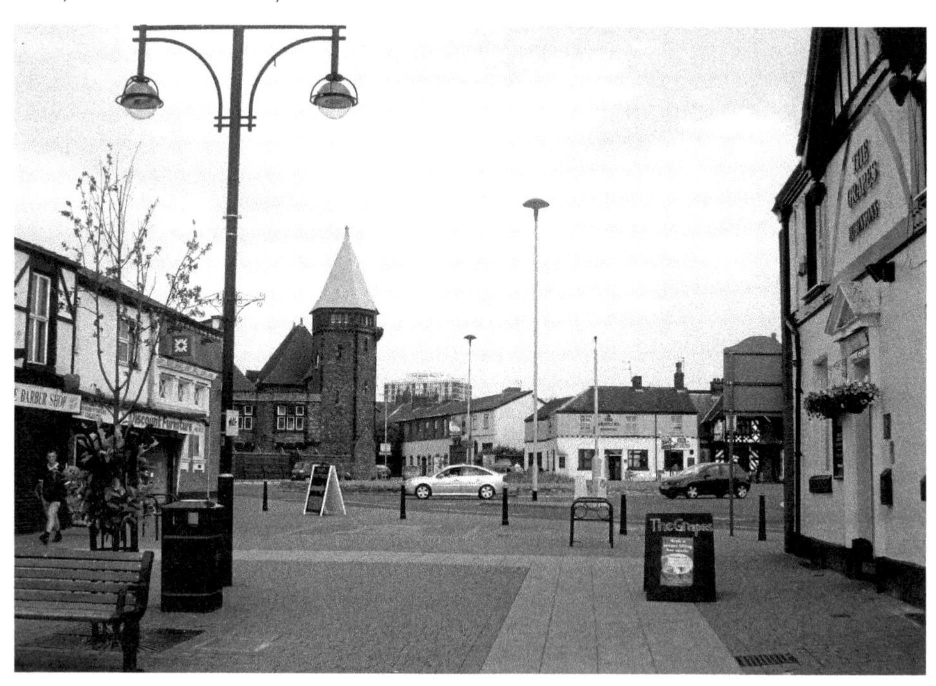

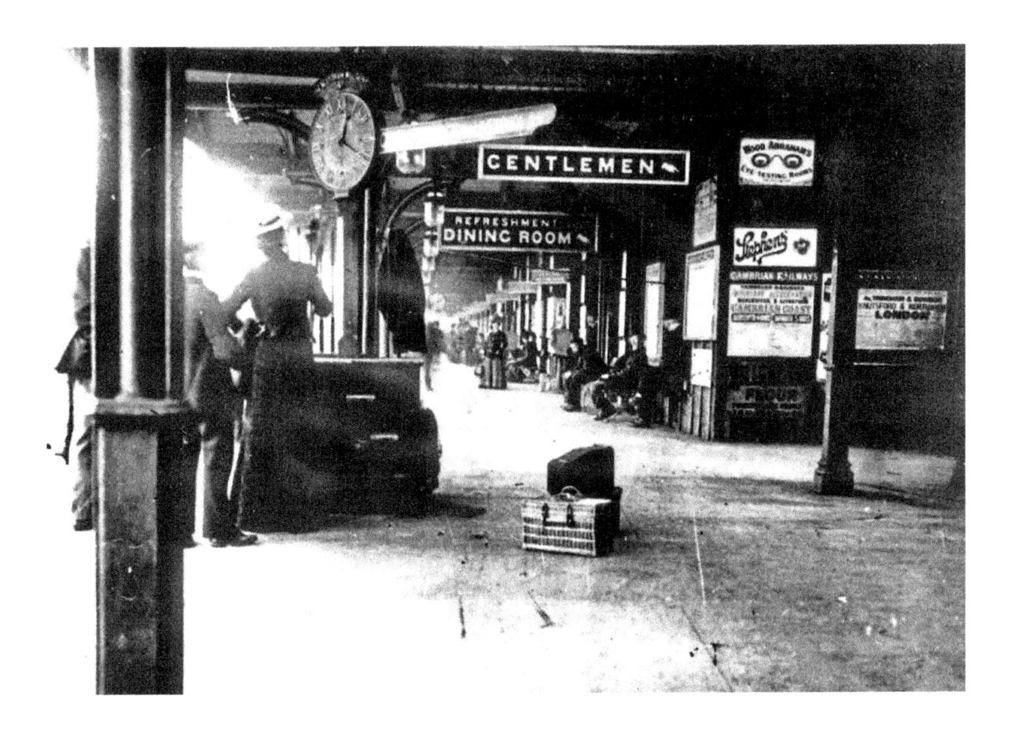

Edgeley Station

Stockport Edgeley station opened in 1842 on completion of the viaduct and was enlarged in the 1880s. On Platform 2, before the Great War, a group of passengers, wait to board the train. Their luggage is placed nearby, and they look anxiously at the departure clock. How they would have been amazed to see a Virgin Pendolino gliding into the station instead of a noisy steam engine! Fortunately the gentlemen's toilet remains, as do the signs for the refreshment room, but the reduction in advertisements is surprising in our increasingly consumerist society.

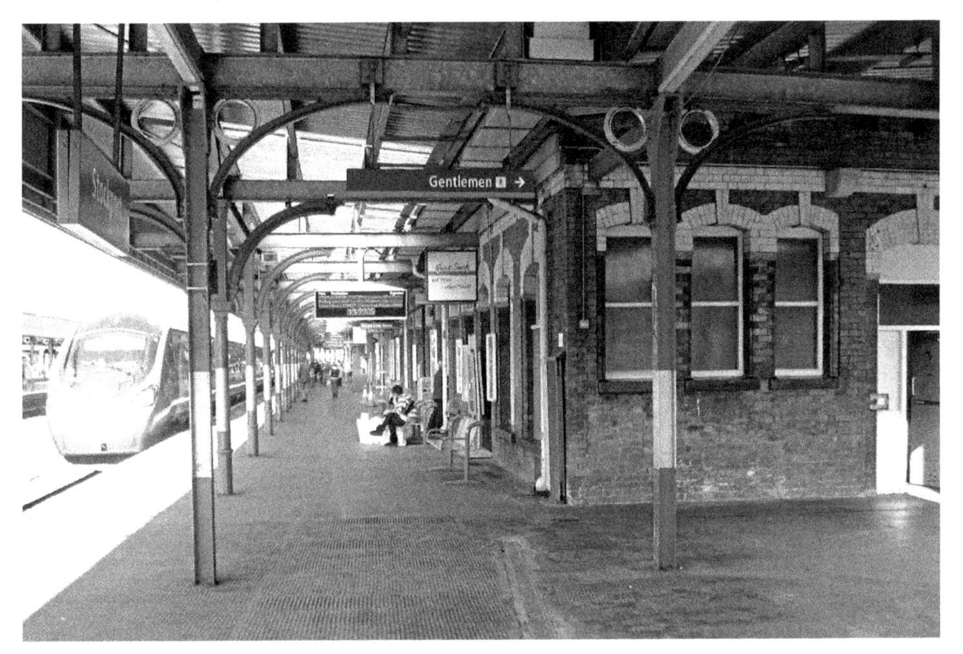

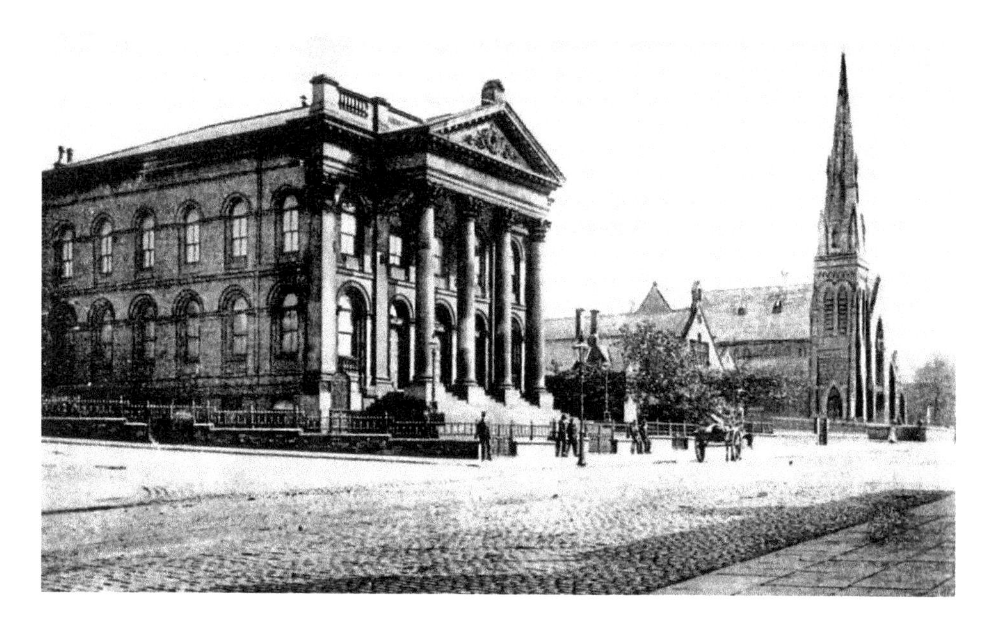

Mount Tabor Chapel

Mount Tabor Chapel was opened in 1869 on the corner of Edward Street at a cost of over £9,000, and it could seat 9,000 worshippers. In the mid-1800s there was no organised education for children and many churches took on this vital need. At Mount Tabor there were thirty-eight teachers for its Sunday school. Changes in Stockport's population distribution meant that the congregation disappeared to the suburbs and by 1955 Mount Tabor closed its doors for good. Exactly 100 years later it was demolished to provide a relaxing paved area, with only the capitals of the columns as a reminder.

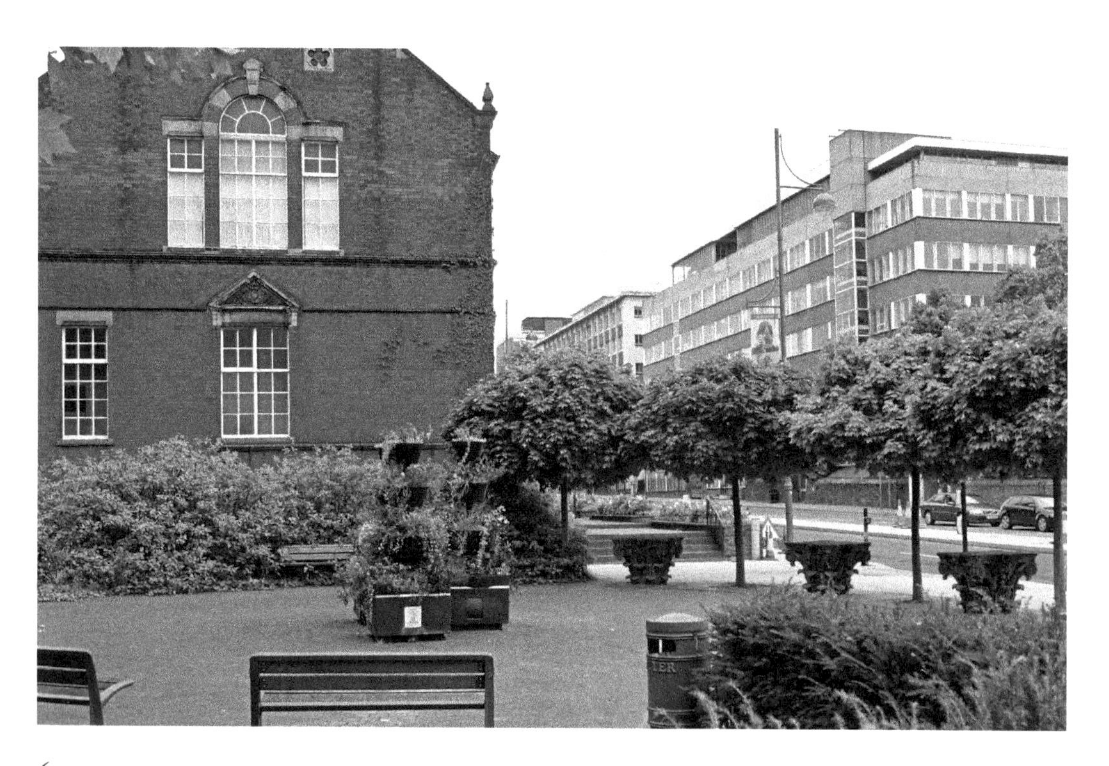

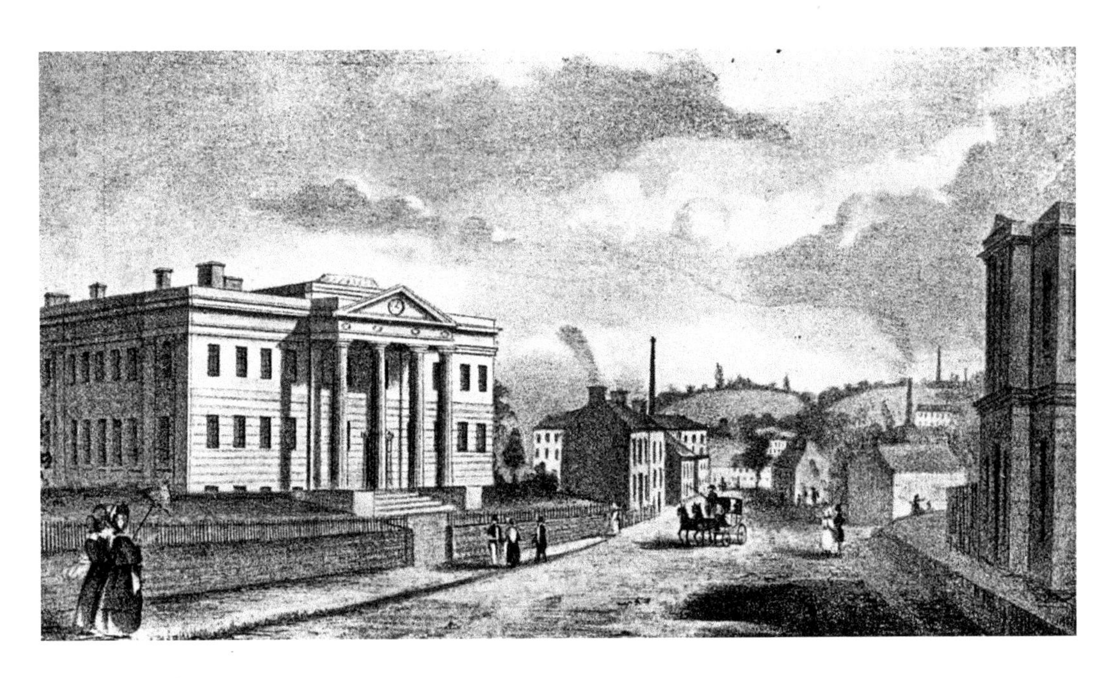

The Infirmary

As we have seen, the Stockport Dispensary first operated out of the Thatched House and later moved to Daw Bank. However, the pressure of rising industrialisation meant better facilities were needed. Money was raised by bazaars and public subscription and an infirmary was built on land, donated by Lady Vernon, fronting the new Wellington Road. Extended many times, it ceased to be a hospital in 1996 and after some uncertainty was converted into offices. Considered one of the finest Georgian buildings in Stockport, it is deserving of its Grade II listing and blue plaque.

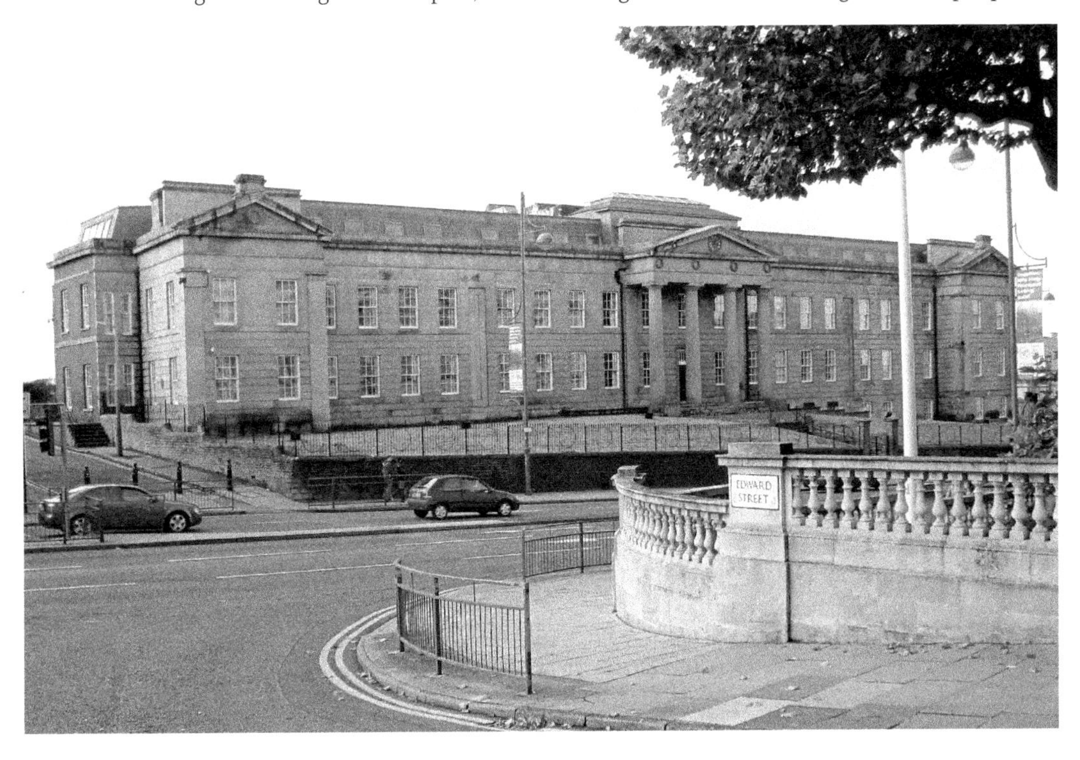

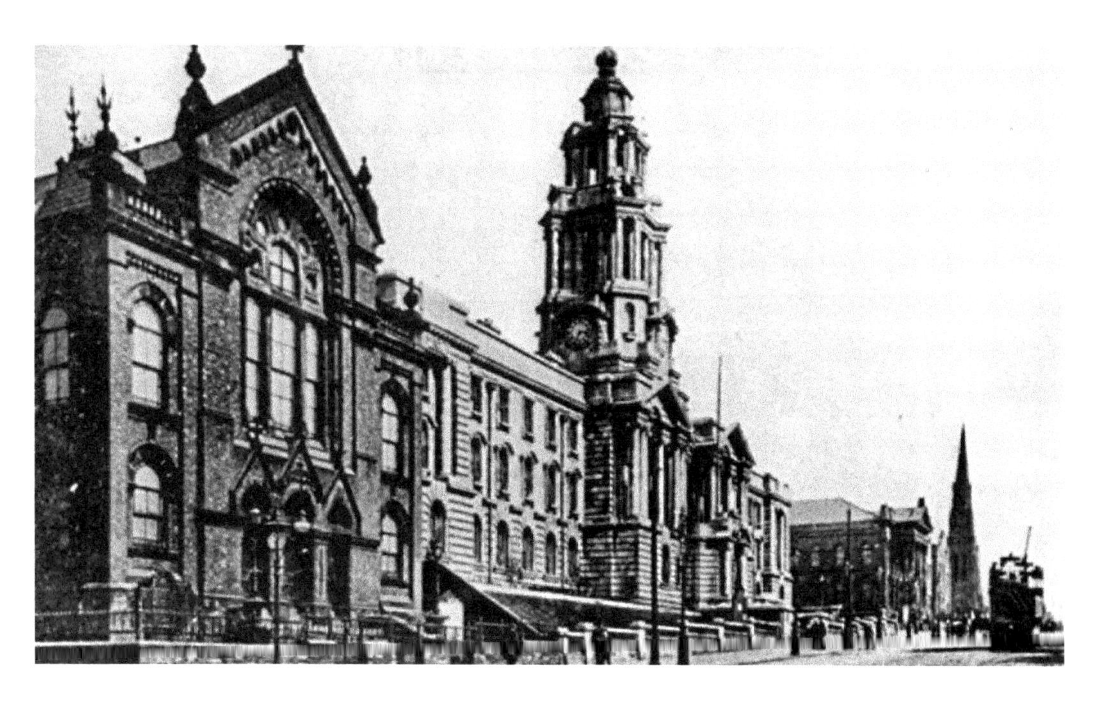

Town Hall

It is hard to imagine a town without a town hall, but for nearly sixty years after the Stockport Improvement Act, the power to build one had lain dormant. The site of the national school on Wellington Road was chosen and a competition was arranged for the best design. The winning designer was Sir Arthur Brumwell Thomas, and with the demolition of the school, work commenced at an estimated cost of £60,000. Opened in 1908 by the Prince and Princess of Wales, it has always been known as 'the Wedding Cake'.

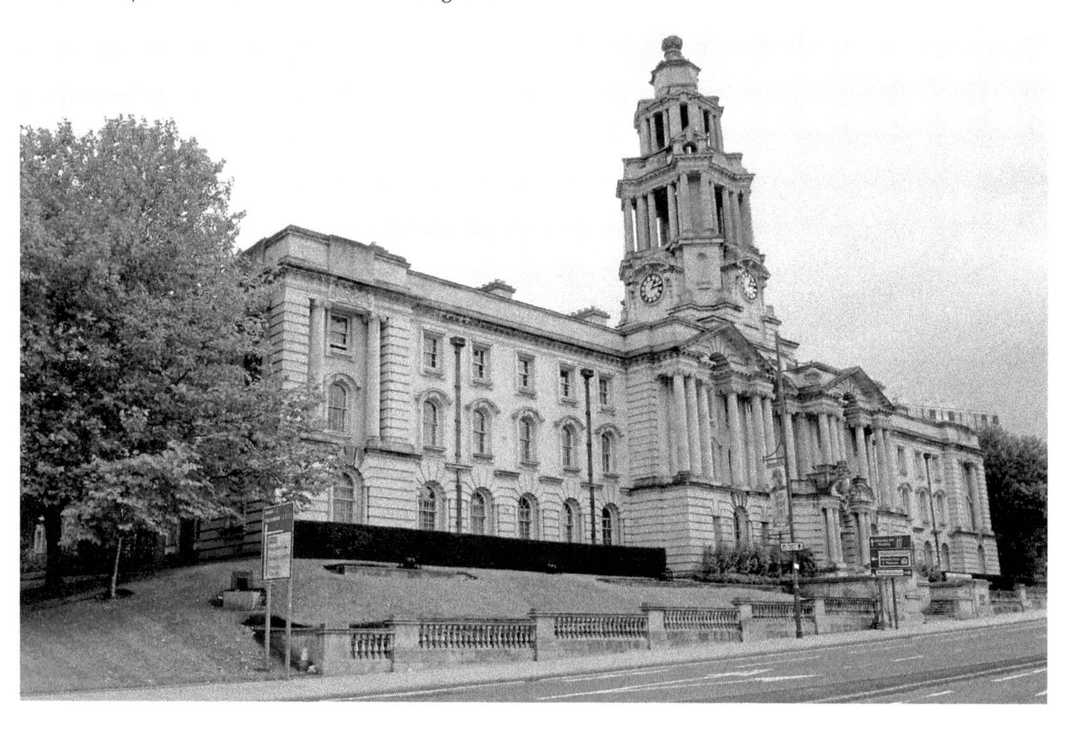

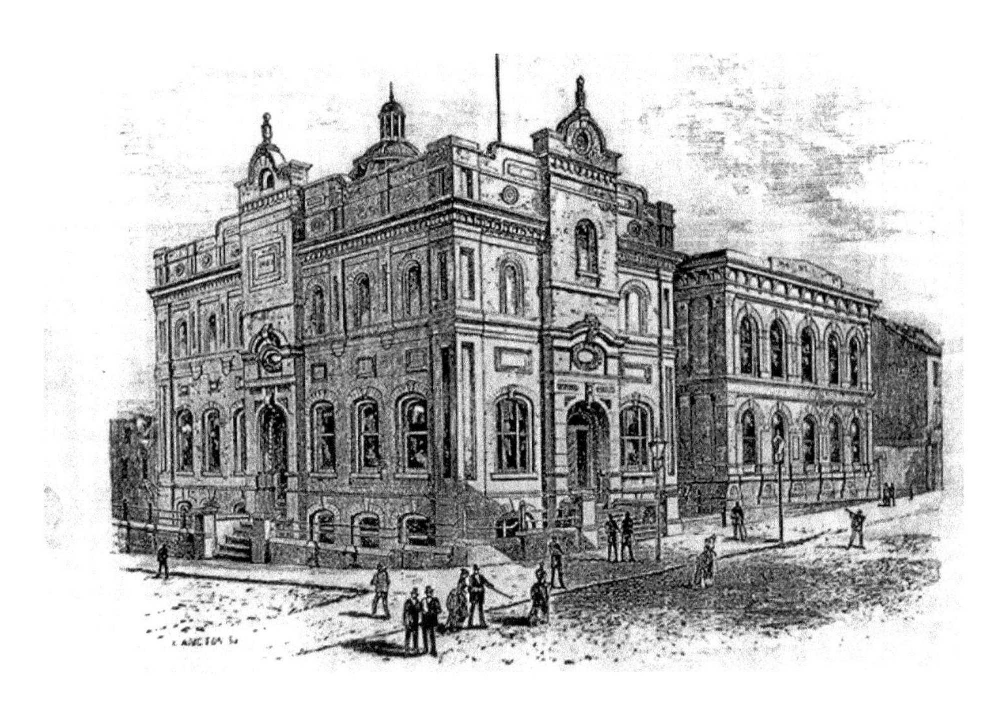

Central Library

On the corner of St Petersgate once stood the Mechanics' Institute, which opened in 1862 after a chequered history of different locations in the town. Opened by Lord Stanley, it boasted a reading room, library and lecture theatre, but was destined to have a short life. Stockport's free library was originally opened above the Produce Hall in the Market Place, but despite enlargements outgrew its premises. In 1912 a gift from Andrew Carnegie paved the way for a new facility and the institute was demolished to make way for Stockport Central Library.

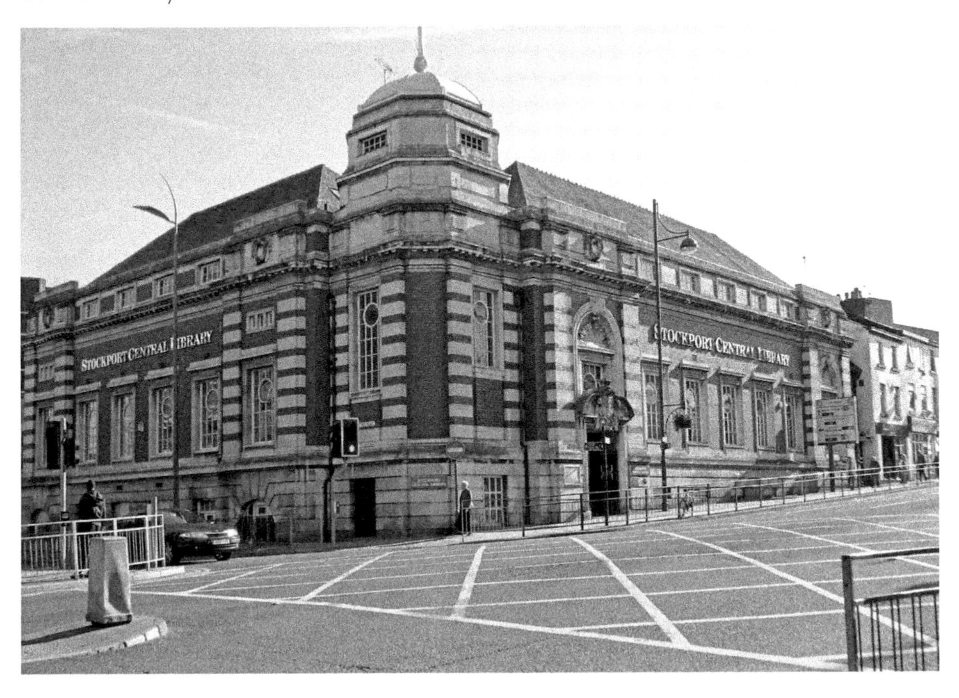

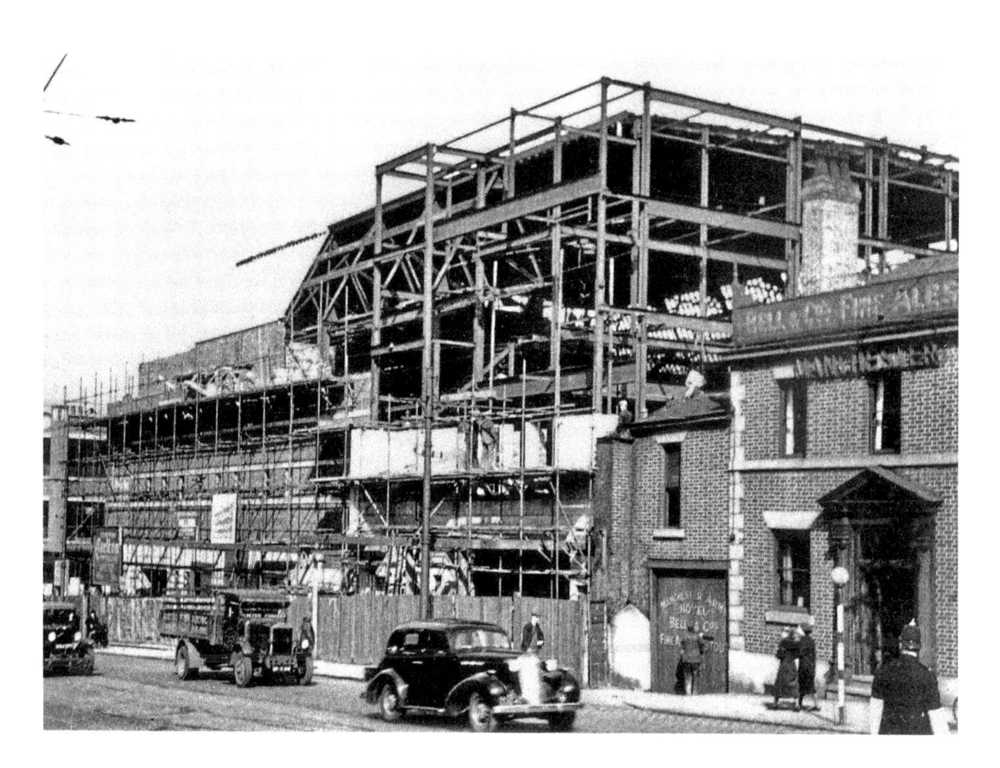

Essoldo Cinema

One of the last cinemas to be built in Stockport was the Carlton, seen here under construction in the late 1930s. It later became the more well-known Essoldo. In the time before traffic lights, a member of Stockport Borough Police, complete with white armbands, controls the busy St Petersgate junction. Next to the new cinema, the traditionally named Manchester Arms still plies its trade, but now as the trendier Cobdens wine bar. Ironically, the new glass office block is now occupied by BSkyB, whose product – television – almost killed the cinema.

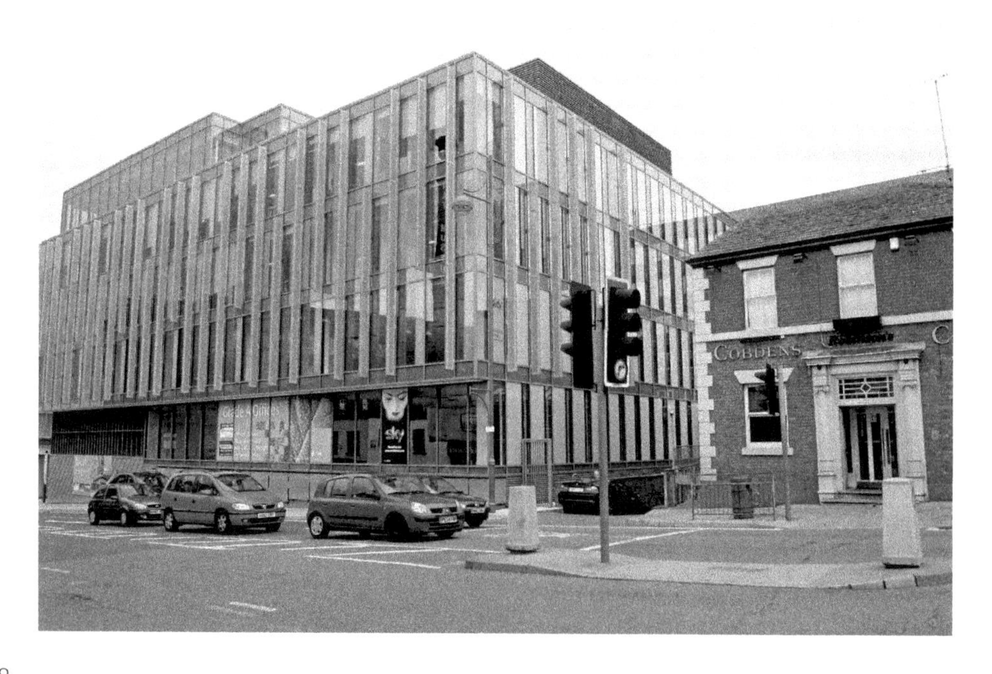

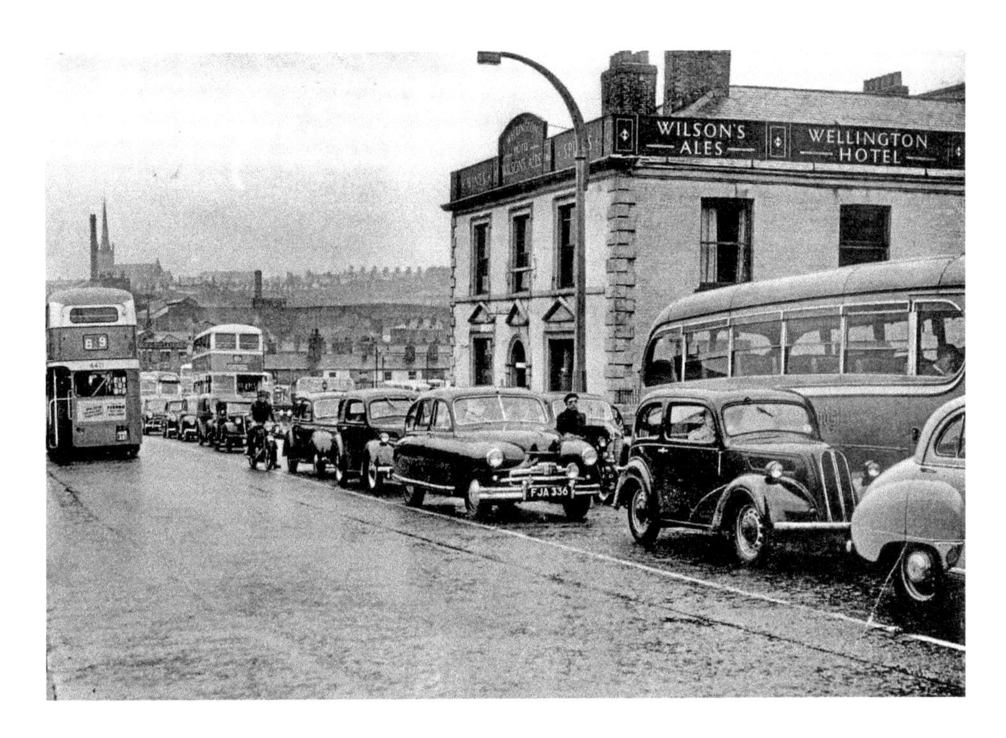

Wellington Inn

The new bypass, Wellington Road, crossed the Stockport–Warrington Turnpike at this point and the two-level Wellington Inn was built to serve as what we would now call an interchange. The inn was located just after the Wellington Bridge tollgate and all London-bound stagecoaches stopped here, making connections with the east–west traffic below. Until the opening of the M6, Wellington Road was a section of the main route from north to south and was often snarled up with vehicles, as seen here on a dismal day in the 1950s. Today the historic inn lies unused, a victim of changing times.

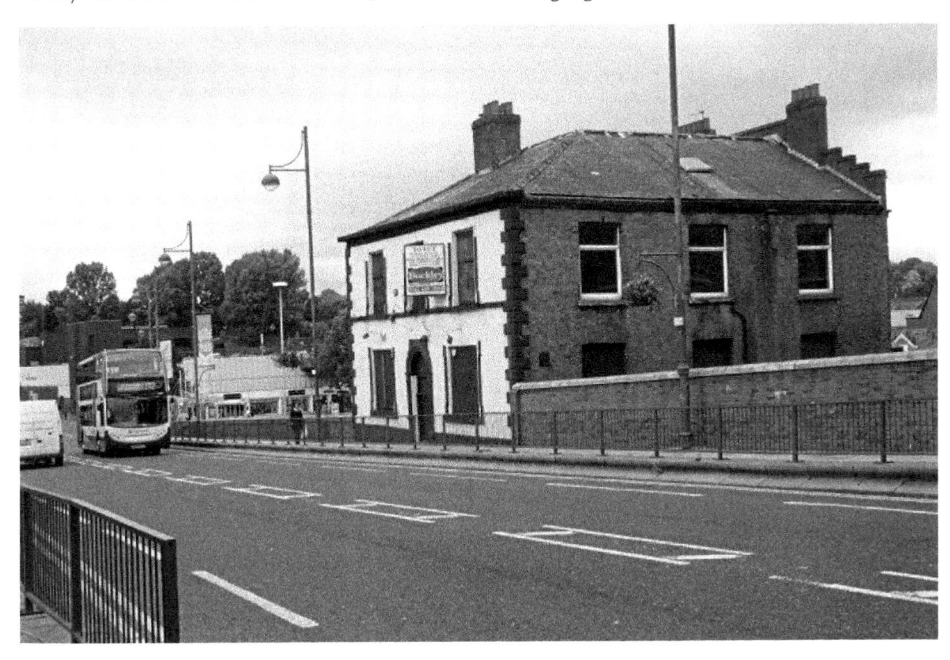

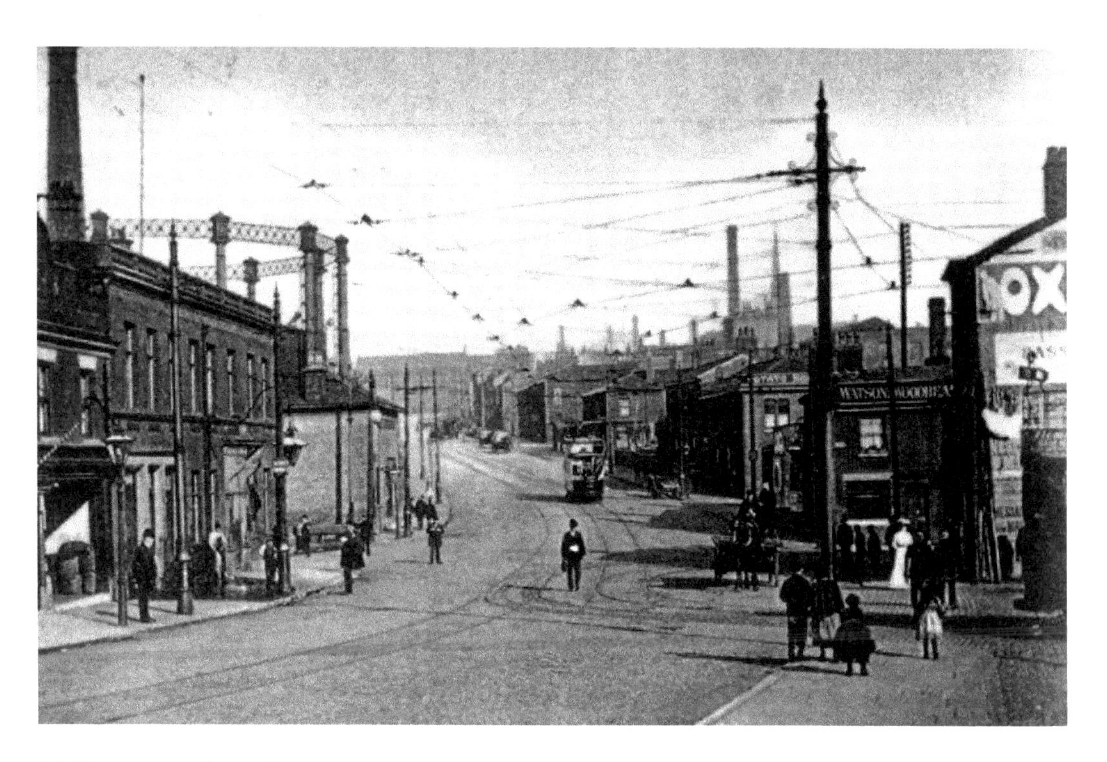

Wellington Road North

There is a wealth of interest in this 1910 photograph. A tram sways down the hill by the old gasworks and will shortly pass a horse and cart taking refuge by the kerb. Strange to our eyes is the way pedestrians wander around in the road – today they are all fenced in. On her way to the shops on Princes Street is a very elegant lady dressed in white. In those days your clothes reflected your station in life. Only the George on the corner of Heaton Lane remains, although its magnificent lamp has disappeared.

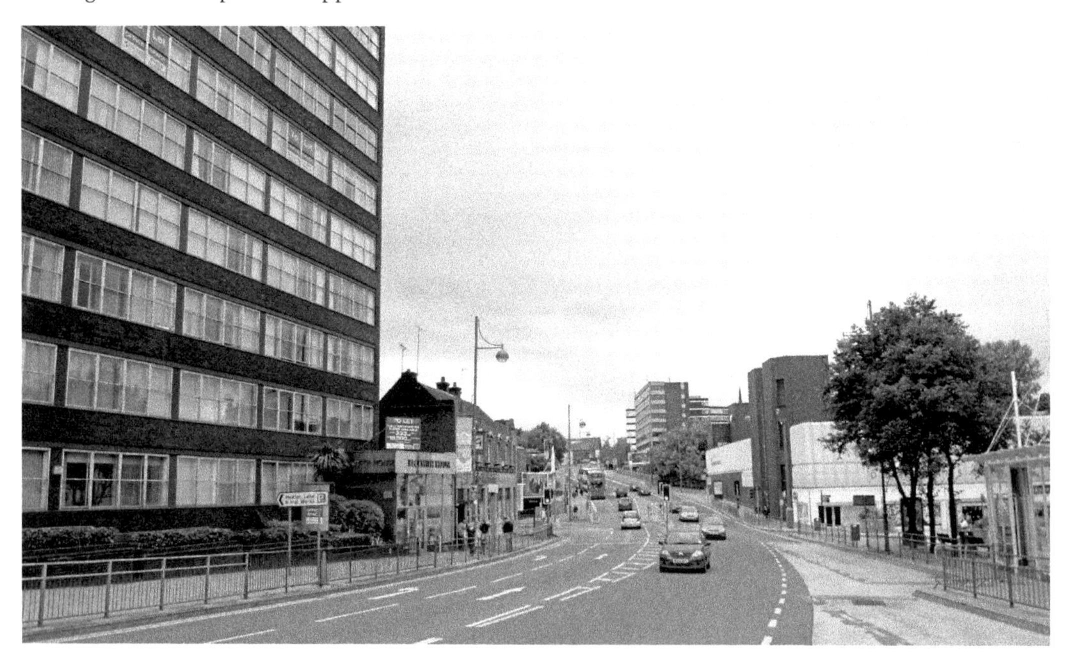

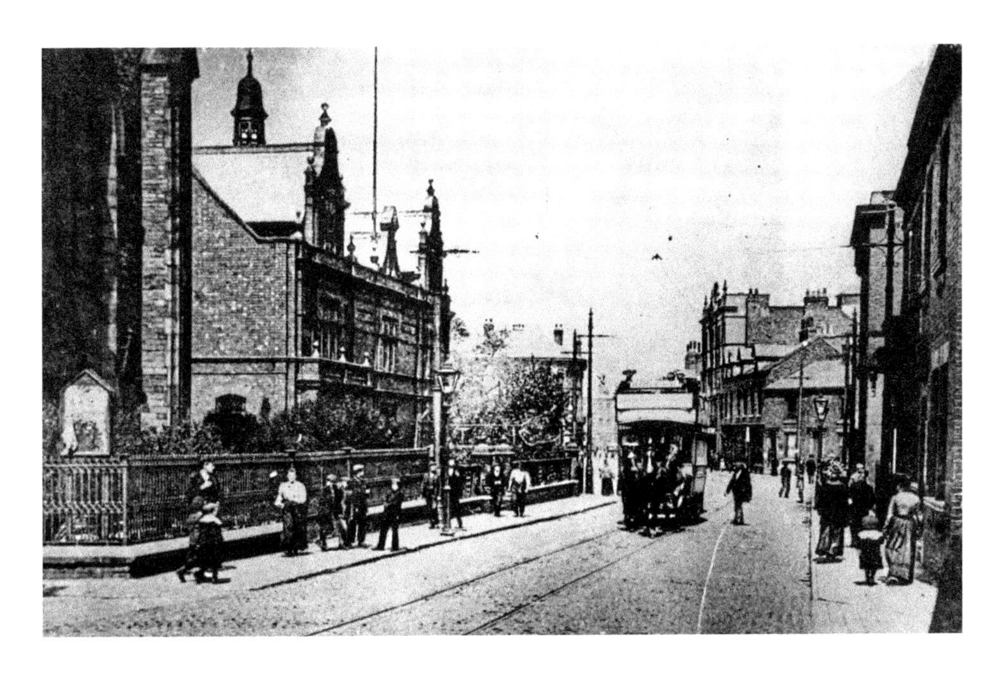

St Petersgate towards St Peter's Square

This photograph was taken around 1904, in the final years of horse-tram operation. Under the new trolley wire, a tram has chain horses attached to help it climb out of the Mersey Valley towards Hazel Grove. On the left is St Petersgate School, its bulk hiding the municipal swimming baths. The old St Peter's Rectory stands beyond the trees. Today, new office development has swept away these old buildings, but, as can be seen, St Petersgate remains as busy as ever.

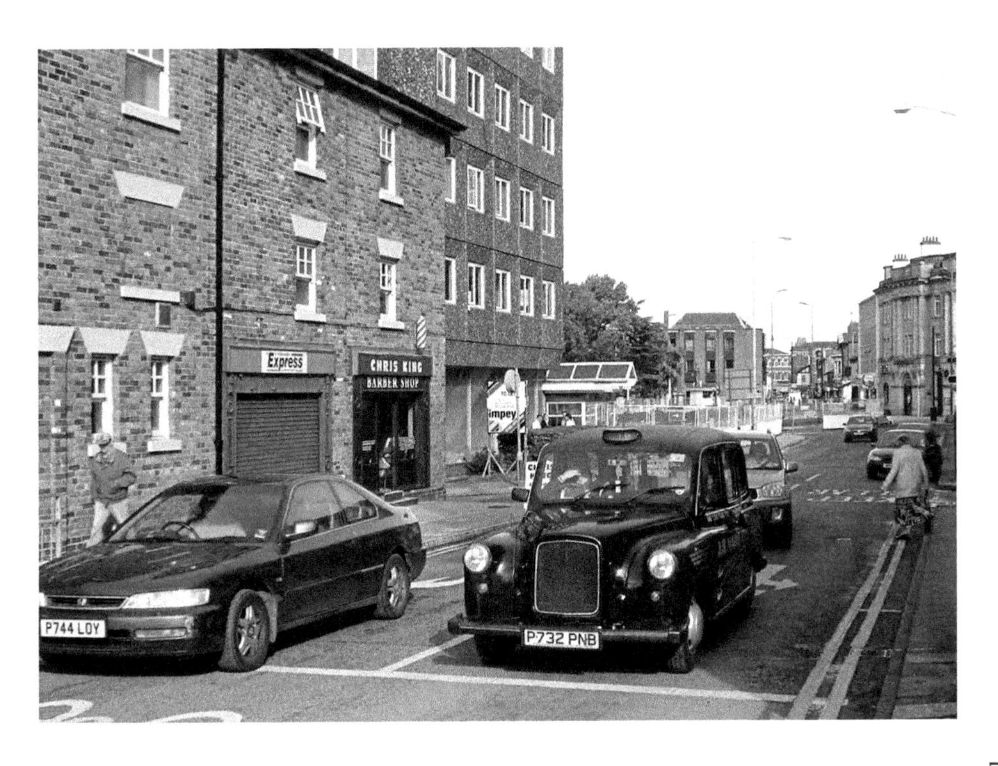

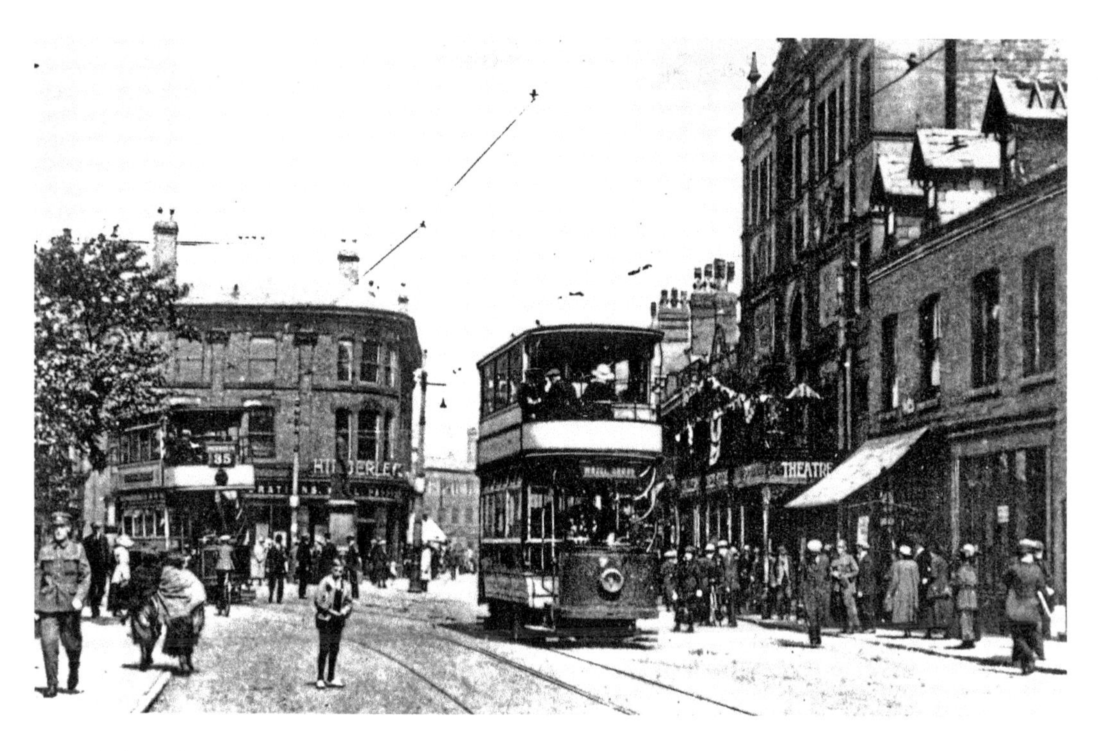

St Peter's Square

Part of the way along, St Petersgate opens into St Peter's Square. The uniformed soldier dates the picture to near the end of the First World War. On the corner, Hidderley's wallpaper emporium was a well-known business in the town; it is now replaced by the Co-operative Bank. Between the two trams it is possible to see Stockport's only outdoor statue, that of its most famous MP, Richard Cobden, who helped to repeal the Corn Laws. Today the square has been imaginatively remodelled and gives the ambience of a continental piazza.

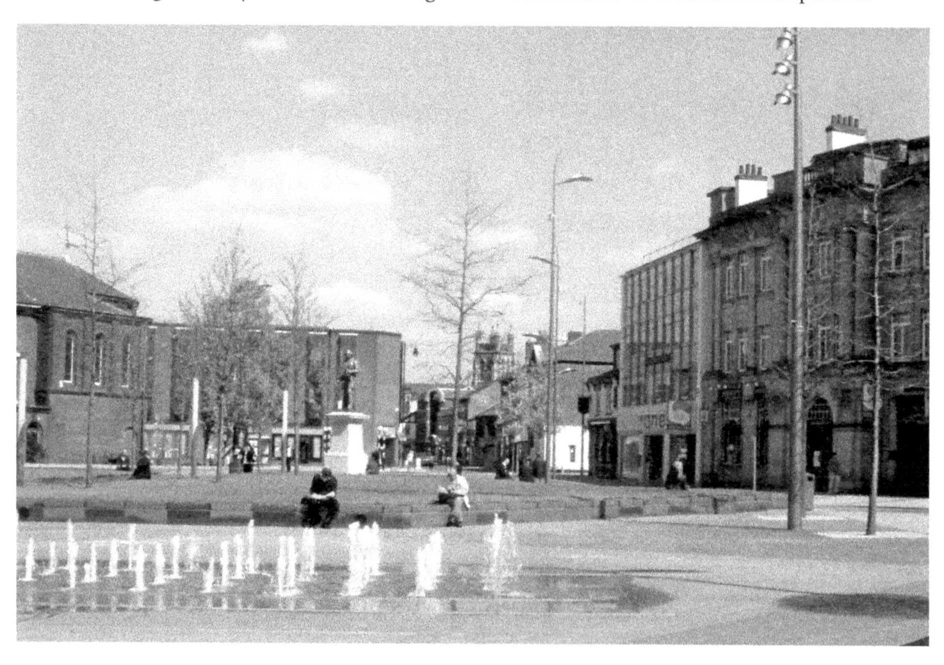

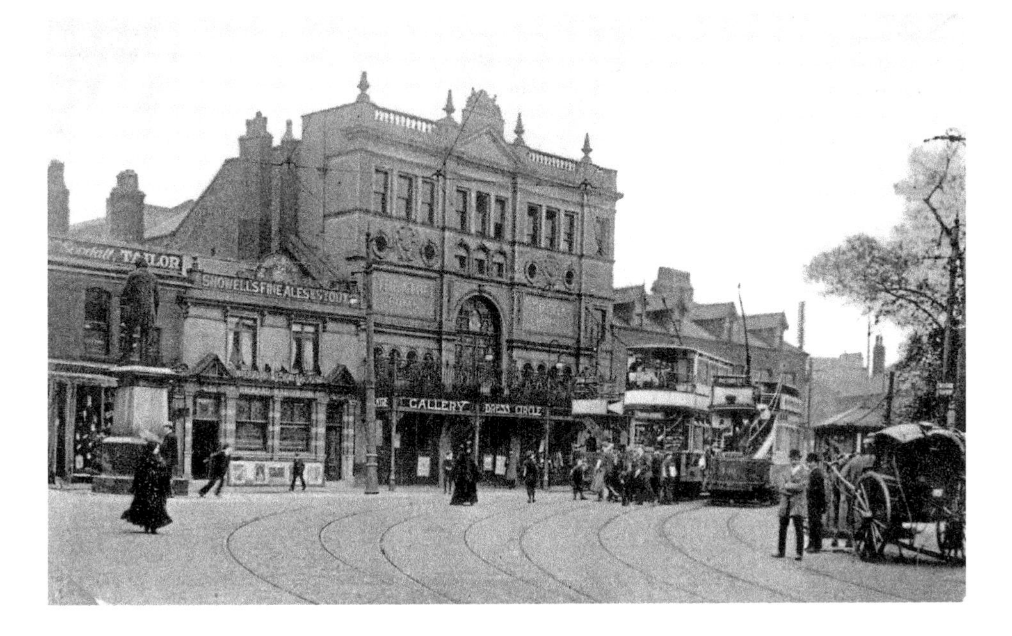

Theatre Royal
Stockport's premier theatre was opened in 1869 and, as seen here, it was rebuilt after a fire in 1888. Alas, it has now been replaced by a grim office block. Stars such as Dan Leno, Harry Lauder and Charlie Chaplin performed on its stage. Next to the theatre, but surviving fire and change, stands the Imperial Hotel, now called the Square Tavern. Its former owner, Showell's, was one of the four main breweries in Stockport. The square, equipped with a cabbies' hut on the right, was a transport hub.

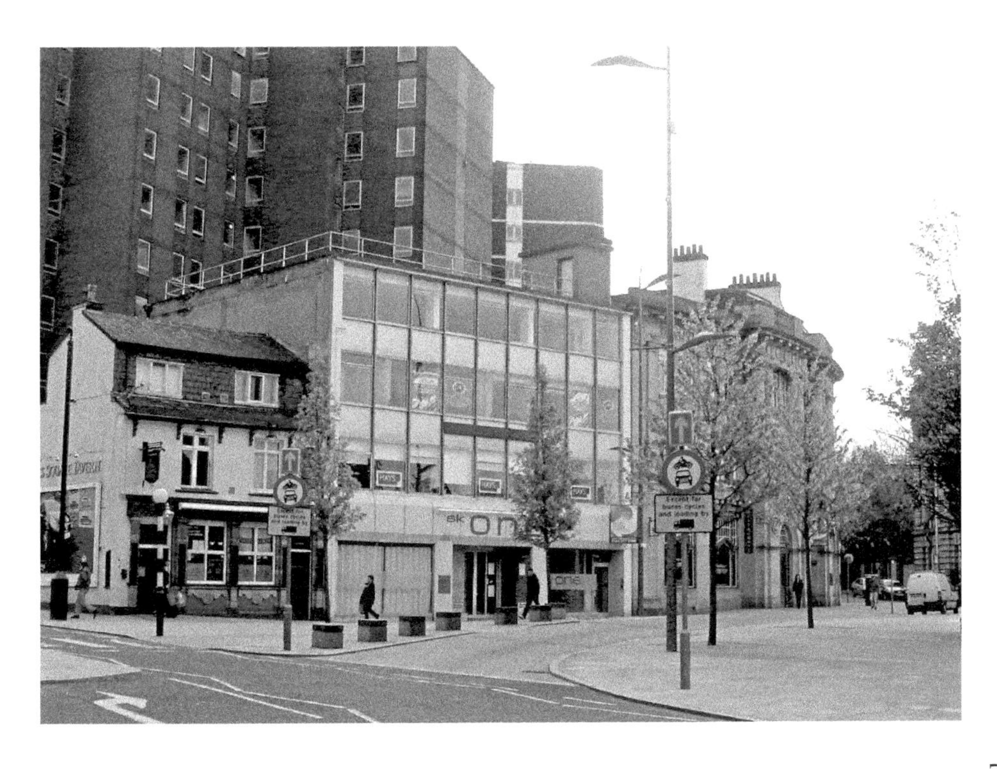

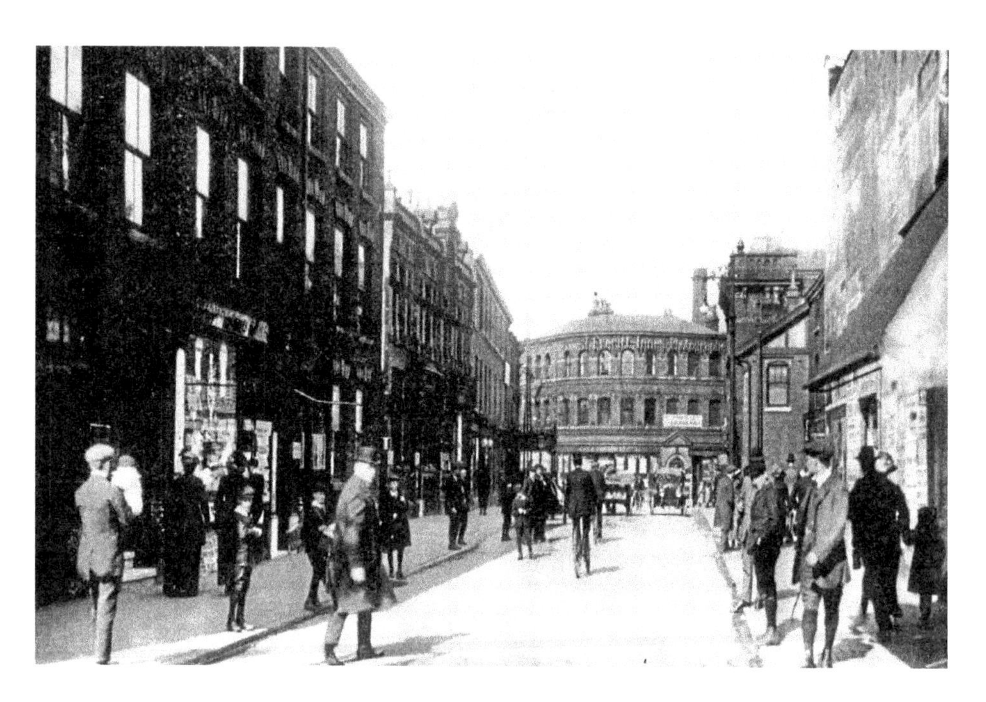

St Petersgate towards the Market

This busy street is still lined with shops, offices and public houses. Above, the rare appearance of a motor car splits the attention from the camera but has not stopped pedestrians using the road. Many of the buildings featured in the earlier view still remain, including the distinctive curved front of the office on the corner of High Street. It is a shame that modern shops are suffering in the depression and are littered with 'To Let' signs.

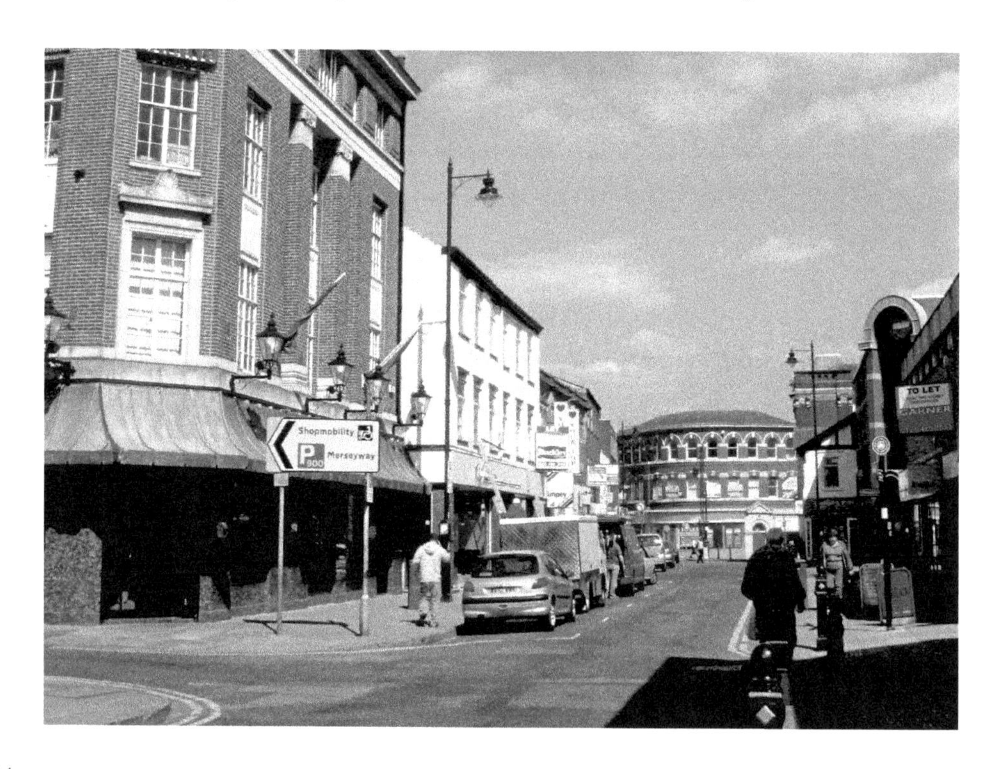

Empire Theatre and St Petersgate Bridge

Opposite High Street was another Stockport theatre, the Empire. Its frontage was so squeezed between shops and the Egerton Arms, whose distinctive lamp stands out, that it needed another entrance off High Bankside. A short distance away, beyond the ornate street light, are the parapets of St Petersgate Bridge. When opened in 1868, it gave level access to the Market Place, saving the use of two flights of steps. Today the rather special lamp columns on the bridge parapet remain, as does the Egerton Arms, its lamp replaced by a satellite dish.

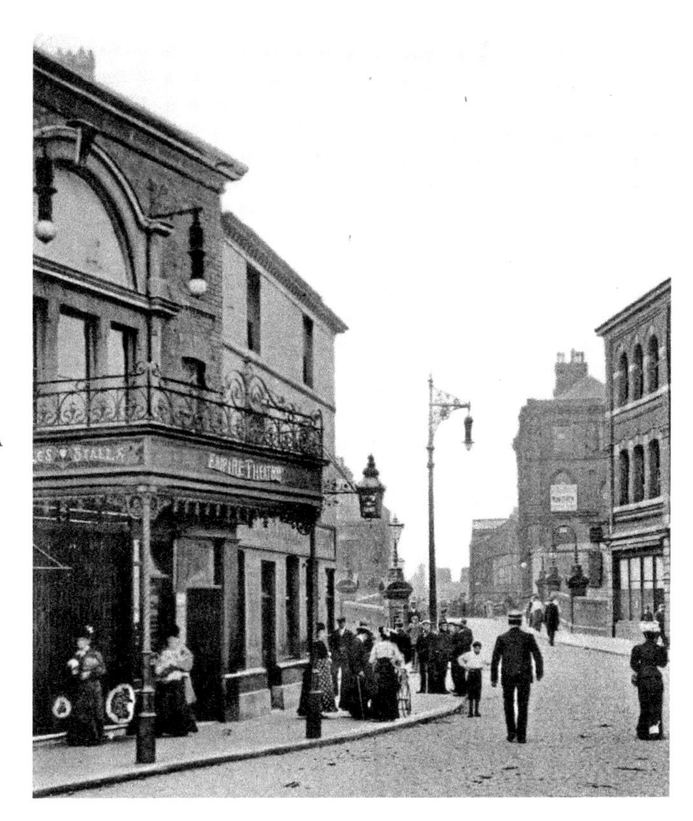

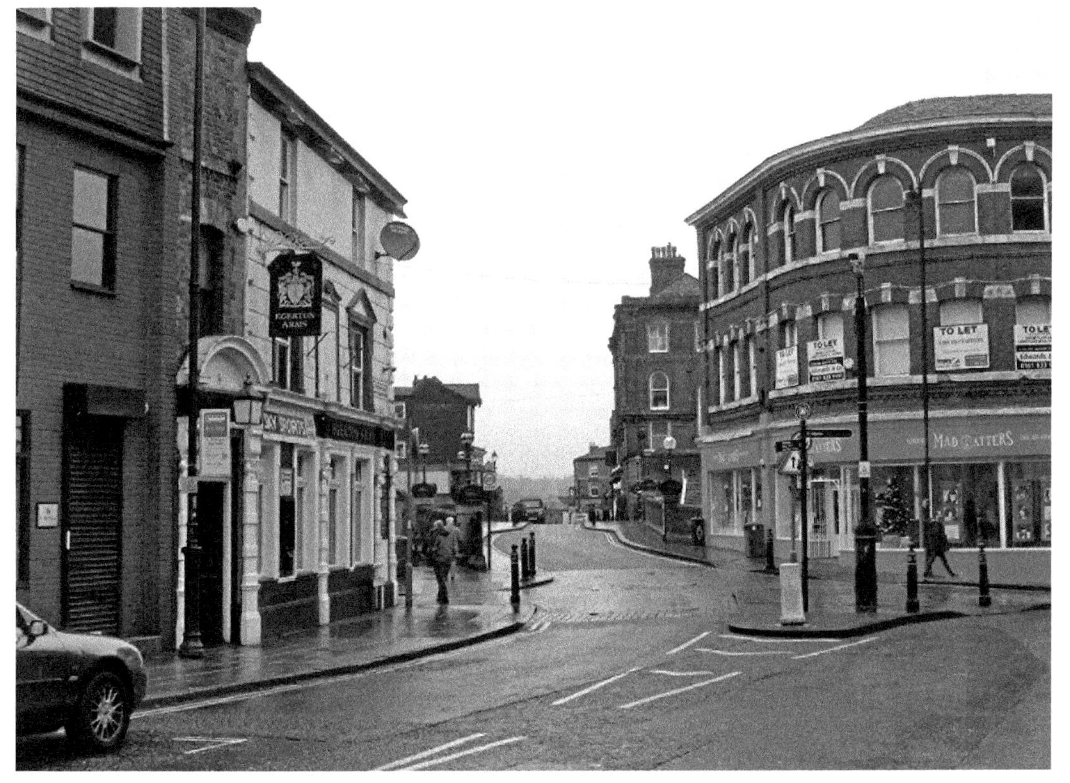

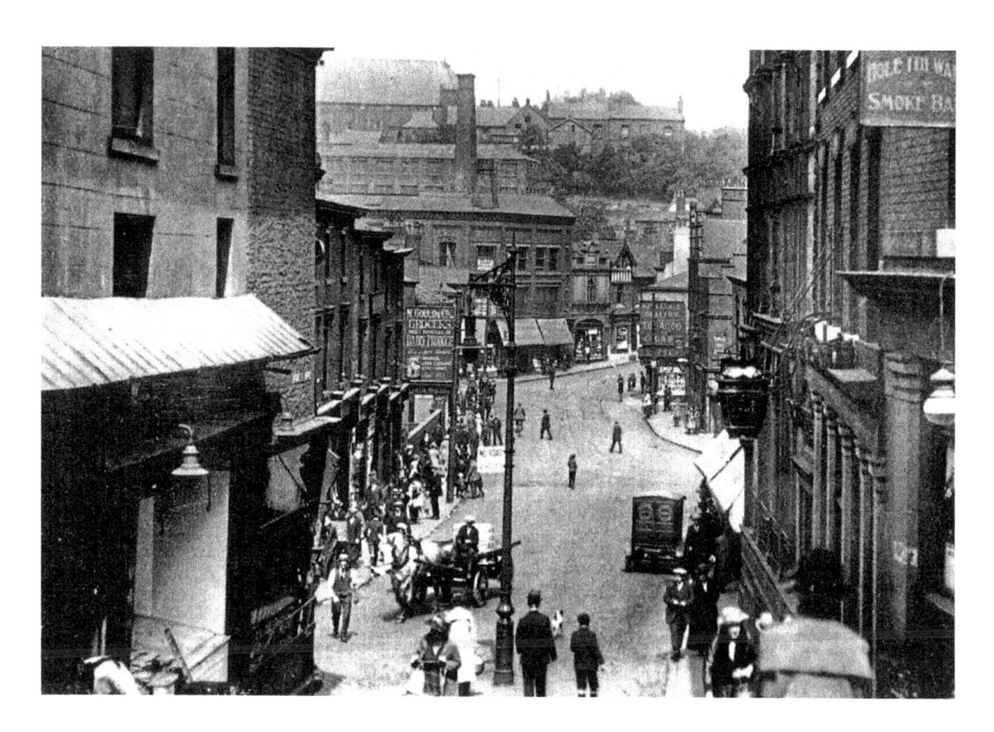

Looking Down Bridge Street Brow

This brow rises steeply up from Bridge Street to the Market Place and was once called Brierley Brow. On the right was the strangely named Hole in the Wall, once the King's Arms. Across the street there is a shop that has traded as a fishmonger for over 140 years, ever since the coming of the railway. The dray horse makes a fine sight delivering goods in the town. It is so much more pleasant than the blue transit van of today.

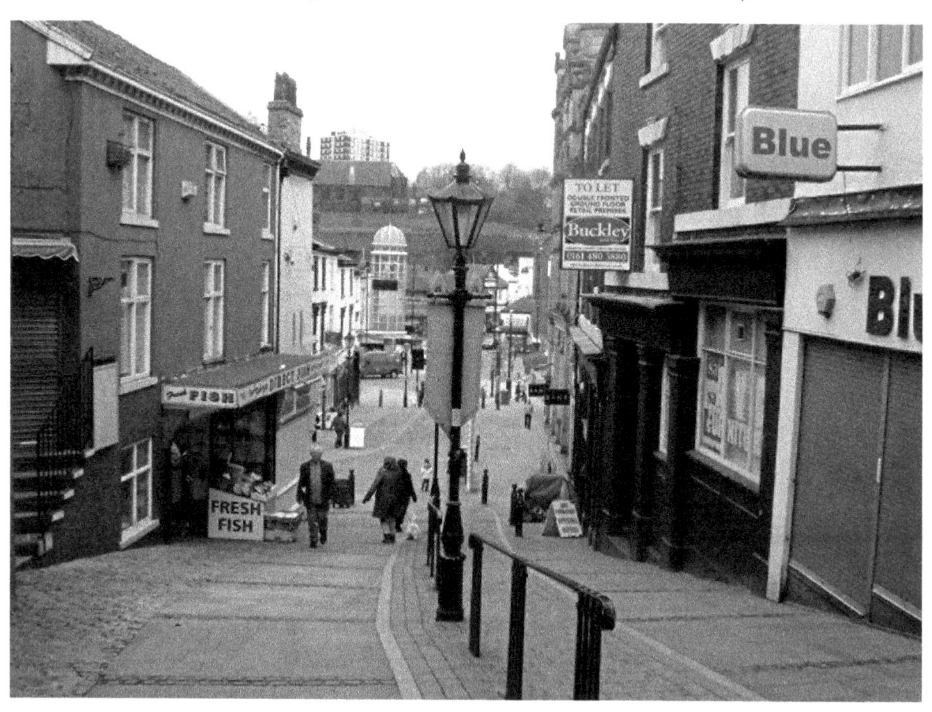

Looking Up Bridge Street Brow

This brow has seen little change to its buildings in the hundred years or so between these photographs. The climb is still one of the most breathtaking access routes into the Market Place. It is a conservation area and the council's effort to replicate the lamp standards should be applauded. It is also pleasant to see the old Boots Cash Chemists as a new specialist sweet emporium, Mr Simms Olde Sweet Shopp, which certainly enhances the 'old town' atmosphere.

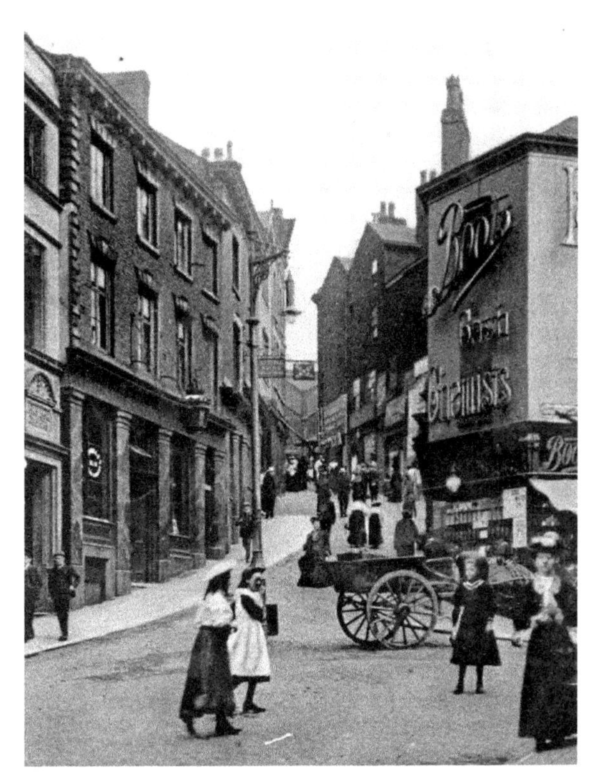

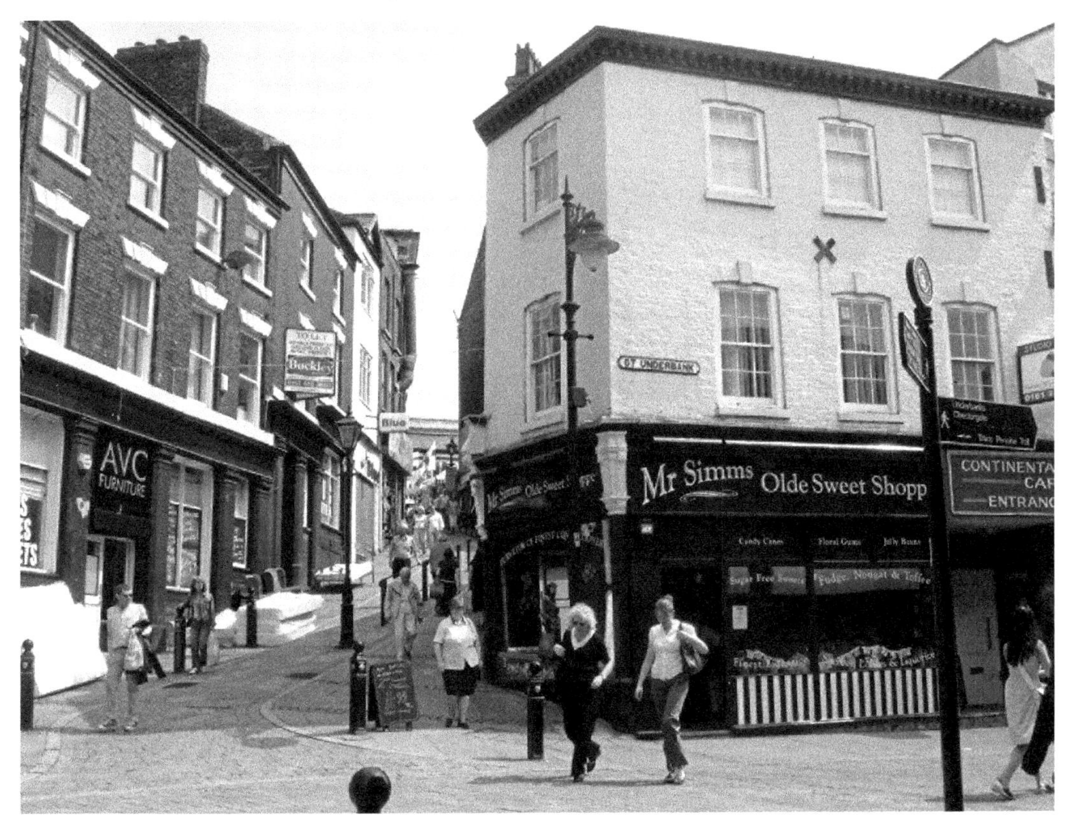

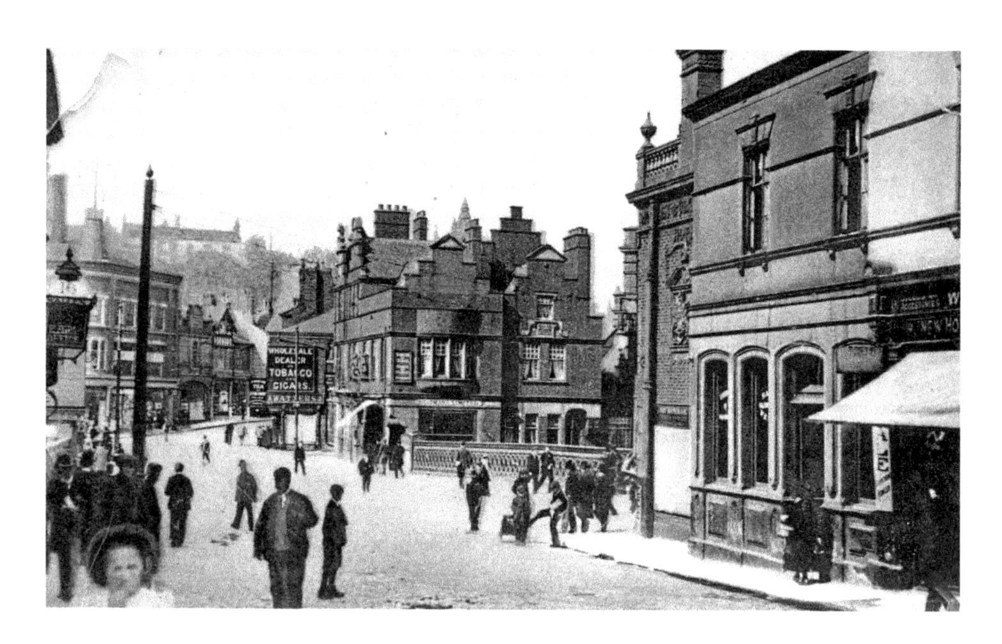

Lancashire Bridge

The ford across the River Mersey was a key element in the founding of Stockport. It was replaced by a bridge, first mentioned in 1282 and originally called Stockport Bridge. This was the scene of a skirmish in the English Civil War. It was later demolished in an attempt to stop Bonnie Prince Charlie during the Jacobite rebellion of 1745. Straddling each side of the rebuilt bridge and its ornate parapet were two of Stockport's most famous inns, the Buck and Dog and the Warren Bulkeley. Now, apart from some distant property, all has changed. Even the bridge has disappeared beneath the Merseyway development.

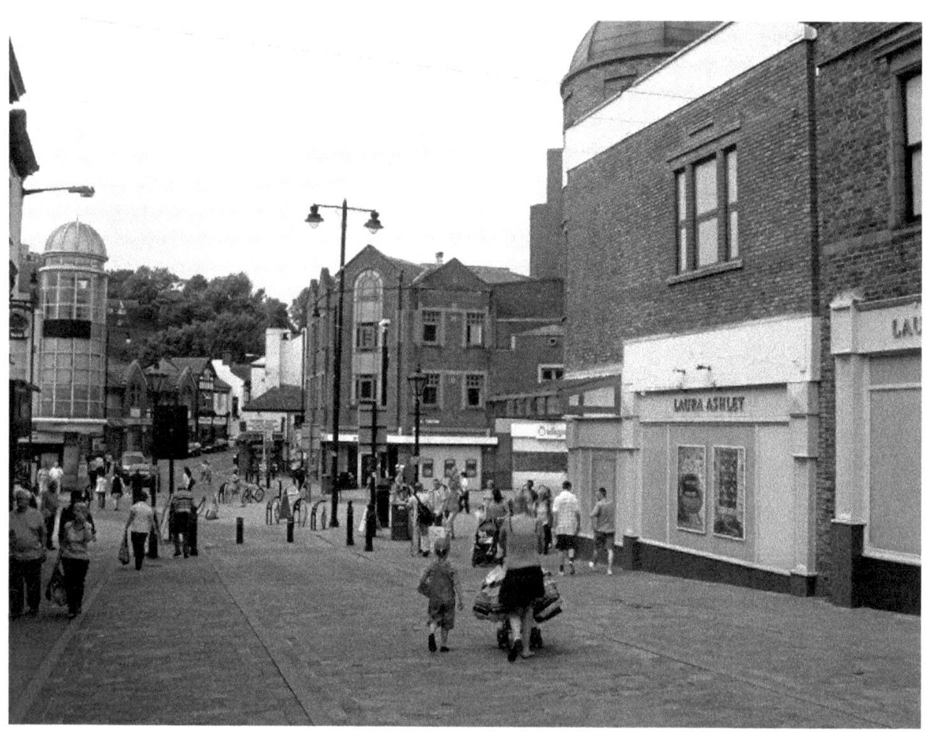

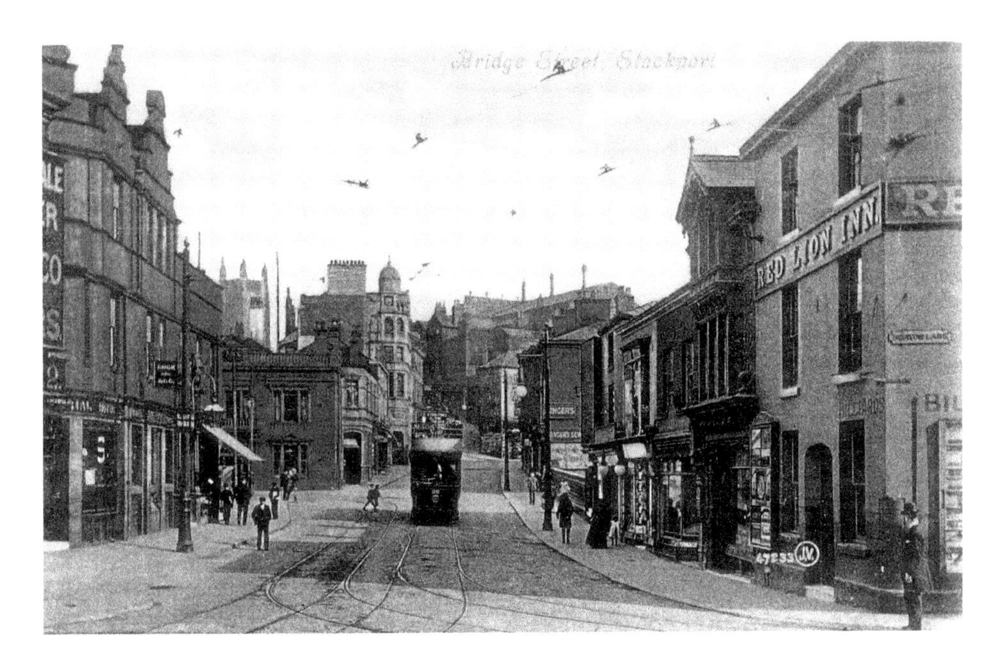

Tiviot Dale

This photograph looks back over Lancashire Bridge in the early 1900s as a tram from Hyde slows to turn left into Heaton Lane, which in 1908 would become Prince's Street in honour of the Prince of Wales' visit to open the town hall. A nice touch on the day of his visit was the newly made street nameplate dropping down to cover the old one as he passed. Despite the changes brought about by the Merseyway development, looking up Bridge Street Bow some elements of the old town remain.

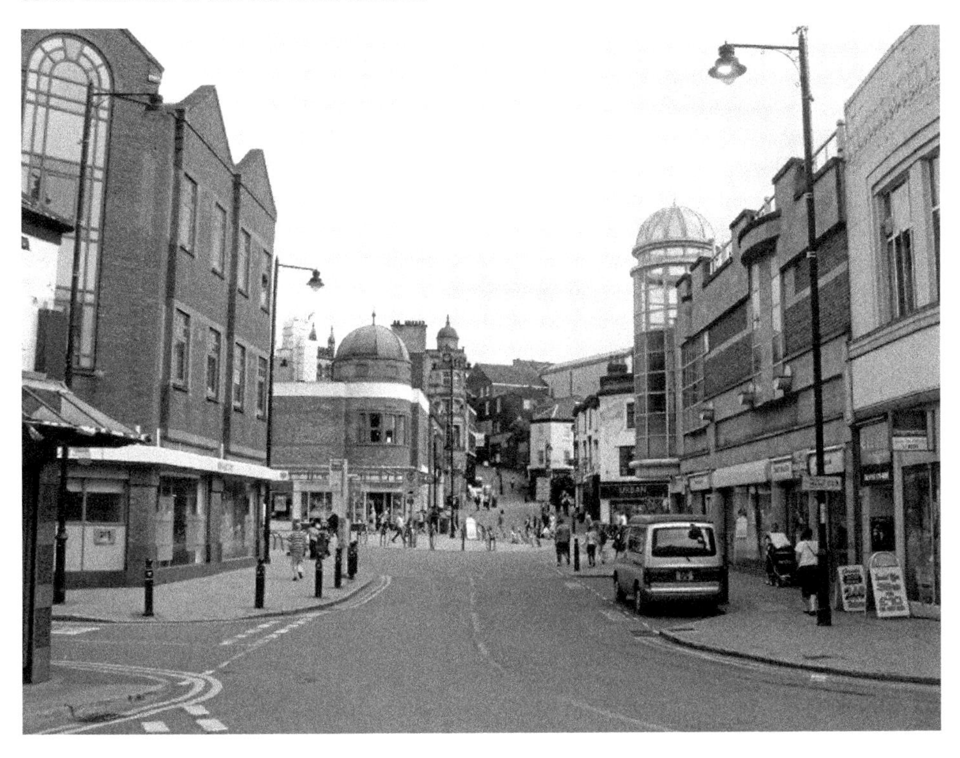

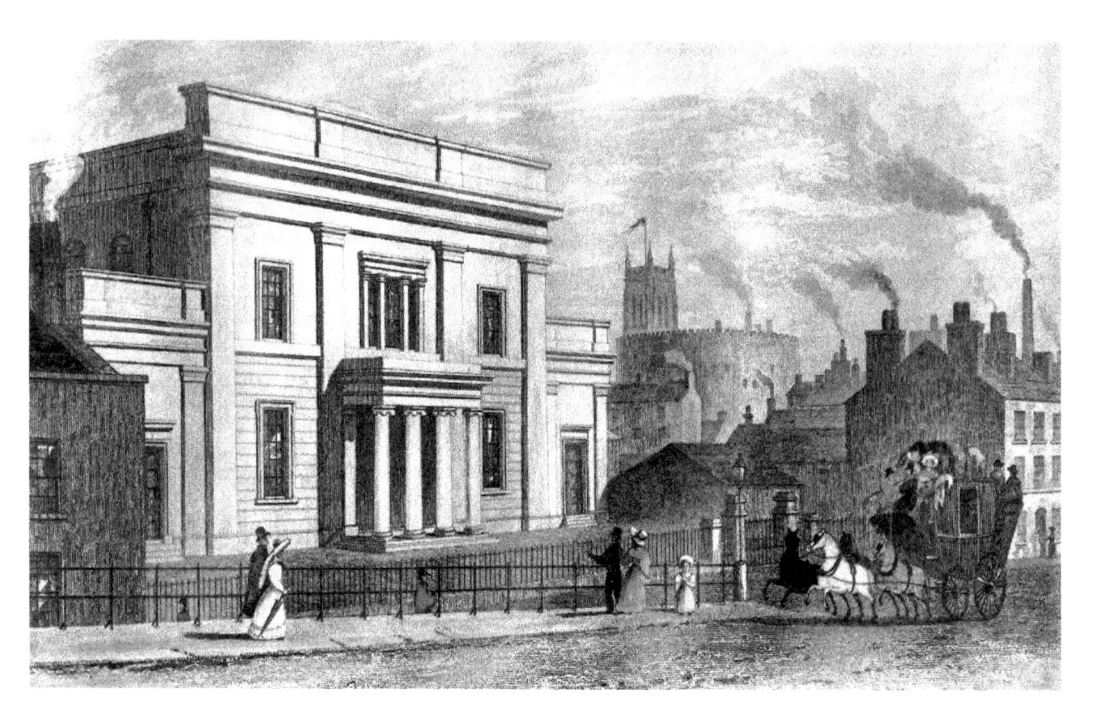

Tiviot Dale Methodist Church

The steepest descent into Stockport was from Manchester. To ease the gradient, the Turnpike Trust engineered a new road down to Lancashire Bridge in 1794. In the old print we can see the Methodist church, opened in 1826 and located at the bottom of the road. Beyond stands the tower of St Mary's and the fortress-like bulk of Stockport's first powered cotton mill. Today the road has been bisected by the new link road and the church has been demolished for an office development, but the gateposts stand defiant in a commercial world.

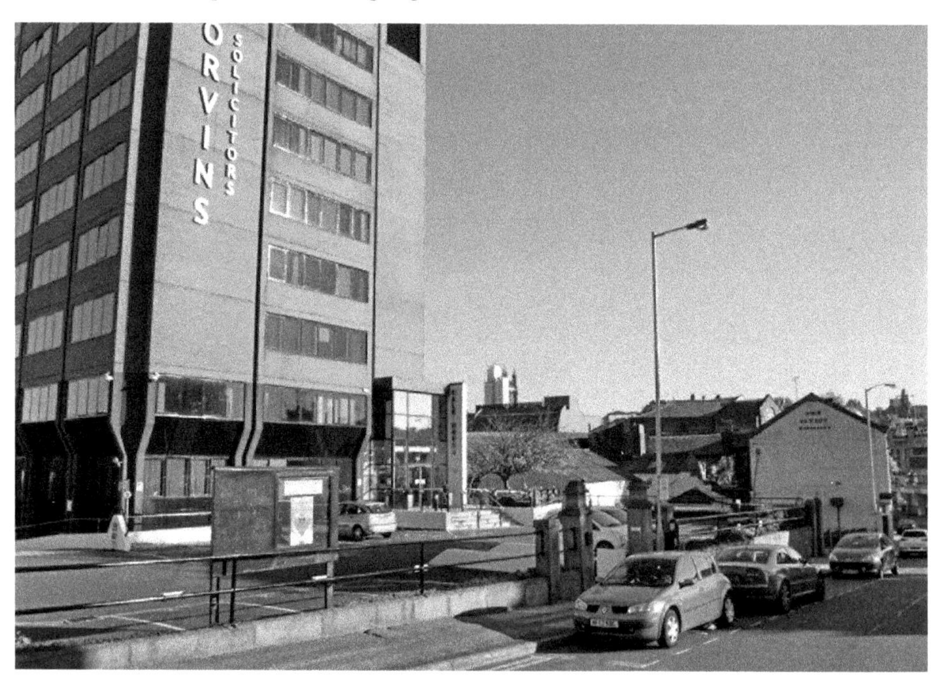

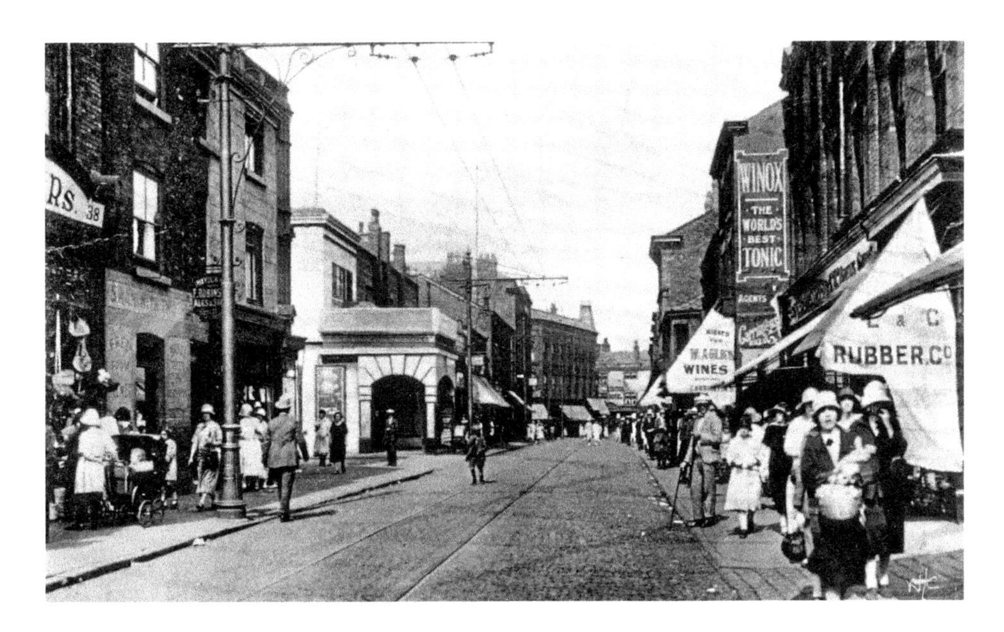

Prince's Street

As mentioned earlier, the road was named Prince's Street after the Prince of Wales' 1908 visit. It has always been an important thoroughfare to the west, from Lancashire Bridge. In this photograph from the 1920s, it is evident that shopping was as well catered for on this street as it is now. On the left is the Swan with Two Necks, which is happily still serving the town, although now in a continental fashion, thanks to pedestrianisation. The Palladium cinema's large foyer once made a grand statement, but it was closed in 1956 and its frontage was replaced with a rather soulless glass-fronted modern shop.

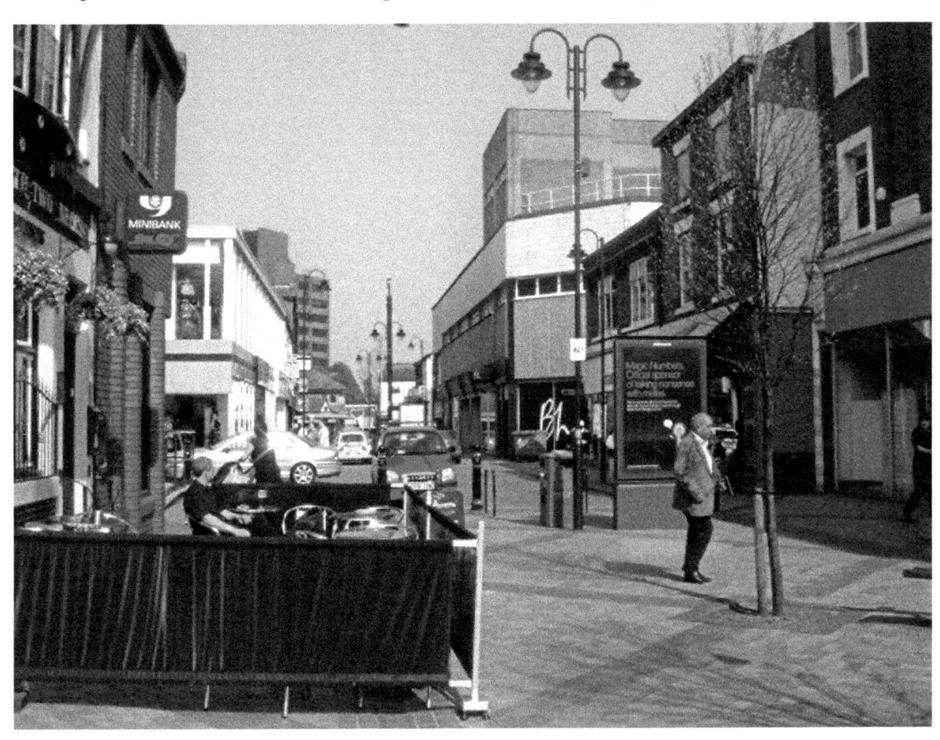

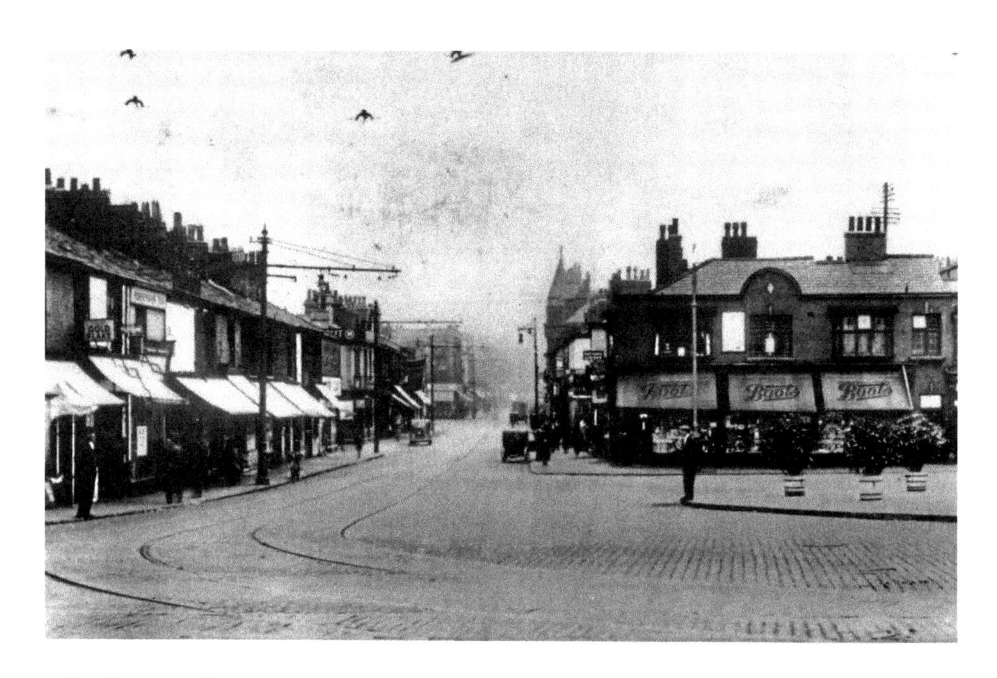

Prince's Street from Mersey Square

This photograph, taken before the Second World War, shows a remarkably quiet view of Prince's Street compared with that of the previous page; perhaps it is early morning. The cobbled surface was a feature of the roads until the demise of the trams, and in wet weather it could be lethal for cyclists. Talking of which, when did you last see a bicycle parked on its pedal at the kerb? In today's picture the outline of older properties can still be seen behind the modern buildings and bridge. Unfortunately one of Stockport's main shopping streets has a less inviting aspect today.

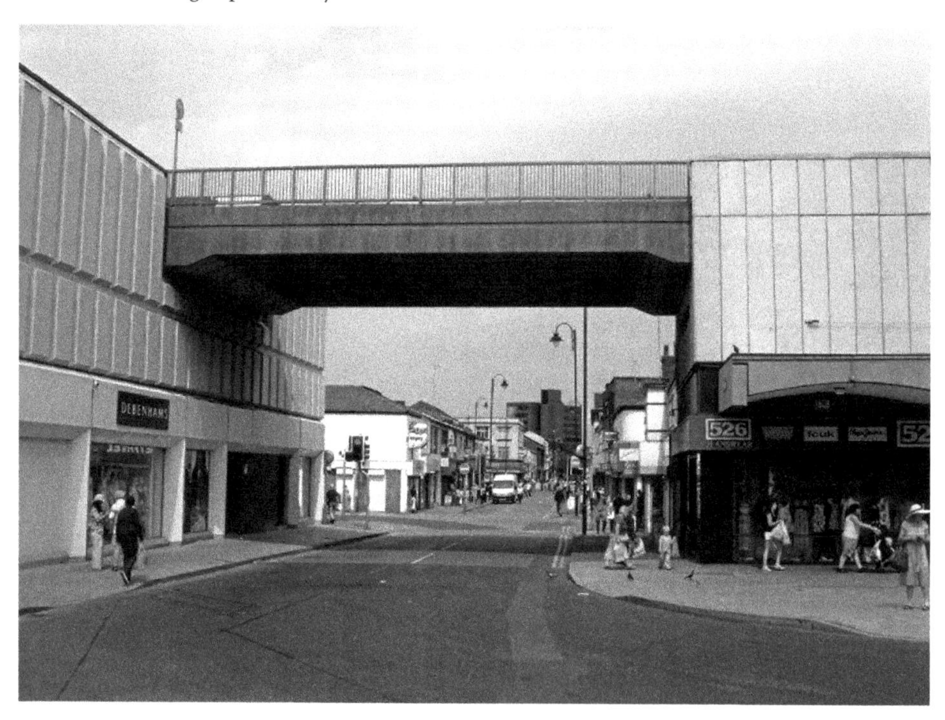

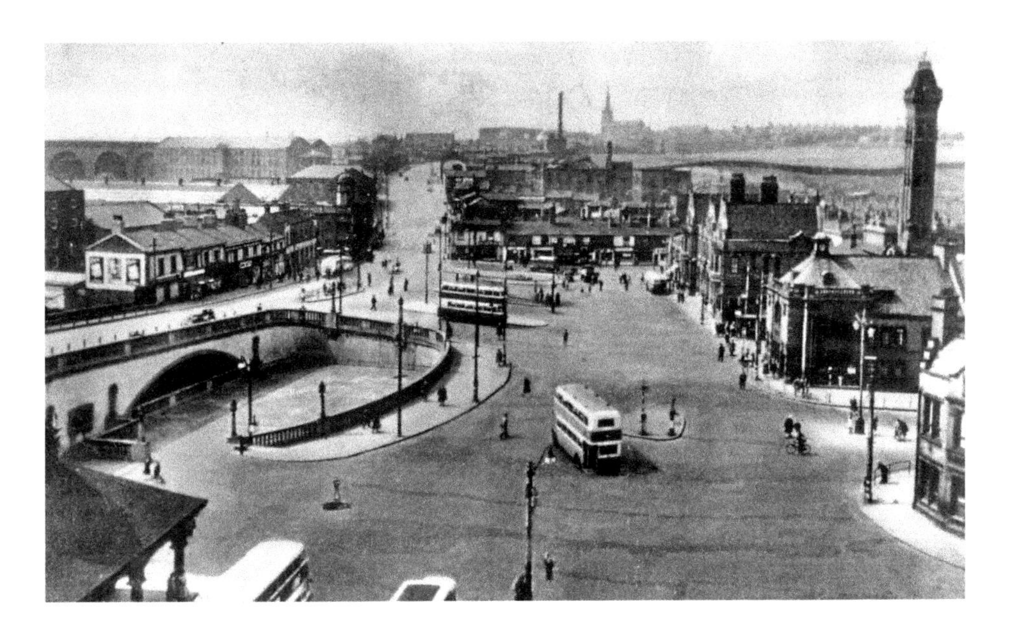

Mersey Square

This photograph, taken in the early 1950s, is full of interest. Notice the blackout lines on the lamp posts, which really show the importance of Mersey Square as a transport hub. On the left, Wellington Road leads towards Manchester, past the strangely named Bear Pit. It was built over the River Mersey and opened in 1935. To the right the hose-drying tower of the fire station stands out. Today only the Bear Pit can be recognised. However, the name of the office block, Beckwith House, remembers Howard Beckwith, Stockport's fire chief, who perished near this spot in 1926.

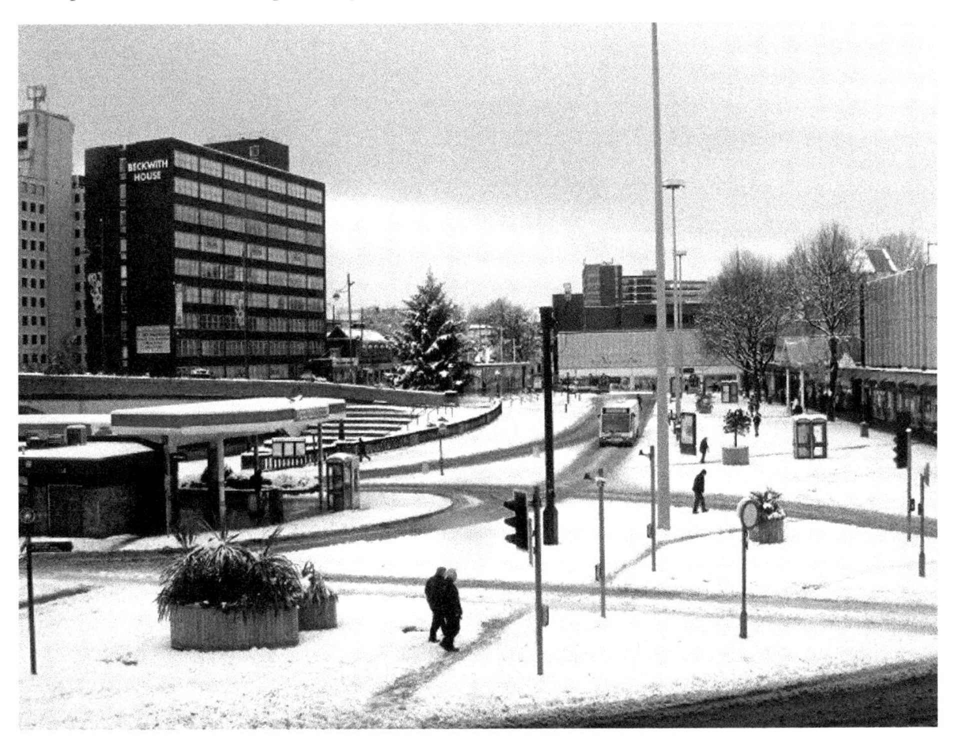

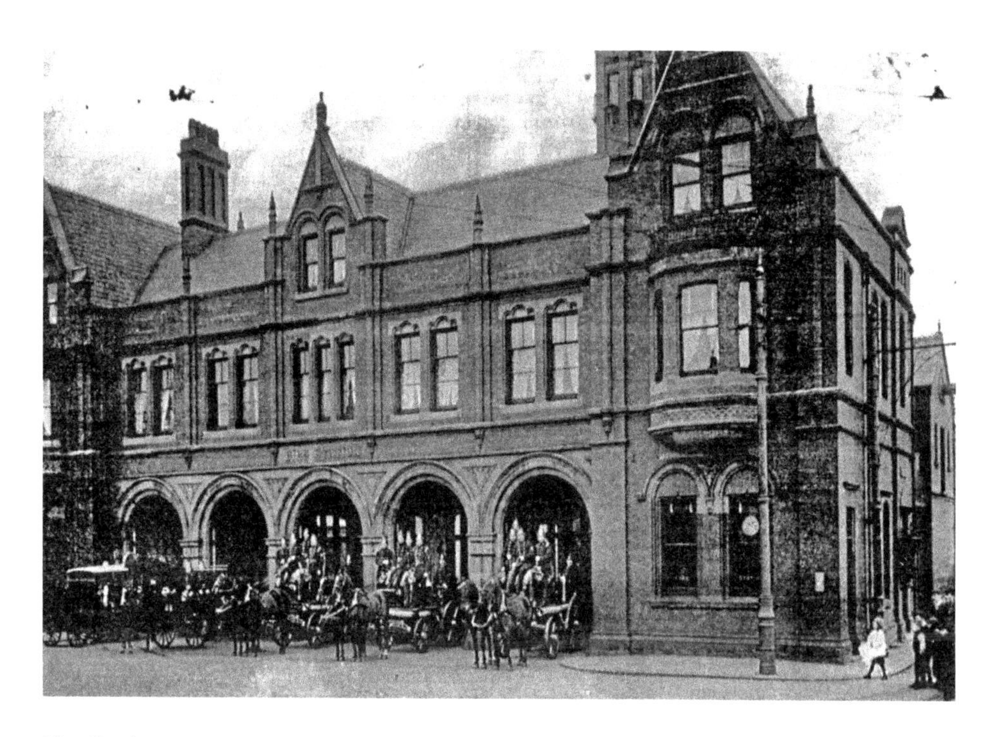

Fire Station

Stockport Fire Brigade moved from Corporation Street into the new fire station on Mersey Square in 1902 and this fine assembly of horse-drawn fire appliances outside the station seems to be 'on parade' in about 1906. The brigade received its first motorised appliance in 1910 and it was this later machine that was involved in the fatal crash and plunged off the roadway. The relocation of the fire brigade out of town in 1967 allowed the Merseyway shopping complex to have the impressive frontage shown on the later picture.

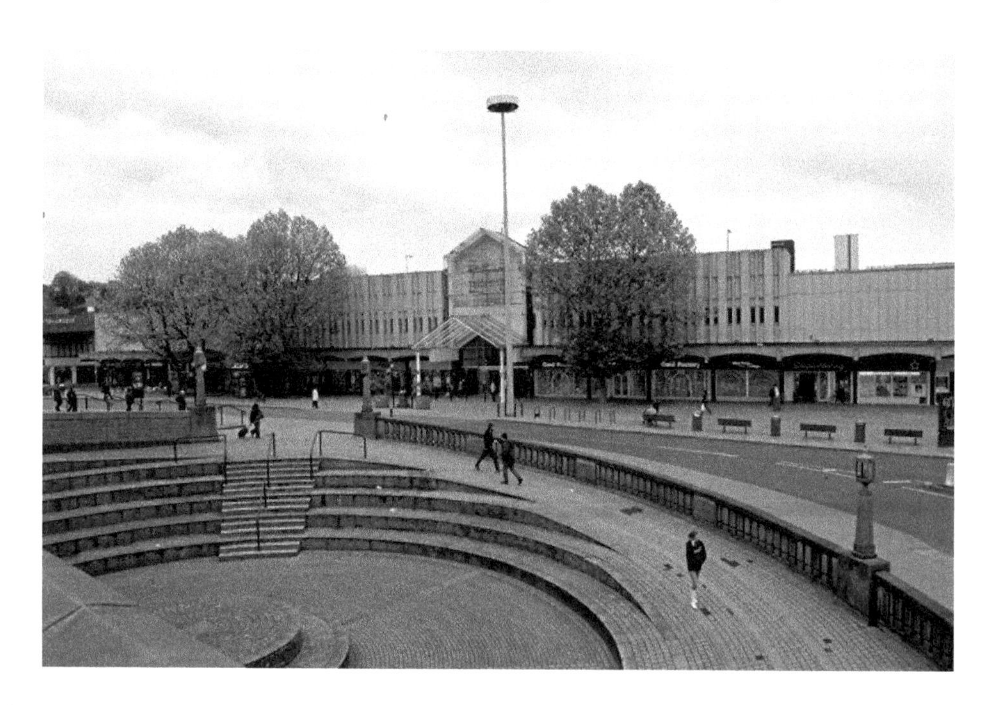

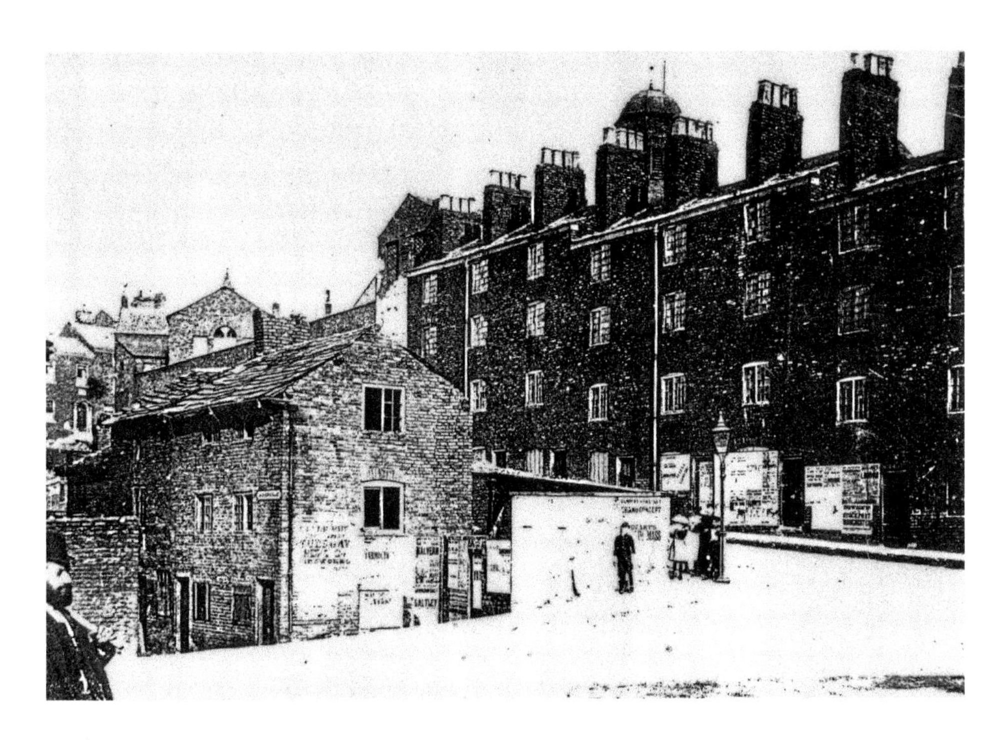

Rock Row

Providing access to St Peter's Square from Mersey Square and once called Petty Carr Green, Rock Row was the sight of many a travelling steam fair with merry-go-rounds and coconut shies. The poor housing was demolished to make way for distinctive warehouses with shops beneath, and only the tower of St Peter's church appears on both pictures. The Plaza cinema, opened in 1932, was saved from closure by a group of volunteers and thanks to grants and other funding its spectacular art deco design has been restored, making it a fabulous venue for the arts in Stockport.

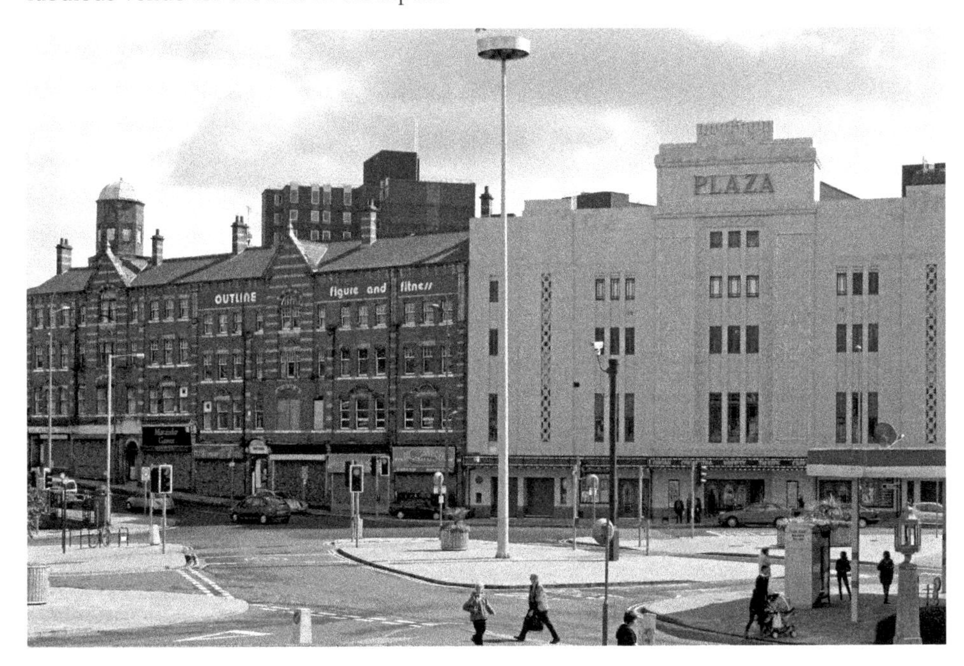

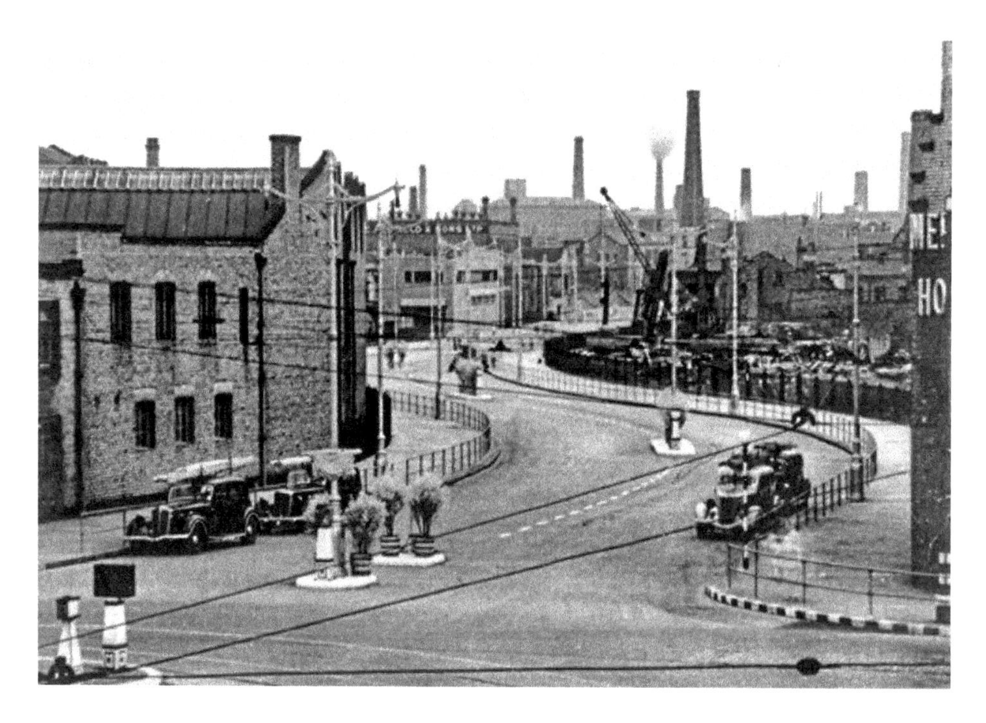

Merseyway

Traffic through Stockport in an east–west direction became an increasing problem after the First World War and a bold solution to the situation was to construct a new road, called Merseyway, on concrete arches over the river. Opened in 1940, it never became a main highway and in 1964 the roadway formed the basis of the Merseyway Shopping Precinct. It is amazing to think that the shopping development could swallow up the road with only the Mersey Hotel, to the side, standing as a reminder.

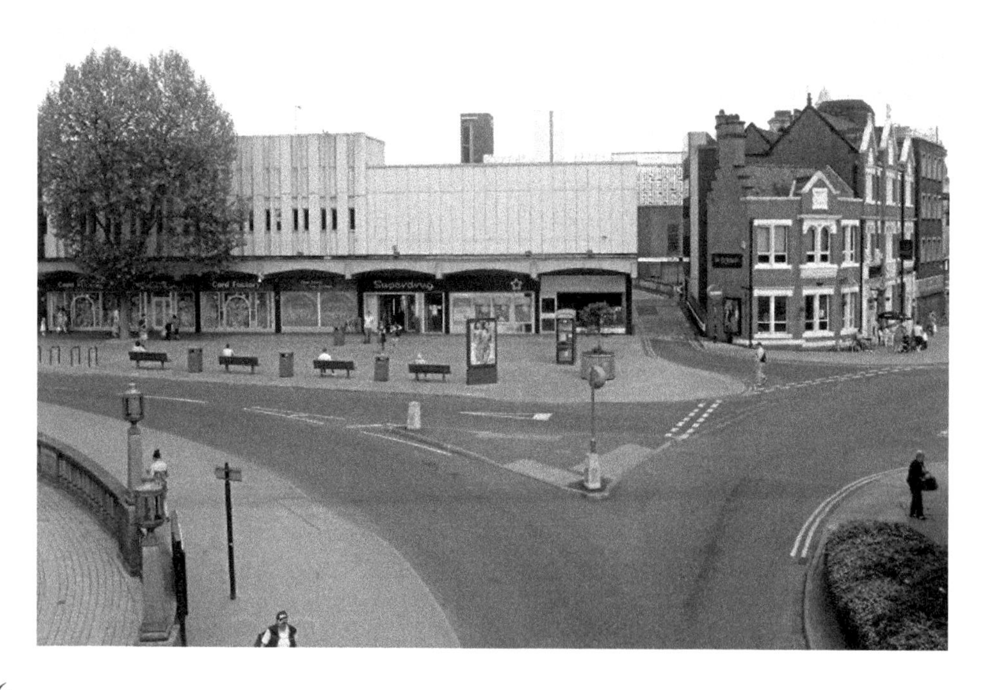

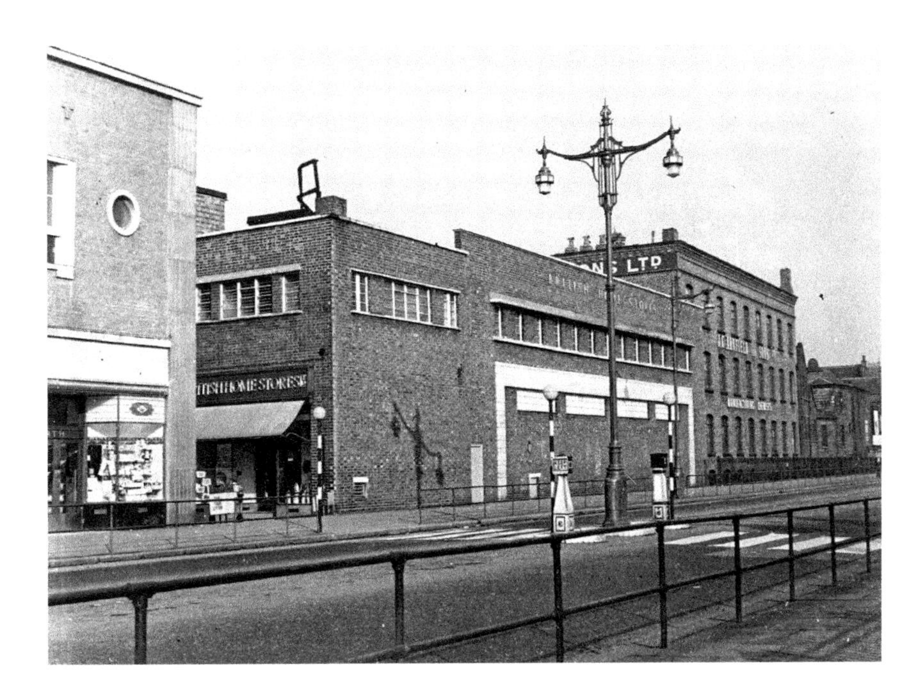

Merseyway

Built along the backs of some large existing stores on Prince's Street, Merseyway allowed these businesses to open entrances on the new road. When the shopping development was built, these store entrances became one side of the precinct. The Merseyway development at last joined the two halves of the town's shopping culture, which had previously been divided by the River Mersey. It is one of the oldest shopping precincts in the North West and, probably due to constant modernisation and upgrading, remains one of the most popular.

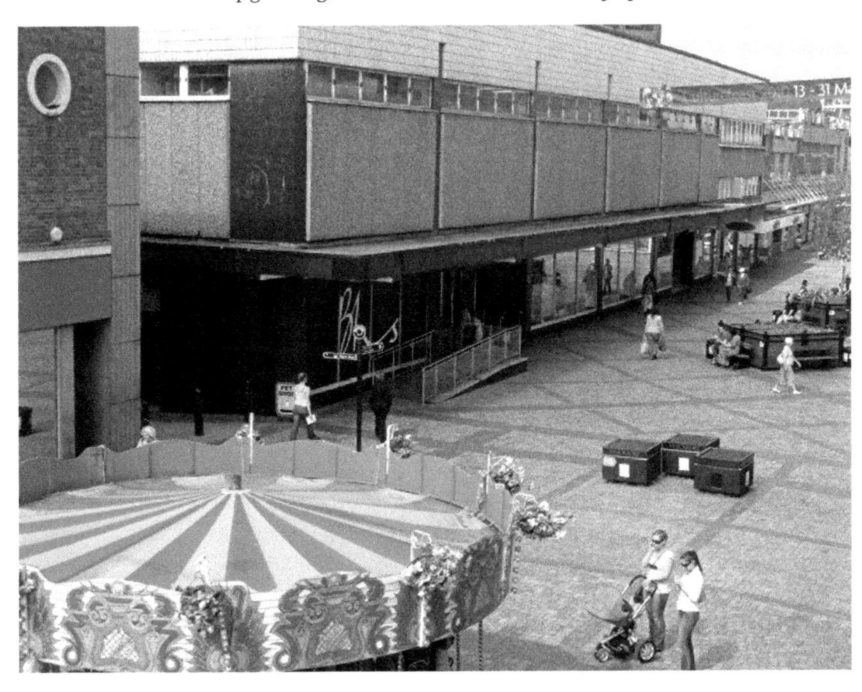

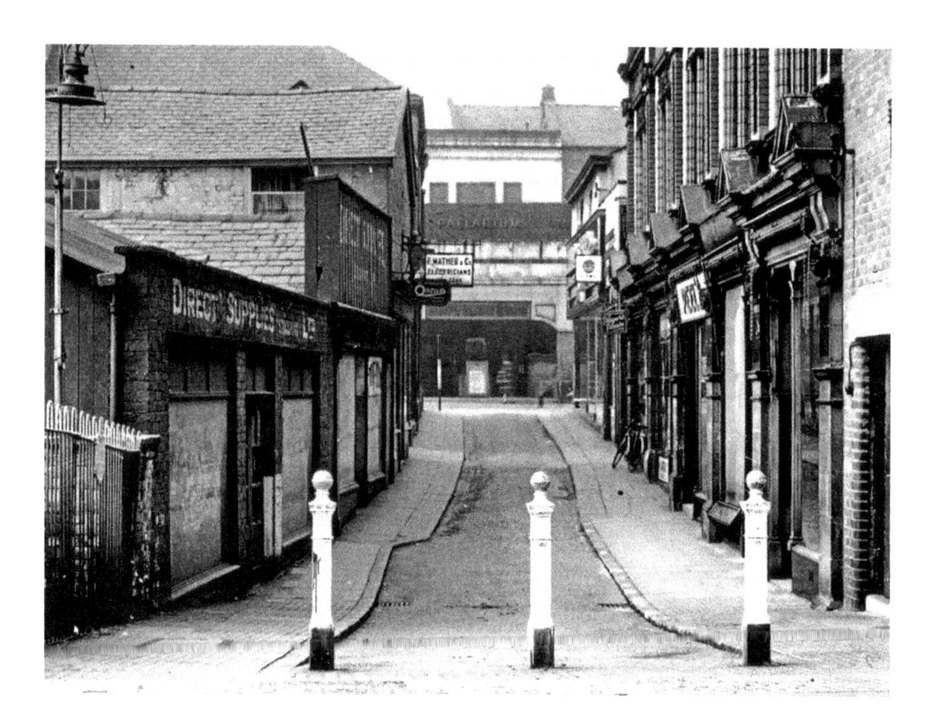

Union Road

With its bridge over the river, Union Road was one of the few ways of crossing between the two sides of the town and was always popular with shoppers. Earlier we featured the Cheshire side of the roadway, but across the bridge on the Lancashire side it opened onto Prince's Street and the previously mentioned Palladium cinema. The road is still used today by shoppers, but the mural on the side of British Home Stores is often not noticed. This wonderful artwork, in relief, depicts in several panels the history of Stockport from its earliest times.

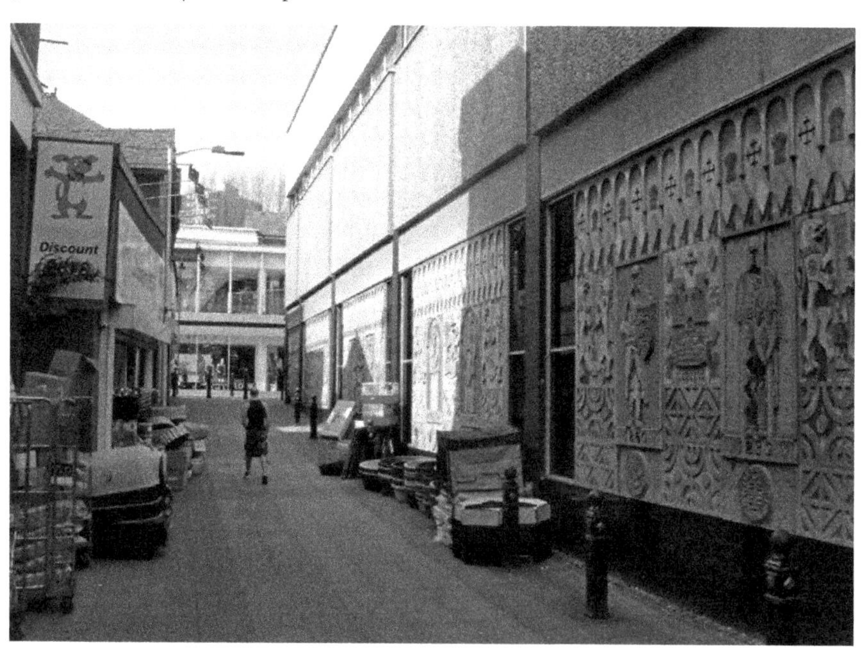

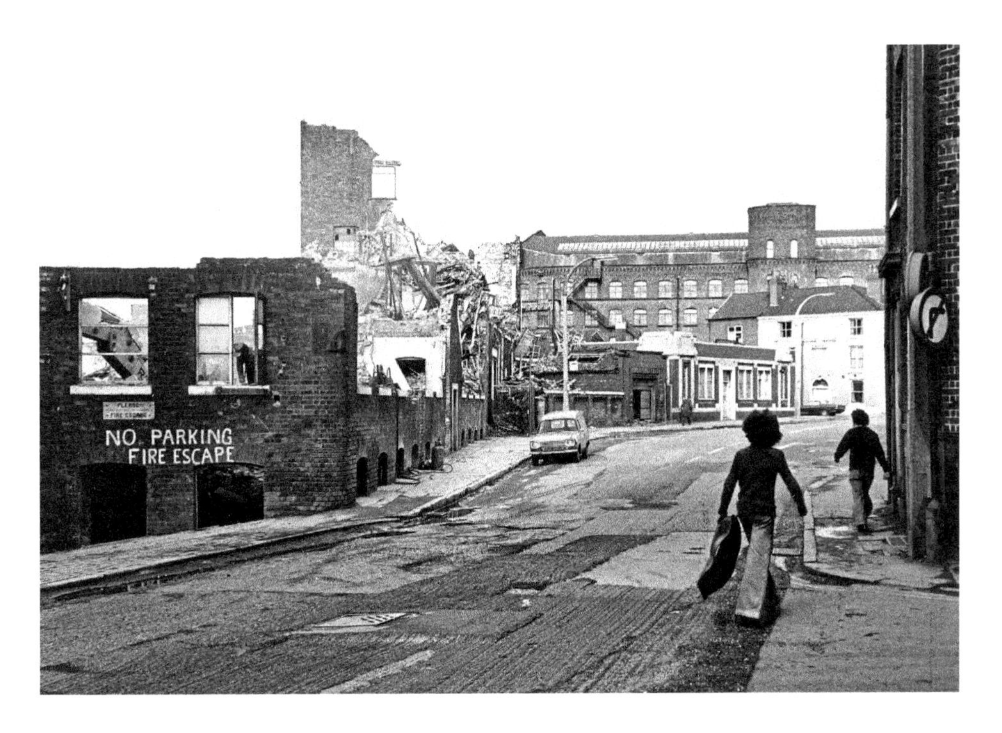

Warren Street

This street was named after the Warrens, who for many years were Lords of the Manor of Stockport. In the earlier picture of about 1970, a brave soul has parked his van next to the site of the Park Mills demolition. The country's second silk mill opened here in 1732. It was taken over by the Marsland family, converted for cotton production, and became one of the largest mills in the town. Its machinery was originally powered by four giant waterwheels, whose outlets can still be seen behind Sainsbury's.

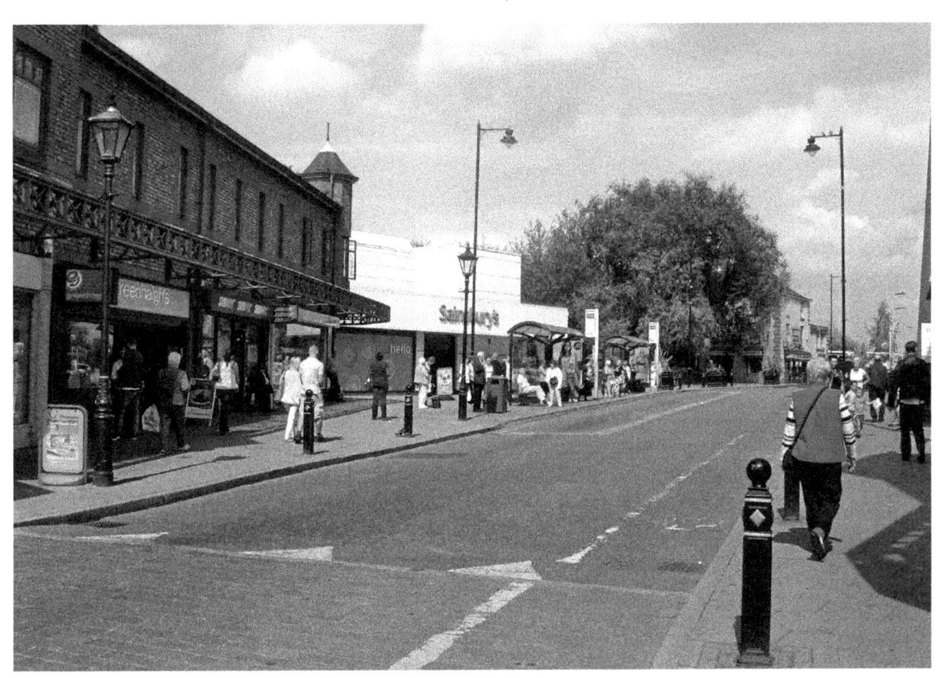

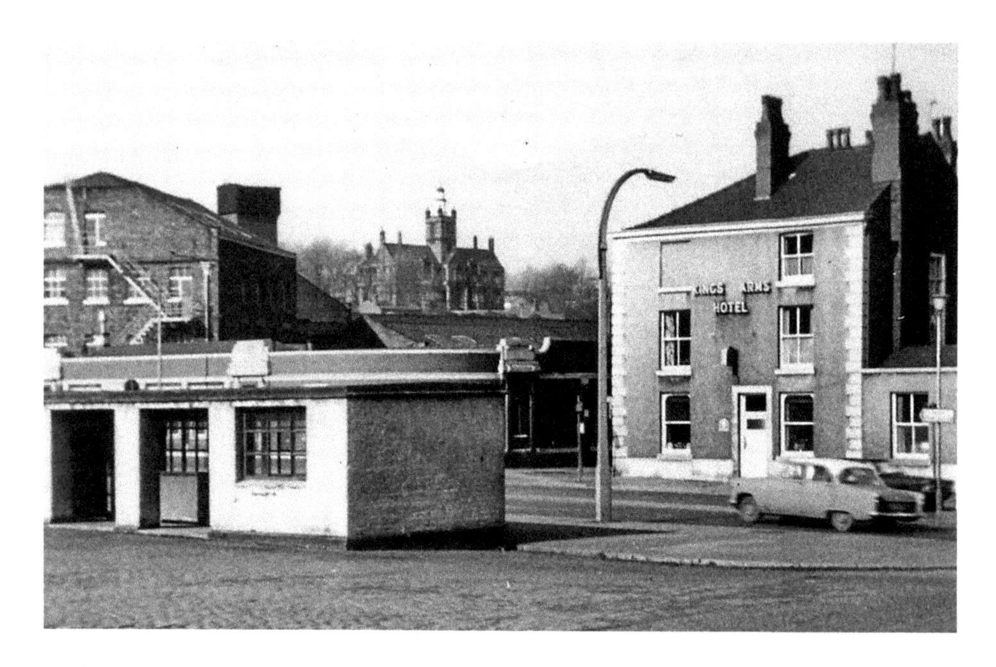

Andrew Square

The Kings Arms, like many public houses, closed and now trades as a shop. Andrew Square served many bus routes, hence the rather large and uninspiring waiting shelter. In the distance, but today hidden by trees, stands the imposing Pendlebury Hall, now an old people's home. The hall was a gift to the town by former mayor Sir Ralph Pendlebury, and provided a home and support for the orphans and poor children of Stockport. The buggy-pushing mum would be concerned to know that beneath her feet is situated a large natural cavern, part of a geological fault.

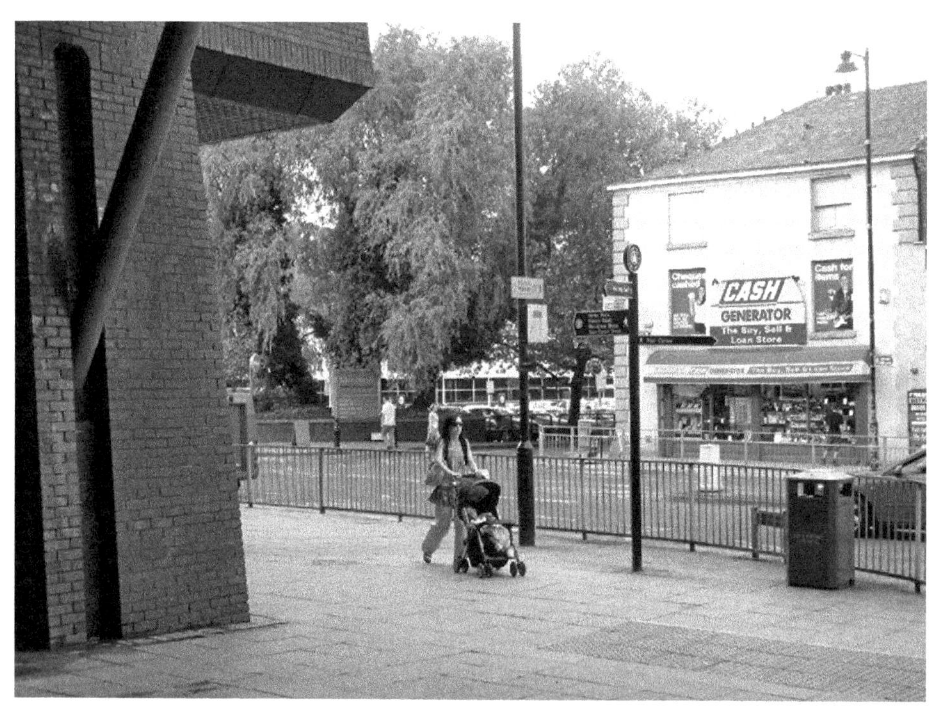

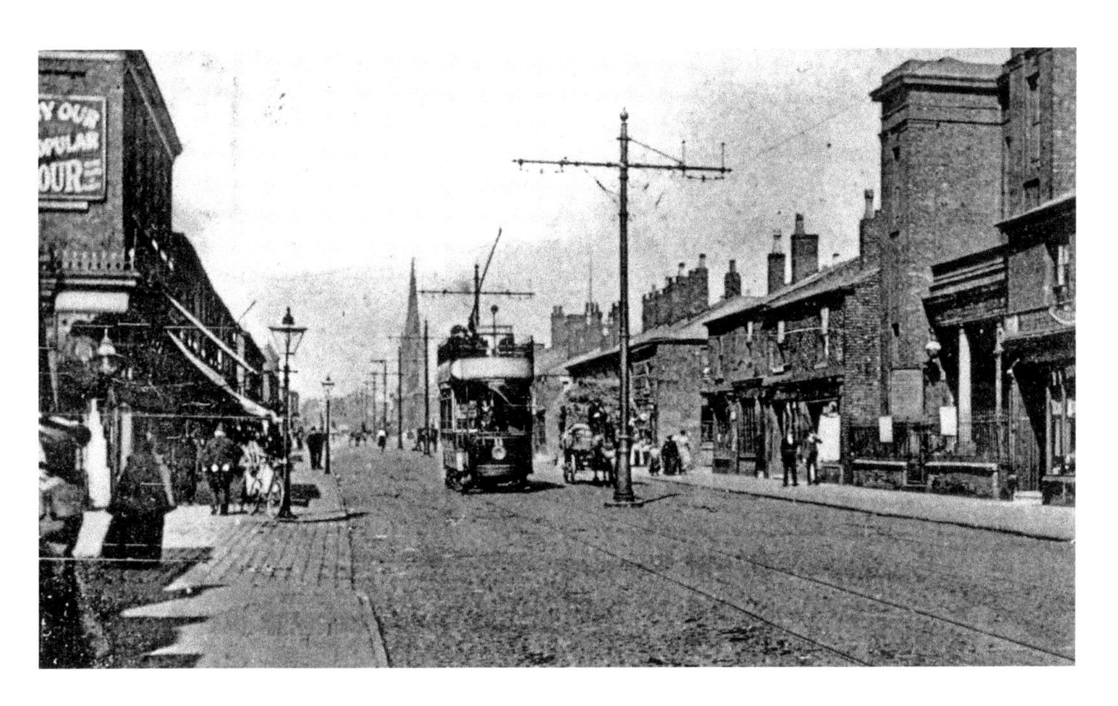

Great Portwood Street

All the property on the right of this road has been swept away for the Peel Centre retail park. The new god, consumerism, in the form of a Comet outlet, replaces the Methodist chapel. Beyond the tram and pointing to the sky is another victim of the demolition men, the spire of St Paul's church. The church was consecrated in 1851 and barely lasted a hundred years. It is surprising how much the planting of trees and hedges has improved our townscapes by softening the outlines of modern buildings.

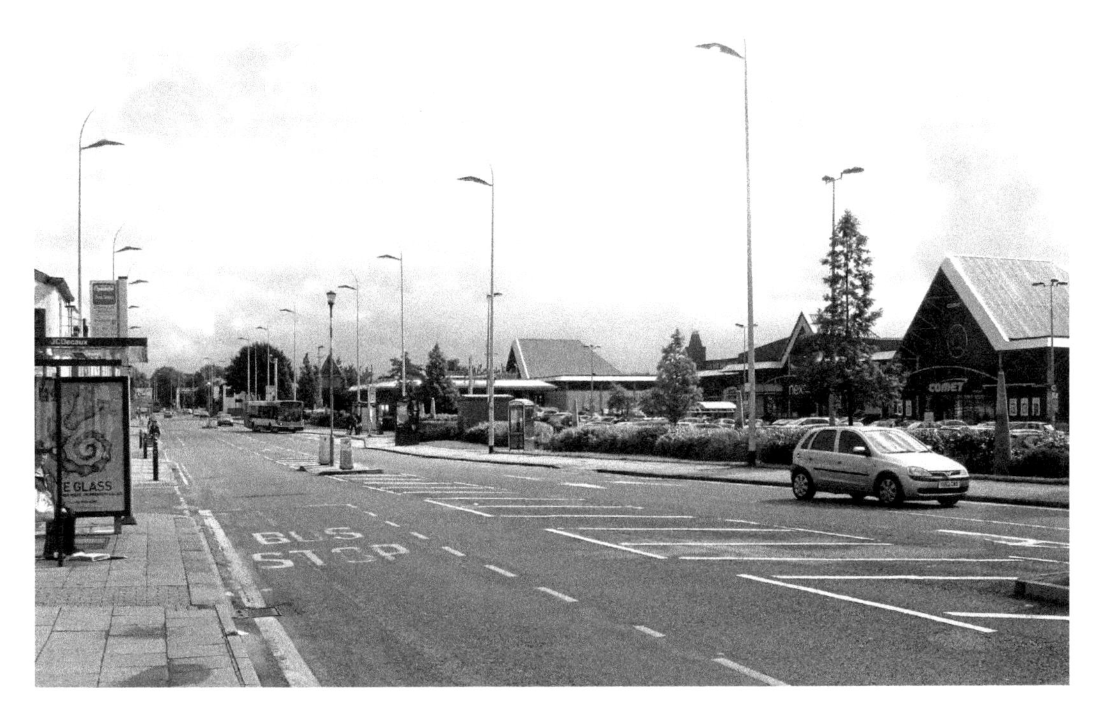

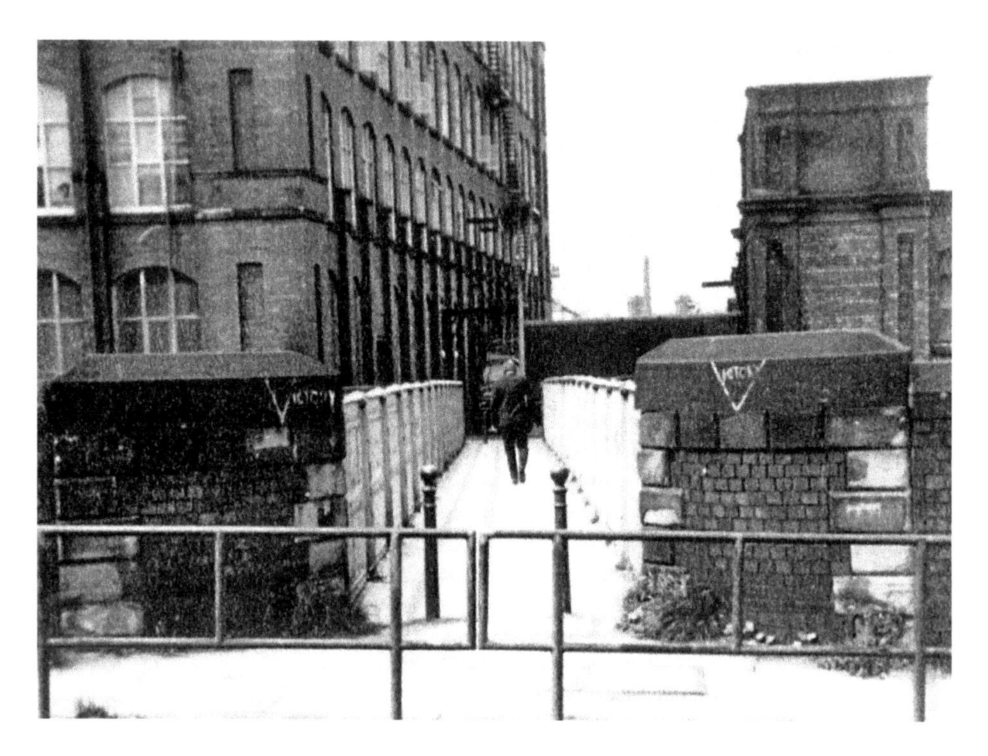

Captain's Bridge

This footbridge was erected by cotton mill owner Peter Marsland to allow his workers access to their place of work. Originally constructed in wood, it was later replaced with an all-metal bridge, as shown in the black-and-white photograph. Of interest is the 'victory' graffiti, painted by patriotic Stopfordians all over the borough, which dates our picture to the Second World War or soon after. Today St Mary's Way, part of the motorway access, crosses the river at the same place and replaces Captain's Bridge and so leaves our lonely pedestrian enduring the fumes and the noise of endless traffic.

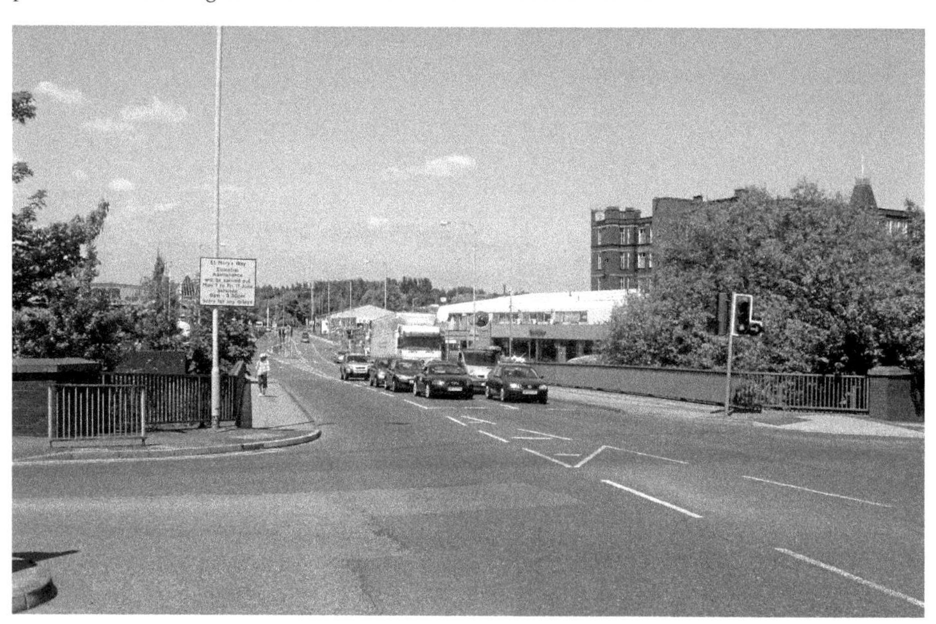

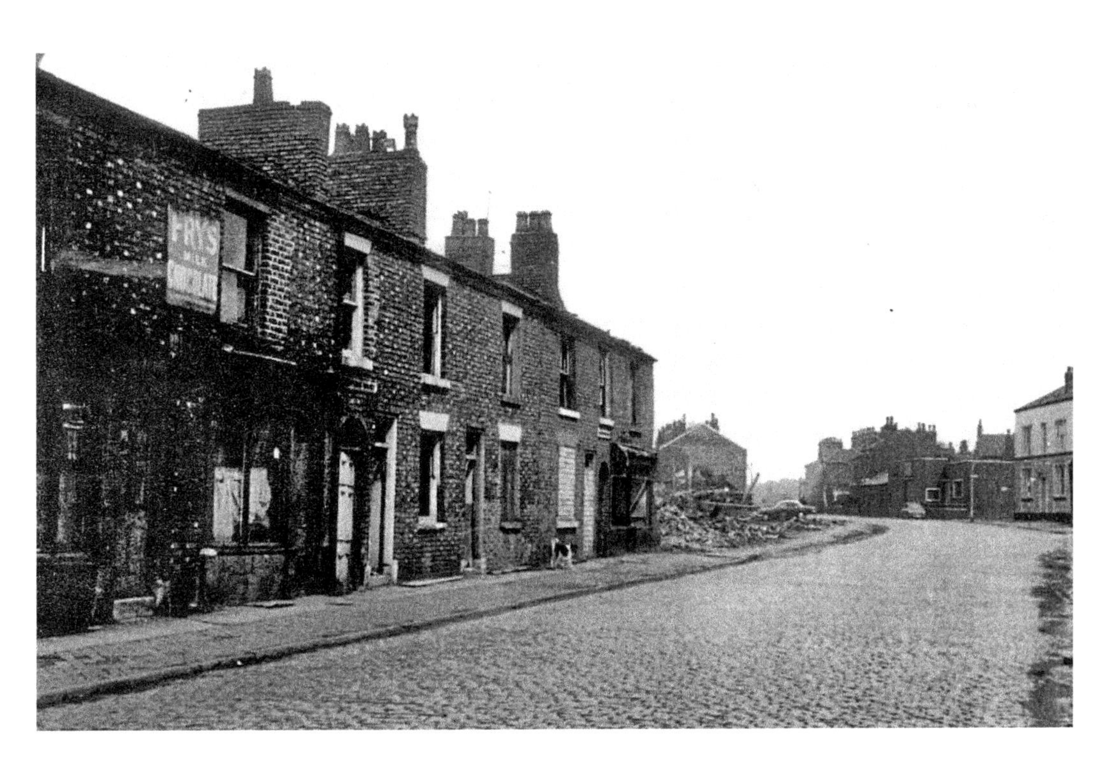

New Bridge Lane Looking East
The houses on the whole of the left side are in the process of demolition due to slum clearance policy and yet the property on the right remains virtually intact. The white building was once the home of the Coppock family and later became the Stanley Arms, the centre of the Stockport Chartist movement. Enamel advertising signs fastened to walls and fences, like the one for Fry's chocolate above the old shop, were once a common sight. Before central heating, coal fires needed chimneys – just look how many there were on the old houses.

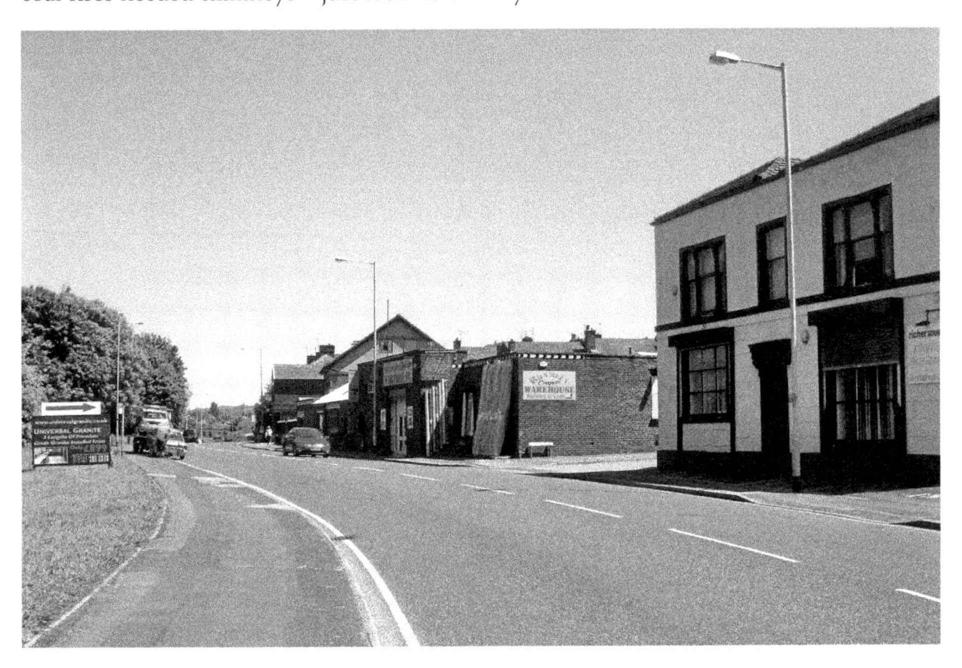

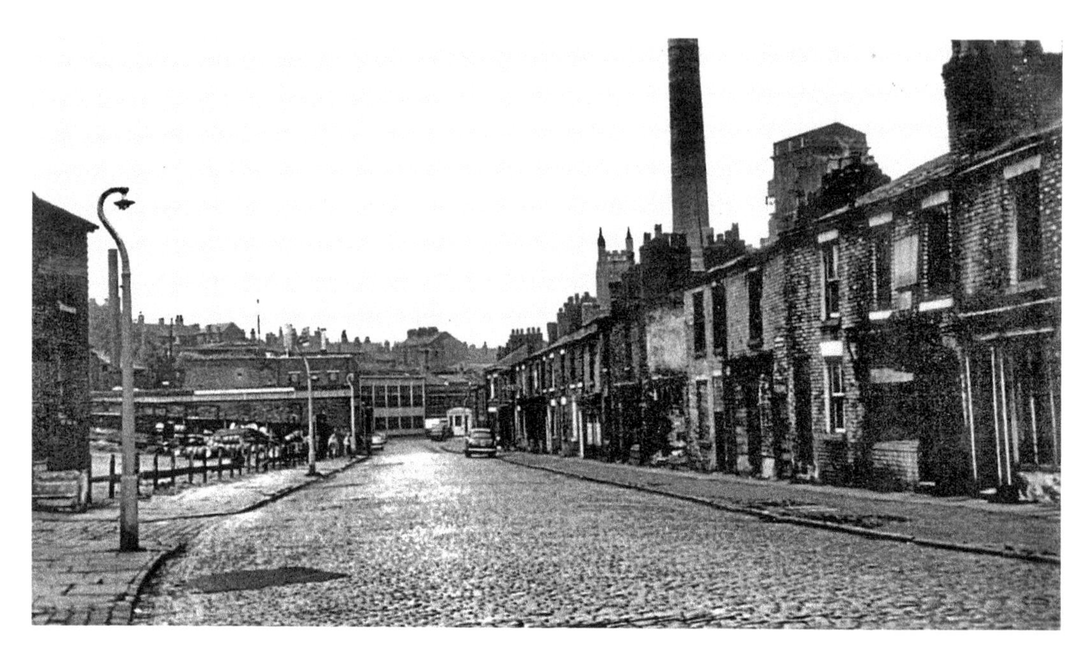

New Bridge Lane Looking West

Looking the other way towards the town centre, the skyline is dominated by the chimney and cooling tower of Stockport Power Station, with the tower of St Mary's church at a lower level. At the end of the road, the more modern steel-framed building belonged to the Cornbrook Chemical Co., at one time one of the many manufacturers in the town producing dyes for the textile industry. Now the cobbles are buried and the properties demolished, replaced by the large structure on the left, a Bingo Hall, a sign of the times.

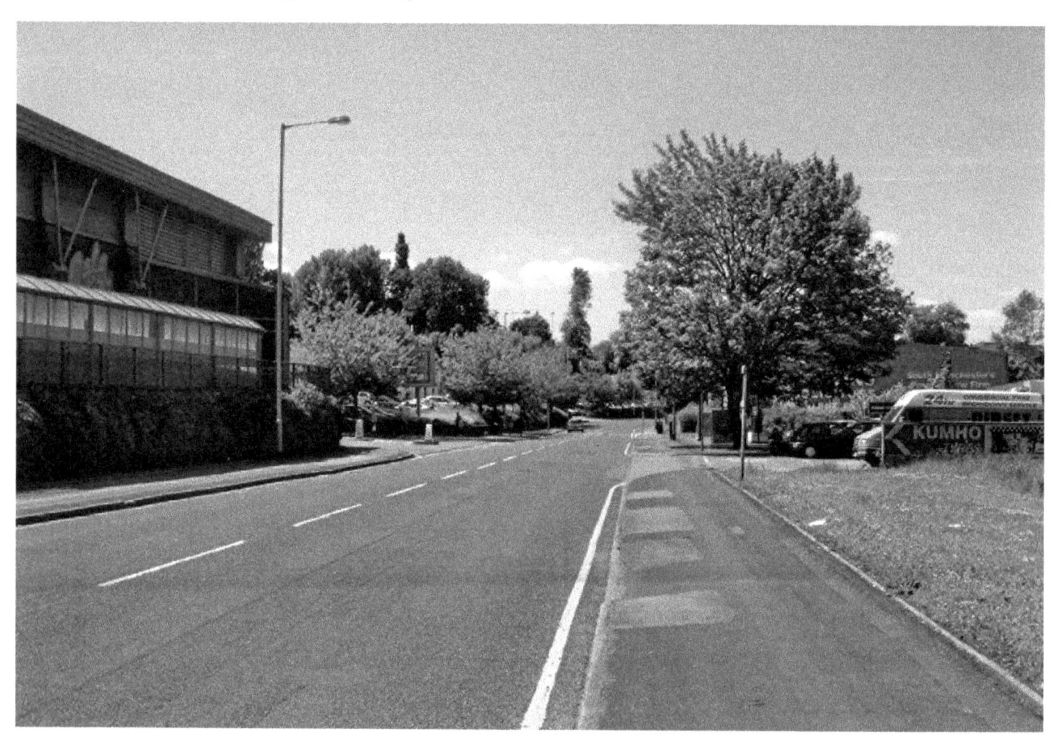

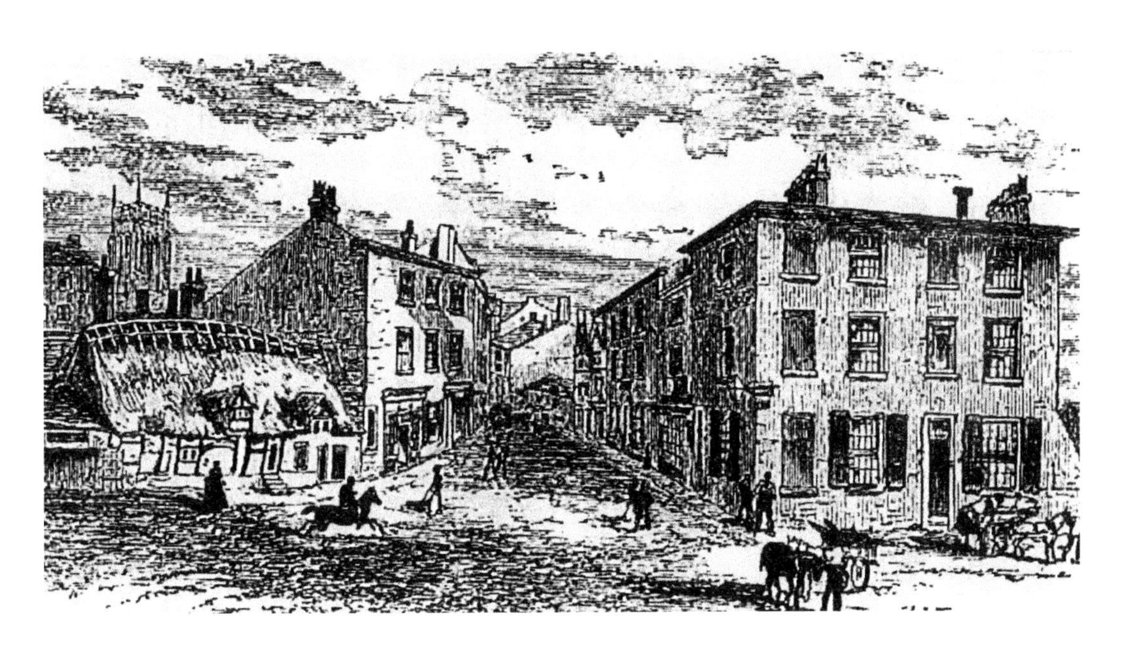

Arden Arms

Millgate starts at the end of New Bridge Lane and, on the lower corner before it rises up to the market, stands the Arden Arms, one of the least modernised pubs in Stockport. It was first recorded as Ye Blew Stoops in 1709 and was even then described as 'ancient'. Across the road, an old property with a wood frame and thatched roof represents the most common type of building in Stockport. Today the 'Arden' still serves its customers well and is noted for its excellent cuisine.

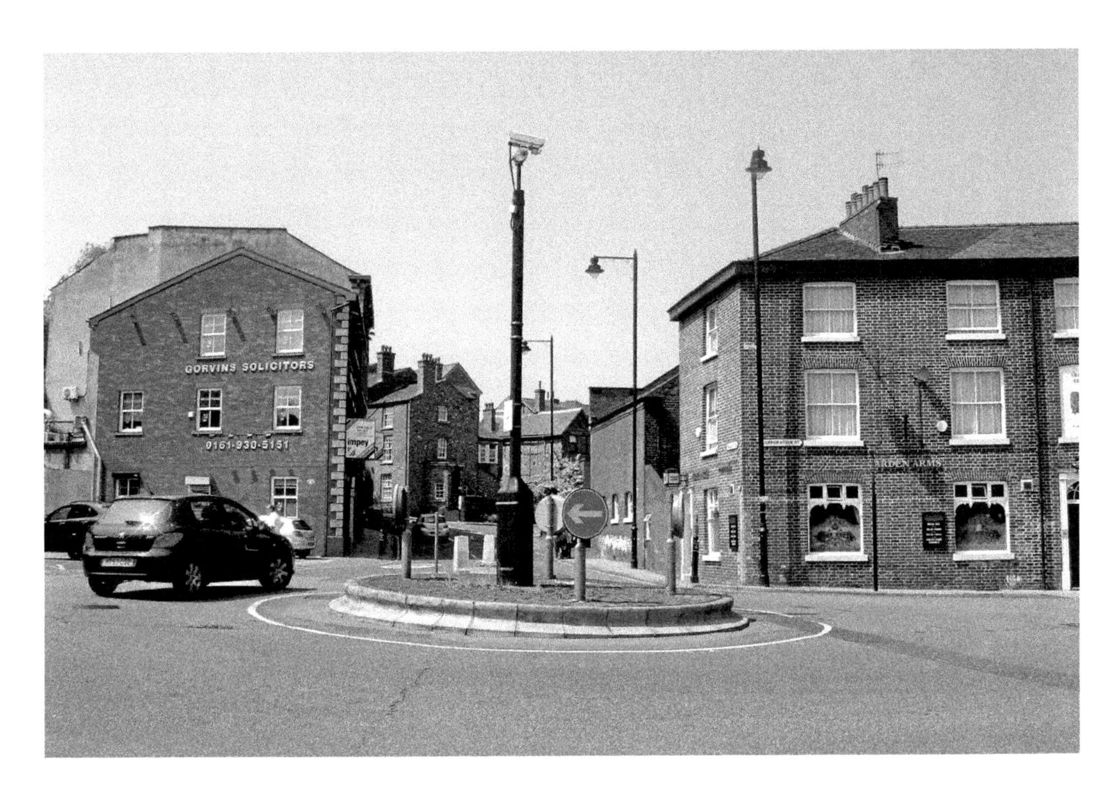

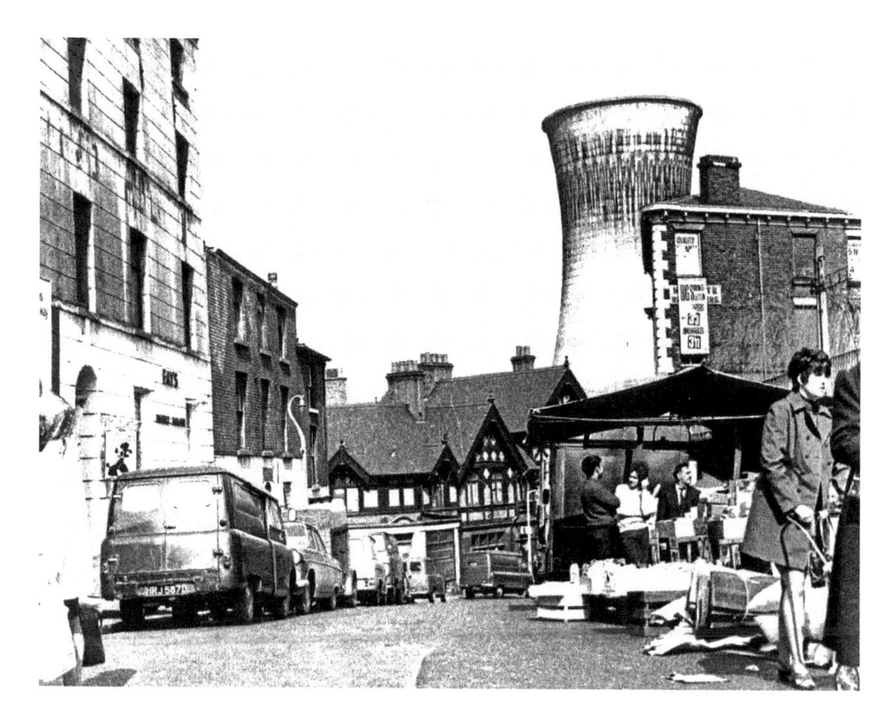

Millgate

This view down Millgate shows the ugly reinforced-concrete cooling tower of the now-closed power station, thankfully a thing of the past. As the name suggests, this was the road down to one of the town's water-powered cornmills by the river. Until recent years the market was so popular that the stall-filled road was closed to traffic, and the traders took advantage and parked their vans there. The row of buildings on the left once hosted five pubs but they have now been replaced by houses of the award-winning Shawcross Fold regeneration.

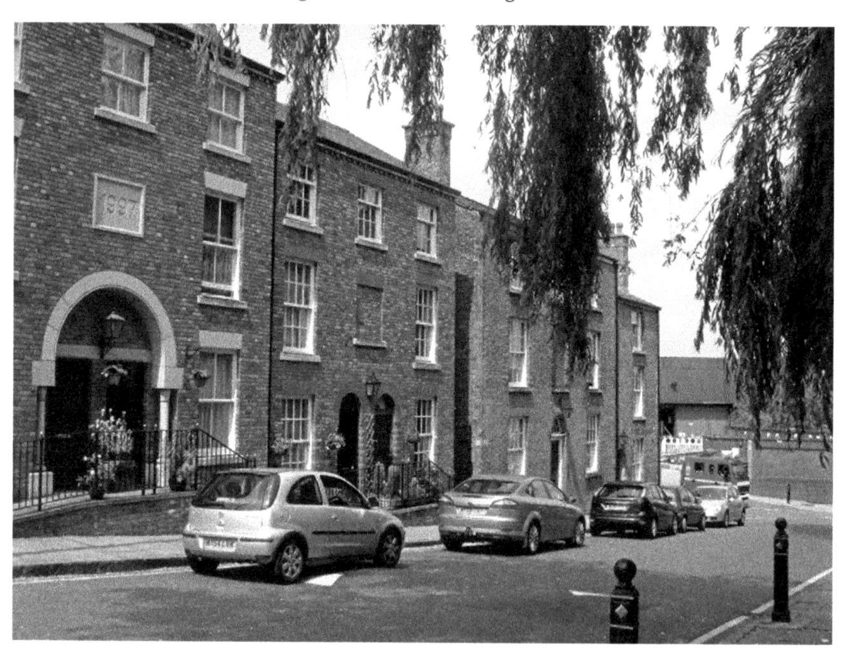